DISABILITIES AND THE LIFE COURSE

RESEARCH IN SOCIAL SCIENCE AND DISABILITY

Series Editors: Sharon N. Barnartt and Barbara M. Altman

Recent Volumes:

RESEARCH IN SOCIAL SCIENCE AND DISABILITY
VOLUME 14

DISABILITIES AND THE LIFE COURSE

EDITED BY

HEATHER E. DILLAWAY
Illinois State University, USA

CARRIE L. SHANDRA
State University of New York at Stony Brook, USA

And

ALEXIS A. BENDER
Emory University, USA

United Kingdom – North America – Japan
India – Malaysia – China

Emerald Publishing Limited
Howard House, Wagon Lane, Bingley BD16 1WA, UK

First edition 2023

British Library Cataloguing in Publication Data
A catalogue record for this book is available from the British Library

ISBN: 978-1-80455-202-5 (Print)
ISBN: 978-1-80455-201-8 (Online)
ISBN: 978-1-80455-203-2 (Epub)

ISSN: 1479-3547 (Series)

Printed and bound by CPI Group (UK) Ltd, Croydon, CR0 4YY

ISOQAR certified
Management System,
awarded to Emerald
for adherence to
Environmental
standard
ISO 14001:2004.

ISOQAR
REGISTERED
Certificate Number 1985
ISO 14001

INVESTOR IN PEOPLE

CONTENTS

LIST OF FIGURES

LIST OF TABLES

LIST OF CONTRIBUTORS

Alexis A. Bender	Emory University School of Medicine, USA
Célia Bouchet	Centre for Research on Social Inequalities (CRIS) and Laboratory for Interdisciplinary Evaluation of Public Policies (LIEPP), Sciences Po, France
Mathéa Boudinet	Centre for Research on Social Inequalities (CRIS) and Laboratory for Interdisciplinary Evaluation of Public Policies (LIEPP), Sciences Po, France
Tess Bowles	Emory University, USA
Robyn Lewis Brown	University of Kentucky, USA
Fiona Burke	State University of New York at Stony Brook, USA
Kiera Chan	Emory University, USA
Heather E. Dillaway	Illinois State University, USA
Nancy G. Kutner	Emory University, USA
Scott D. Landes	Syracuse University, USA
Kenzie Latham-Mintus	IUPUI, USA
Louise C. Palmer	Virginia C. Crawford Research Institute, Shepherd Center, Atlanta, Georgia, USA
Anna Penner	Pepperdine University, USA
Anne Revillard	Centre for Research on Social Inequalities (CRIS) and Laboratory for Interdisciplinary Evaluation of Public Policies (LIEPP), Sciences Po, France
Carrie L. Shandra	State University of New York at Stony Brook, USA
Hillary Steinberg	AJ Drexel Autism Institute, USA

ACKNOWLEDGMENTS

We would like to thank all of our colleagues who donated their time to serve as peer reviewers for pieces in this volume and provided valuable feedback to the authors. We also would like to thank Kiera Chan and Riley Hunt for their assistance with the final edits for the volume. Collectively, we also thank all study participants showcased in this volume for sharing their stories with our esteemed colleagues so we can understand their lived experiences across the life course. Finally, we thank Barbara M. Altman, Sharon N. Barnartt, Allison C. Carey, and Sara E. Green for leading the charge on this book series and allowing us to be part of the legacy.

INTRODUCTION: DISABILITIES AND THE LIFE COURSE

Heather E. Dillaway, Carrie L. Shandra, Kiera Chan and Alexis A. Bender

AUTHOR BIOGRAPHIES

Heather E. Dillaway, PhD, is a Professor of Sociology and Dean of the College of Arts and Sciences at Illinois State University. Her research focuses on women's experiences of menopause and midlife, and the reproductive health experiences of women with physical disabilities. Her research on women's experiences of physical disability appears in a range of journals and book volumes, including *Sex Roles, Disability Studies Quarterly, Disability and Health Journal, American Journal of Occupational Therapy, The Journal of Spinal Cord Medicine, Research in Social Science and Disability*, and *The Oxford Handbook on the Sociology of Disability*. She also coedited a special issue of *Gender & Society* on intersectionality, gender and disability.

Carrie L. Shandra, PhD, is an Associate Professor in the Department of Sociology at Stony Brook University. Her research focuses on work (broadly defined) and life course inequalities in the United States, particularly as they occur during the transition to adulthood and among individuals with disabilities. She has held fellowships from the Russell Sage Foundation, Sciences Po, the National Institute on Disability, Independent Living, and Rehabilitation Research, and the National Academy of Education/Spencer Foundation. Select work has appeared in *Social Forces, Journal of Marriage and Family, Social Science Research*, and *Sociological Perspectives*.

Kiera Chan, MPH, is a senior research interviewer and research associate in the School of Medicine at Emory University. She is a qualitative researcher whose work centers around stigma, chronic illness, patient care, and women's empowerment. She aims to progress patient-centered care via research, advocacy, and community engagement. She applies a sociological lens toward public health topics by studying the social determinants of health and illuminating key barriers

Disabilities and the Life Course
Research in Social Science and Disability, Volume 14, 1–10
ISSN: 1479-3547/doi:10.1108/S1479-354720230000014001

in the healthcare system. She conducts both global and domestic research emphasizing the role of stigma in health among vulnerable populations. She currently works on patient-centered care related research on topics of HIV, substance use, dementia, and disability.

Alexis A. Bender, PhD, is an Assistant Professor in the Department of Medicine at Emory University. Dr. Bender completed her PhD in Sociology with a concentration in family, health, and the life course and an interdisciplinary certificate in gerontology. Her research broadly focuses on aging with disability and chronic disease with an emphasis on relationships over the life course. Dr. Bender is a fellow in the NIMH-funded UCSD Sustained Training in Aging & HIV Research (STAHR) program and receives funding from the National Institute on Aging and the National Institute on Drug Abuse. Select work has appeared in *The Gerontologist, Journals of Gerontology, Social Sciences, Journal of the American Geriatric Society*, and *Journal of Applied Gerontology*, where she also serves on the editorial board.

INTRODUCTION

Keeping the Focus on Disability

Over 1 billion people – approximately one in six individuals – currently report "significant" disability across the world (World Health Organization [WHO], 2022). In the United States, one in four adults has a disability: 14% of the population reports physical disability, 11% cognitive disability, 6% hearing difficulties or deafness, and 5% vision impairments or blindness (CDC, 2022). Although there is no definitive list, disabilities can be categorized as (1) congenital or acquired, (2) physical, cognitive, or sensory, (3) visible or invisible, and (4) severe, moderate, or mild. Higher rates of disability worldwide are largely attributed to the aging of populations, higher incidence of chronic health conditions and noncommunicable diseases such as cardiovascular disease and diabetes, and greater risk of accidental injuries such as motor vehicle accidents (CDC, 2022). Furthermore, according to the World Health Organization (WHO, 2002), almost everyone will be temporarily or permanently impaired at some point in life because of eventual acquired disabilities (see also Dillaway et al., 2022). Considering the increasing inevitability of disability acquisition across the lifespan and increasing rates of disability in general, it is important to understand how individuals experience disabilities over time and place – particularly because disabilities vary in how they manifest and affect individuals' lives.

The International Classification of Functioning Disability and Health (ICF) defines disability as not just an attribute or fixed property of a person but, rather, a state that results from the interaction between a person and environment (WHO, 2002; see also Naples et al., 2019). Therefore, while disability may be based loosely on the existence of an underlying impairment of some kind, impairment alone does not determine experience (WHO, 2002). Disability studies scholars in the social sciences have tried to keep the focus on disability as the embodied experience of impairment, as well as the structural barriers that individuals with disabilities confront (Mauldin & Brown, 2021; Naples et al., 2019). As different authors note in this volume, individuals with disabilities report discrimination in all areas of their lives: employment, education, healthcare, relationships with others, etc. (Frederick & Shifrer, 2019; MacInnes, 2011; Maroto et al., 2019; Mauldin & Brown, 2021; Naples et al., 2019; Pettinichio et al., 2021; Shandra, 2018; Shifrer & Frederick, 2019). Indeed, individuals with disabilities are "subject to ableist processes that result in their exclusion and marginalization" (Naples et al., 2019, p. 5; see also Frederick & Shifrer, 2019; Pettinichio et al., 2021; Shifrer & Frederick, 2019). This means that disability status is an axis of inequality, similar to race, class, gender, sexuality, and age, that reflects larger systems of oppression (Frederick & Shifrer, 2019; Mauldin & Brown, 2021; Shandra, 2018; Shifrer & Frederick, 2019). As social scientists who seek to deepen our understanding of impairment and disability, we must continue to interrogate how individuals with disabilities navigate embodied experiences and confront macro-level barriers across the lifespan.

A Life Course Perspective

Emerging first in the 1960s, the life course perspective is a theoretical framework developed to examine "continuity and change of human lives in relation to interpersonal, structural, and historical forces" (Elder et al., 2003, p. 4). Sociologists, anthropologists, social historians, demographers, social workers, economists, political scientists, and developmental psychologists, among others, have worked to advance this paradigm across disciplines. They have called attention to myriad topics: the significance of historical events and social change in shaping individual lives; cohort, period, and generational differences in lived experience; varied pathways to adulthood and older age; typical life transitions and turning points; the timing and sequencing of personal events and decisions; and how individuals can employ human agency across the life course (Elder, 1994; Elder et al., 2003; Harrington Meyer, 2014). Life course scholars propose that "depending on the exact life stage, different factors or issues take on differing degrees of importance" and become significant in shaping identity and experience as well as an individual's ability to accomplish certain typical life transitions and trajectories (Dillaway et al., 2022; Elder et al., 2003; Roehling et al., 2001, p. 146). Life course analysis also enables researchers to observe how individuals navigate a particular identity or experience within one single moment as well as to consider how individuals negotiate a particular identity or experience over time (Harrington Meyer, 2014). An emphasis on the life course, therefore, allows us to see the immediate, cumulative, and/or longstanding effects of individuals' and groups' experiences.

As Robyn Brown appropriately notes in this volume, "the life course paradigm is not a single cohesive perspective, but a combination of perspectives guided by ... principles and methodological considerations." As many other authors in this volume also note, a life course lens is guided by four main themes that researchers and practitioners utilize in different ways as they engage in the "long way of thinking" about human lives and social pathways (Elder, 1994, p. 5): (1) "the interplay of human lives and historical times," (2) the timing of life transitions and events, (3) how individuals lead interdependent or "linked lives," and (4) how individuals use agency as they make choices across the lifespan. Elder et al. (2003) detail a fifth theme in later publications, reminding life course scholars that human development and aging are "lifelong processes." In emphasizing timing, transitions, and trajectories, as well as how historical forces and social institutions can shape day-to-day life, life course scholars focus on connections between the macro- and micro-levels of experience and examine both continuity and change in people's identities and experiences across time.

Our Project: Applying a Life Course Lens to the Study of Impairment and Disability

All individuals, with or without disabilities, have storied lives that unfold across time and place. Impairments and disabilities also have varied meanings and implications depending on time, place, and other life contexts. That is, an individual's identity and experience of an impairment or disability at one moment could be quite different from their identity and experience at another moment. At the same time, an entire cohort or generation of individuals with the same type of impairment or disability may face similar lived experiences in key moments, depending on historical context and the opportunities created by technologies, institutions, or policies. Alternatively, individuals could experience the same moment very differently depending on their social locations, types and levels of impairment or disability, past experiences, and current life contexts.

In this volume we aim to broaden the application of the life course perspective to explore the multiple ways in which impairments and disabilities factor across the lifespan and have diverse impacts in assorted life stages. In addition, we aim to highlight how individuals might think about, maneuver, and encounter impairments or disabilities, in a variety of ways depending on time, place, and life contexts. Consequently, the primary purpose of this volume is to expand our knowledge of impairments and disabilities across the life course, both in terms of how they can change in form, meaning, and experience across time and life stage and how certain life course transitions and events can manifest differently or carry new meanings because of impairment or disability status. We hope to prioritize explorations of individuals' lived identities and experiences as well as the macro-level structures that shape these identities and experiences. Finally, we seek to highlight commonalities and differences in identity and experience with special attention to intersecting social locations and the diversity of impairments and disabilities.

Layout of This Volume

As expected, authors in this volume adopt a wide range of methodologies and approaches to studying disability using a life course perspective. Depending on the chapter, the reader will encounter analyses of data drawn from reviews of existing literature, in-depth case studies, individual interviews, and nationally representative survey data. Authors in this volume specifically contribute to our knowledge of the effects of macro-level contexts on individuals' identities and experiences, linked lives, timing and time use, human agency, cumulative disadvantage, and the intersections of disability with other social locations. Overall, all authors expand our understanding of the continuity and change in both identity and experience, and the ways in which a life course lens can improve our considerations of impairment and disability across the life course. We organize the chapters to reflect authors' different foci and contributions. We begin with chapters that are more conceptual, that consider generally how a life course perspective may help us comprehend disability identity and experience. We then move to pieces that explicitly tackle issues of stigma and identity across the lifespan. Later chapters help us understand disability-related educational experiences, the effects of disability on familial relationships, employment trends for people with and without disabilities, spouses' entry into and negotiation of caregiving roles, and interrogations of specific concepts such as diagnosis pathways, spoiled identity, doing disability, policy reception, work precarity, and time use.

We purposely begin our volume with a conceptual chapter by Kenzie Latham-Mintus and Scott Landes, as these authors focus readers on key concepts and themes of the life course perspective. Latham-Mintus and Landes apply Elder et al.'s (2003) five principles to "reconsider" the life course lens while centering disability status as an axis of inequality and paying close attention to macro-level contexts. *Time and place* play a crucial role in the disability experience, including historical period, geographic location, and birth cohort – as well as policies and social movements that expand or restrict opportunities for disabled populations. *Timing and age effects* should consider how disability, timing and duration of disability, and structural ableism shape life transitions, social trajectories, and cumulative dis/advantage. *Agency* is bounded by social policies, institutionalization, and administrative burden, and is inseparable from the concept of *linked lives* and interdependence. Finally, the resilience and adaptation that accompany *lifespan development* should be considered in tandem with the unique social, environmental, and structural contexts faced by people with disabilities. Latham-Mintus and Landes offer both theoretical and methodological suggestions for aging and disability scholars to "better attend" to issues of disability across the life course.

Louise Palmer reviews existing research on multiple sclerosis (MS) to integrate core concepts of life course theory with an intersectional feminist disability perspective – two equally critical frameworks for understanding disability experience. Palmer highlights the dearth of comprehensive research on the variation in MS trajectories and outcomes, especially by social locations such as race, ethnicity, class, gender, sexual orientation, nationality, age, and disability. Introducing the concept of "diagnosis pathways," she suggests that time from symptom onset to diagnosis determines MS illness trajectories, and that these pathways are shaped by overlapping systems of inequality. Certain groups therefore experience delays in diagnosis which create further disparities in health outcomes across the life course. Individuals' abilities to use relationships with others or their own agency to influence the diagnosis process are also shaped by social locations. Palmer draws from the limited research on racial-ethnic disparities in time to MS diagnosis to show readers how to discern the effects of macro-level inequalities on health outcomes across time. This author ultimately explains how we might miss the importance of this variation in diagnosis pathways if we are not pairing a life course lens with an intersectional perspective. In this way, Palmer illustrates the flexibility of life course theory, in that it can be easily paired with other conceptual frameworks to understand disability and chronic health experiences.

We next turn to issues of disability identity and the French national context with Célia Bouchet and Mathéa Boudinet's chapter. These authors present data from 65 biographical interviews from two separate qualitative studies to examine how individuals with disabilities affiliate and identify with different social groups as they interpret reasons for the disadvantages they face over time. Respondents in this study invoke their disability as a primary cause of negative experiences in a variety of circumstances. In particular, interviewees who had been labeled as "disabled" for a longer period of time were socialized to understand that this identity is more salient than other social locations such as gender or race. However, those who acquired a disability later in life often attributed negative experiences primarily to another social location or identity. The authors also track certain "turning points" in the ways that participants make connections between their identities and the inequalities they face. For example, Bouchet and Boudinet propose that participants reinterpreted the underlying causes of disadvantages they faced as they learned more about their own intersecting social locations and the history of macro-level inequalities over time. Most participants still named a single identity and affiliation as the primary cause of a negative experience, however, even if they defined their experience as based in multiple social locations. This chapter allows readers to contemplate the ways disability identity might be more or less salient over time and how certain types of socialization and education may affect one's sense of identity. These authors also help us understand the reasons why the concepts of time, agency, and linked lives matter, and why and how disability identity and experience might vary across the life span.

Furthering our understanding of disability identity and experience in particular life stages, Nancy Kutner and Tess Bowles interview young adults living with kidney failure about dimensions of young adult development. While all individuals, regardless of disability status, must make the transition "to and from young adulthood," Kutner and Bowles' participants were dependent on medical treatments to manage their conditions. These treatments, in turn, impacted independent living, regular employment, and community involvement – three indicators of "successful" development reported by participants. From their interviews, Kutner and Bowles identify the theme of perceived condition-related stigma and apply Goffman's (1963) notion of spoiled identity, discussing how "different" participants felt in comparison to those without chronic conditions. Finally, they show how participants felt isolated from peers, with limited opportunities to share experiences and identify with others. The authors note that relationships with others and participation in specialized "transition clinics" or other developmentally appropriate programming may benefit young adults who might have difficulty making "on-time" life course transitions because of disabling chronic conditions.

Hillary Steinberg's chapter is an additional analysis of disability identity and performance, yet with attention to how individuals "do" disability and gender simultaneously within ableist environments. This author uses a life course approach to illuminate how early socialization to gender expectations and ableist expectations may have implications for how individuals with disabilities perform gender and disability in later life stages. Specifically, Steinberg focuses on how interviewees, regardless of gender, learn that ableist expectations encourage "feminine" behavior. While some (especially women and nonbinary individuals) may explicitly resist performing gender in feminine ways, such as worrying about others' discomfort over their own when dealing with a disability in a public space, all interviewees reported knowing that emphasized femininity is expected of them. Additionally, interviewees who identified as men also noted the benefits of emphasized femininity in interactions with others about their disabilities. Data presented in this chapter confirm that expectations for gender and disability performance cannot be separated. Steinberg also proposes that living with disability is, itself, a gendered process that impacts both gender and disability identity and performance in all life stages. In reviewing this chapter, then, readers will understand the ways in which different macro-level structures intersect to enforce certain gendered behaviors among those who confront ableism across the lifespan.

Anne Revillard subsequently emphasizes the importance of thinking about how macro-level forces – in this case, changes to disability-related educational policy in France – impact individuals with disabilities on the micro-level. That is, the author clarifies that the study of policy making and policy change must include an evaluation of how policy is received by the individuals targeted by such policy. Studying policy reception through qualitative interviews with individuals born and schooled in different time periods, Revillard shows that policies can have differential effects on individuals depending on personal contexts and one's ability to enact agency. In analyzing the narratives of a woman born in 1942, in the era of separate schooling, and a man born in 1985, in a period of school integration, Revillard compares and contrasts the ways in which policy both limits and expands individuals' opportunities. Thus, public policies have "both a constraining and an enabling effect on individuals." Studying policy reception via a life course lens means focusing on the micro-level effects of policy-making across time periods, cohorts, and generations. Revillard outlines the complexities in studying how macro-level forces impact individuals across time and place.

Anna Penner applies the life course concepts of linked lives and social pathways to evaluate the long-term impact of disabilities – specifically, the effects of growing up with a disabled sibling. Penner utilizes nationally representative survey data to examine the likelihood of college completion among individuals with a disabled sibling, finding that women with disabled siblings are less likely to complete college than women without disabled siblings. However, having married parents eradicates this gap in college completion. Penner indicates that there are invisible costs of having a child with disability within a family unit, but the exact impact on family members varies by social location and parents' relationship status. Readers are reminded that applying the concept of linked lives to the lived experience of disability means studying the effects of disability on both those with disabilities and those within their social networks.

Also concentrating on the effects of disability on the family unit, Alexis Bender explores couples' transitions after one partner incurs a spinal cord injury. Following 18 couples through rehabilitation care and the subsequent transition home, Bender examines how the noninjured partner becomes involved in caregiving and the types of caregiving roles they adopt. She tracks how couples enter, negotiate, and adjust to or exit caregiving relationships across time, and finds three main groups of caregivers in the process: naturalized, constrained, and resistant. Bender examines how healthcare institutions (particularly rehabilitation settings), social class and employment status, and gendered cultural constructions of women as caregivers all influence couples' transitions to the caregiving relationship. Data presented in this chapter reaffirm how important it is to pay attention to the relationships between individuals with disabilities and their partners and/or caregivers, as well as the influence of those in healthcare settings. Bender further urges us to pay attention to individuals' social locations as well as the macro-level ideologies that shape people's perceptions of disabilities and their impacts. Inevitably, individuals and couples will experience disability and life course transitions and trajectories differently depending on these external factors.

Robyn Lewis Brown uses longitudinal, nationally representative data to consider how individuals with disability experience cumulative disadvantage in two types of outcomes: work precarity and involuntary job loss. Results for the first outcome indicate that having a disability in 1986 was positively associated with work precarity (as measured by job and income insecurity) after the start of the Great Recession. Further, people with disabilities who experienced early income insecurity were more likely to experience later income insecurity than people without disabilities. Results for the second outcome show that having a disability in 1986 increased the hazard of involuntary job loss two decades later. Finally, the adverse effects of early job precarity on later job loss were significantly larger for people with disability, compared to those without disability. People with disabilities are disproportionately impacted by early work precarity, despite the passage of the Americans with Disabilities Act during the study period. Brown argues that quantitative researchers must attend to continuity and change over time when studying people with disabilities. In considering both age and period effects across five waves (and 26 years) of data, Brown is able to decipher the employment consequences of living with a disability more fully than with cross-sectional data alone.

Finally, Carrie Shandra and Fiona Burke also use nationally representative survey data to consider how daily time in activities of daily living, instrumental activities of daily living, and other social activities varies by age, gender, and disability status. Thus, they quantify the "disability gap in time use" and consider "when in the life course – and by how much – [individuals] experience differences in activities." Shandra and Burke remind us that, while there is a burgeoning time use literature, much of it does not consider disability, and researchers that do attend to it often "treat disability as having constant effects on daily activities over the life course or over particular life stages." Thus, these authors urge other researchers to use a life course lens to complicate analyses of time use, the effects of impairment and disability, and lived disability experience at different life stages. In addition, their analyses make it clear that we must recognize the importance of intersectional analysis; unless we pay simultaneous attention to other social locations such as age and gender, we cannot develop a comprehensive understanding of the connections between time use and disability experience across the lifespan.

CONCLUSION

Together, the chapters in this volume exemplify the possible range of applications of a life course perspective when studying impairment and disability. Authors question the connections between macro- and micro-level influences, the effects of age, cohort and period effects, the intersections of different social locations and axes of inequality, continuity and change in identity and experience, relationships between individuals with and without disabilities, the extent to which individuals have agency, and the effects of impairment and disability over time. Different chapters also explore varied life transitions, such as the transition to and from young adulthood, the transition to living with a spinal cord injury, the transition to a caregiving role, college completion, involuntary job loss, pathways to diagnosis of chronic illness, and the experience of transitioning from separate schooling to mainstreamed educational environments. Finally, multiple chapters explore the varied consequences of living with disability and chronic illness, such as differential health and educational outcomes, impacts on family relationships, job precarity and job loss, impacts on sleep and other activities of daily living, and changes in identity and behavior over time. Finally, the principles inherent in a life course approach are intertwined throughout this book, as many authors evaluate the impact of historical contexts, the timing of life transitions, the interdependence of individuals, and the importance of human agency.

This volume has implications for researchers, practitioners, and others interested in disability studies. A life course lens forces us to think about impairment and disability as a long-term and ever-changing experience, not just an outcome or a cause. Adopting this perspective on disability also encourages us to think about how varied and complex disability identity and experience can be. There are infinite ways to apply a life course lens across the social sciences. We hope to see more of our peers adopt the "long way of thinking" (Elder, 1994) about impairment and disability.

REFERENCES

Centers for Disease Control (CDC). (2022, October). *Disability impacts all of us: Infographic.* https://www.cdc.gov/ncbddd/disabilityandhealth/infographic-disability-impacts-all.html

Dillaway, H., Mashrah, A., Marzolf, B., Fritz, H., Tarraf, W., & Lysack, C. (2022). Women's reproductive trajectories after spinal cord injury: A life course perspective on acquired disabilities. In R. L. Brown, M. Maroto, & D. Pettinicchio (Eds.), *The Oxford handbook on the sociology of disability* (pp. C19.S1–C19.N4). Oxford University Press. https://doi.org/10.1093/oxfordhb/9780190093167.013.19

Elder, G. H., Jr. (1994). Time, human agency, and social change: Perspectives on the life course. *Social Psychology Quarterly, 57*(1), 4–15. https://doi.org/10.2307/2786971

Elder, G., Jr., Johnson, M. K., & Crosnoe, R. (2003). The emergence and development of life course theory. In J. T. Mortimer & M. J. Shanahan (Eds.), *Handbook of the life course* (pp. 3–19). Handbooks of sociology and social research. Springer. https://doi.org/10.1007/978-0-306-48247-2_1

Frederick, A., & Shifrer, D. (2019). Race and disability: From analogy to intersectionality. *Sociology of Race and Ethnicity, 5*(2), 200–214. https://doi.org/10.1177/2332649218783480

Goffman, E. (1963). *Stigma: Notes on the management of spoiled identity.* Prentice-Hall.

Harrington Meyer, M. (2014). *Grandmothers at work: Juggling families and jobs.* New York University Press.

MacInnes, M. D. (2011). Altar-bound? The effect of disability on the hazard of entry into a first marriage. *International Journal of Sociology, 41*(1), 87–103. https://doi.org/10.2753/IJS0020-7659410105

Maroto, M., Pettinicchio, D., & Patterson, A. C. (2019). Hierarchies of categorical disadvantage: Economic insecurity at the intersection of disability, gender, and race. *Gender & Society, 33*(1), 64–93. https://doi.org/10.1177/0891243218794648

Mauldin, L., & Brown, R. L. (2021). Missing pieces: Engaging sociology of disability in medical sociology. *Journal of Health and Social Behavior, 62*(4), 477–492. https://doi.org/10.1177%2F00221465211019358

Naples, N., Mauldin, L., & Dillaway, H. (2019). From the guest editors: Gender, disability, and intersectionality. *Gender & Society, 33*(1), 5–18. https://doi.org/10.1177/0891243218813309

Pettinicchio, D., Maroto, M., & Lukk, M. (2021). Perceptions of Canadian federal policy responses to COVID-19 among people with disabilities and chronic health conditions. *Canadian Public Policy, 47*(2), 231–251. https://doi.org/10.3138/cpp.2021-012

Roehling, P. V., Roehling, M. V., & Moen, P. (2001). The relationship between work-life policies and practices and employee loyalty: A life course perspective. *Journal of Family and Economic Issues, 22*(2), 141–170. https://doi.org/10.1023/A:1016630229628

Shandra, C. L. (2018). Disability as inequality: Social disparities, health disparities, and participation in daily activities. *Social Forces, 97*(1), 157–192. https://doi.org/10.1093/sf/soy031

Shifrer, D., & Frederick, A. (2019). Disability at the intersections. *Sociological Compass, 13*, e12733. https://doi.org/10.1111/soc4.12733

World Health Organization. (2002). *Towards a common language: The international classification of functioning, disability, and health (ICF).* The World Wide ICF Network. https://cdn.who.int/media/docs/default-source/classification/icf/icfbeginnersguide.pdf?sfvrsn=eead63d3_4. Accessed on October 22, 2021.

World Health Organization. (2022, December). Fact sheet: "Disability." https://www.who.int/news-room/fact-sheets/detail/disability-and-health

INTEGRATING THE SOCIAL AND POLITICAL DIMENSIONS OF DISABILITY INTO LIFE COURSE THEORY

Kenzie Latham-Mintus and Scott D. Landes

AUTHOR BIOGRAPHIES

Kenzie Latham-Mintus, PhD, FGSA, is an Associate Professor of Sociology in the School of Liberal Arts at IUPUI. She received a PhD in Sociology from the University of Florida in 2011. Her research interests include health and aging with an emphasis on disability as well as chronic illness. Much of Latham-Mintus' research focuses on identifying and understanding health disparities among older adults. In 2017, she was selected as a Fellow of The Gerontological Society of America (GSA). Dr. Latham-Mintus serves on several journal editorial boards including *The Journals of Gerontology, Jounal of Social Sciences*, and *Journal of Aging and Health*.

Scott D. Landes, PhD, is an Associate Professor of Sociology and Faculty Associate in the Aging Studies Institute. He received a PhD in Sociology from the University of Florida in 2014. Informed by his interest in medical sociology, aging and the life course, and disability theory, the majority of his research focuses on health and mortality trends across the life course for disabled people, and for veterans. His other primary research focus addresses the intersections of disability and social theory.

ABSTRACT

The purpose of this chapter is to reconsider the five principles of Elder et al.'s (2003) life course theory while centering disability status as an axis of inequality. We use existing research from the fields of the sociology of disability, disability studies, and aging and the life course to reflect on ways in which each life course principle can better attend to the experiences of disabled people. We start with the

Disabilities and the Life Course
Research in Social Science and Disability, Volume 14, 11–28
Copyright © 2023 Kenzie Latham-Mintus and Scott D. Landes
Published under exclusive licence by Emerald Publishing Limited
ISSN: 1479-3547/doi:10.1108/S1479-354720230000014002

principle of time and place and discuss how cohort and period effects facilitate a deeper understanding of disabled people's experiences historically. Next, we analyze the principle of timing with an emphasis on cumulative disadvantage to establish how disability status is an axis of inequality that contributes to the accumulation of social disadvantage and intersects with other axes of inequality (e.g., race, class, and gender). Then, we discuss the two principles of agency and linked lives and employ the concept of "bounded agency" to describe how ableism limits the agency of disabled people. Finally, we examine the principle of life-span development and discuss how adaptation and resilience are contextual and an ordinary part of human experiences. We conclude by offering recommendations for both life course and disability scholars to consider in hopes of broadening our theoretical and empirical knowledge about the lives of disabled people at every stage of the life course and the mechanisms by which resources are stratified by disability and age.

Keywords: Ableism; aging; cumulative advantage/disadvantage; disability; life course theory; age–period–cohort effects

Disability is a common and consequential part of the life course that is, perplexingly, often ignored by life course scholars. Increases in life expectancy over the past century mean longer lives, but typically with chronic health conditions and/or disability (Engelman & Jackson, 2019; Lee et al., 2020). According to the Centers for Disease Control and Prevention (CDC, 2020), 26% of adults in the United States, or 61 million people in the United States, are disabled, with variation in prevalence by age group, sex, and race-ethnicity. In wealthy nations, social, economic, and medical advancements have resulted in extended life expectancies for people with intellectual or developmental disabilities, with the average age at death reaching the 60s for people with intellectual disability, and mid- to late 50s for people with Down syndrome or cerebral palsy (Landes et al., 2021). Thus, the evidence is clear that a growing share of individuals can anticipate aging with disability. Yet, as an area of inquiry, disability across the life course remains severely underdeveloped. This is puzzling as disability experiences are punctuated by age-related variation and inequalities, topics of research typically addressed by life course scholars. The purpose of this chapter is to address this gap by reimaging existing life course theory through a disability lens.

Disability in old age is a common experience, yet the experiences of those who acquire impairment in later life compared with those who were born with or developed disability in early life are quite distinct (Bogart et al., 2018). Disability status is an axis of inequality, similar to other axes such as race, class, and gender that reflect larger systems of oppression (Mauldin & Brown, 2021; Shandra, 2018). Disabled people experience discrimination in all domains of life; employment, college graduation, and marriage rates are all lower for people with disabilities (MacInnes, 2011; Maroto et al., 2019; Shandra, 2018). Because individual resources (e.g., power, wealth, and opportunities) are stratified by disability, people who are born with a disability or acquire disability early in life experience more cumulative disadvantage over their lifetime (Clarke & Latham, 2014; Shuey & Willson, 2022; Verbrugge et al., 2017).

Aging scholars frequently examine these phenomena but do so without considering how disability experiences vary across the life course. Furthermore, aging and disability scholars often view disability through different conceptual frameworks. Gerontologists and aging scholars typically apply a medicalized model of disability that conceptualizes disability as part of the normative aging process, ignoring the social and political dimensions of disability, while disability scholars – who emphasize the political and social dimensions of disability – often neglect the role of timing and the experiences of people who acquire disability in old age (Kahana & Kahana, 2017). A lack of dialogue among these scholars leads to an incomplete picture of disability across the life course.

We argue that one reason for this lack of integration is that life course scholarship has ignored disability as an axis of inequality, and therefore, neglected to account for the social and political dimensions of disability within the major theories and frameworks, despite its centrality to key life course concepts. Therefore, the purpose of this chapter is to reexamine the five principles of life course theory (see Elder et al., 2003) while centering disability status as an axis of inequality. To do so, we use existing research from the fields of the sociology of disability, disability studies, and aging and the life course to reflect on ways in which each life course principle can better attend to the experiences of disabled people. We believe that this chapter provides a roadmap for scholars to better account for disability across the life course. In addition, it provides a needed critique of traditional interpretations of life course principles through the lens of disability, thereby improving dialogue between aging/life course and disability scholars.

AN OVERVIEW OF LIFE COURSE THEORY

After four decades of work in the area, Elder (1998) first outlined the four principles (a few years later, a fifth principle was added) of life course theory in the late 1990s. Broadly, life course theory focuses on understanding the interrelationships among sociohistorical structure and change, time, and human agency (Elder, 1994, 1998). Elder (1998) viewed life pathways as one of the more intriguing areas of study – noting that life transitions (e.g., entering school, birth of a first child, marriage) were important aspects of social trajectories. Elder's (1998) first two principles considered the role of time including historical time and place and timing in one's life. These principles underscore that life paths are shaped by sociohistorical forces and *when* someone experiences a life transition matters because the timing influences subsequent transitions and can have long-term consequences (Elder, 1998). The additional two original principles focused on linked lives and agency. Elder (1998) states that individuals live interdependent lives and that choices and actions occur within the "opportunities and constraints of history and social circumstances" (p. 4). In 2003, Elder and colleagues added a fifth principle: the principle of life-span development. It states that "[h]uman development and aging are lifelong processes" (Elder et al., 2003). Taken together, over the past two decades, these principles have laid the foundation for much of contemporary life course scholarship; however, the word disability does not appear in Elder's 1998 or 2003 publication. Looking toward the future of disability and life course scholarship, we reexamine the five principles of life course theory centering disability and make recommendations, including the need for better disability-related measurement and data availability, so that scholars from both fields can expand our collective knowledge about disability across the life course.

TIME, PLACE, AND TIMING

The Principle of Time and Place

The Principle of Time and Place: The life course of individuals is embedded and shaped by the historical times and places they experience over their lifetime. (Elder et al., 2003, p. 12)

According to Elder et al. (2003), "[t]ime operates at both a sociohistorical and personal level" (p. 8). The first principle we discuss focuses on the sociohistorical aspects of time. Elder's (Elder et al., 2003) principle of time and place underscores that individual lives are "shaped" by historical and geographic context. Specifically, Elder et al. (2003) use the concepts of cohort and period effects to describe how historical context influences life pathways; cohort effects represent the unique sociohistorical conditions that people experience based on when they are born, whereas period effects represent the extent to which social changes influence current and successive cohorts in similar ways (Elder et al., 2003). This aspect of the life course has been overlooked in much of the research focused on disability. To illustrate, the most used frameworks for understanding the disability experience within research literature over the past 50 years have been Nagi's Disablement Model (1965), Verbrugge's and Jette's Disablement Process (1994), and the World Health Organization's International Classification of Functioning, Disability, and Death (ICF) (2001), which emphasize individual pathways from pathology to disability with little to no attention paid to sociohistorical and geographical context.

To varying degrees, each of these frameworks attempts to attend to the ways in which corporeal and environmental factors (often combining medical and social models of disability) impact functioning for disabled people. Beyond concerns with the way these frameworks separate the disabled person's bodily experience from the conceptualization of the disability (Barnes, 2016; Shakespeare & Watson, 2010) and prioritize pathology as opposed to self-identification as the starting point for disability, we want to underscore the lack of attention to time and place – specifically related to historical period, geographical location, and birth cohort differences in the disability experience (Glenn, 2004).

This lack of attention to time and place shrouds the heterogeneity present within the disability experience. Scholars should consider possible cohort (variation in experiences based on birth cohort) and period effects (variation in experience based on social and historical conditions) on disability experience (Yang, 2011). In the early part of the twentieth century, the US public policy severely marginalized and abused disabled people through specific policies around institutionalization and forced sterilization, as well as other state and local policies (Carey, 2010; Kristiansen & Bigby, 2005; Nielsen, 2012; Trent, 1994). In addition, even after the deinstitutionalization movement, prior to the passage of the Omnibus Budget Reconciliation Act (OBRA) to reform nursing homes, many disabled people were moved directly and without proper consent from state institutions to nursing homes (Kristiansen & Bigby, 2005; Landes & Lillaney, 2019). Although the scale and severity of these abuses have generally decreased over time, for many countries including the United States, the institutionalization of disabled people in either large- or small-scale residential settings (Rosenthal, 2021) and/or forced sterilization via court order continues today (Griffin, 2018; Rowlands & Amy, 2019).

Other social movements and resulting policies enacted in the latter part of the twentieth century had more beneficial effects (Carey, 2010; Heller & Parker Harris, 2012; Nielsen, 2012; Scotch, 1989; Trent, 1994). The Disability Rights Movement (DRM) which started in the early 1980s advocated for policy changes that protected the rights of disabled people and were at least partially addressed in legislation (Pettinicchio, 2020). The Individuals with Disabilities Education Act (IDEA) enacted in 1975 increased disabled students' access to a free and appropriate education. The Americans with Disabilities Act (ADA) enacted in 1990 prohibited discrimination against disabled people in employment, education, and transportation, as well as other public and private places open to the general public. The Convention on the Rights of Persons with Disabilities (CRPD) which was first adopted by the United Nations in 2006 to promote the rights of disabled people around the globe has been formally ratified by 184 countries to date. The uneven expansion of disability rights across time and nations emphasizes the central premise of this principle – individuals' lives need to be understood within the context of historical time and place.

Each of these policies, for good or ill, had immediate and long-term impacts on the psychological and physical well-being of disabled people. Thus, it is important for researchers to not only understand the history of disability (Nielsen, 2012) but also to consider how each policy may result in cohort and/or period effects that differentiate outcomes among disabled individuals. The recent conceptual work on the "life course cube" by Bernardi et al. (2018) offers a possible pathway forward by positing a time axis as a foundational aspect of life course studies that incorporates life course trajectories and changes in societal structures. We think this may be a good starting point for conceptually understanding how period and cohort effects (along with age effects or individual change over time) are at play in the lives of disabled people. Although demographic research into age–period–cohort trends in disability is well established (see Beller & Epping, 2021), we are only aware of one study that accounts for policy-change-related cohort effects in the disability experience. Landes (2017) demonstrated it is important to account for cohort variation in access to public education when examining the effects of education on mortality outcomes among adults with intellectual and developmental disability. It will be important for future studies to expand this effort and more clearly attend to the ways in which time specified by age, period, and cohort effects factor into outcomes for disabled people.

The Principle of Timing

The Principle of Timing: The developmental antecedents and consequences of life transitions, events, and behavioral patterns vary according to their timing in a person's life. (Elder et al., 2003, p. 12)

The next principle we discuss addresses time at the individual level, which includes age effects. According to Elder et al. (2003), important life events or transitions can take on different meanings for individuals depending on life stage. It is our goal to build upon this principle by examining how disability shapes life transitions, social trajectories, cumulative dis/advantage, and expand upon the relationship between life transitions and identity formation. When discussing life transitions, Elder et al. (2003) provide the example of early transitions (also known as "off time" or nonnormative transitions) into adult statuses, where leaving one's parental home or having children at young ages is associated with poorer mental health. They connect the different timing (and pile up) of life transitions to processes related to cumulative advantages and disadvantages (Elder et al., 2003).

However, life transitions, and the related concept of cumulative dis/advantage, are intimately tied to disability experiences. For example, disabled adolescents and young adults often experience delayed or restricted life transitions due to fewer opportunities (e.g., inaccessible education and work environments) or overprotective guardians (Fyson & Kitson, 2007). To illustrate, Howland and Rintala (2001) interviewed women with physical disabilities about their dating experiences; a major theme was identified as "delayed development of dating behaviors" (p. 47). The women interviewed discussed a lack of perceived romantic interest from peers, physical barriers to dating, inexperience with age-appropriate social skills, and interfering parents as reasons for entering romantic relationships at older ages than their able-bodied peers (Howland & Rintala, 2001). These off-time transitions may contribute to the lower rates of marriage among disabled adults (MacInnes, 2011).

Social trajectories are composed of multiple life transitions and form "long-term patterns of stability and change...that can be reliably differentiated from alternate patterns" (George, 1993). In general, the social trajectories of disabled adults vary in terms of education, work, and family formation, compared with abled adults, which were the foci of Elder's early work. Disabled Americans have fewer opportunities for normative life transitions and experience more off-time transitions, which influence subsequent transitions (e.g., barriers to going and graduating college limit work opportunities) (Stevens, 2019). These differing social trajectories are due to structural ableism – the systemic oppression of disabled people that occurs through social/cultural prejudice and social marginalization (Barnes, 2016; Bogart & Dunn, 2019) – and often reflect unequal life chances and cumulative dis/advantage.

Because disability is an axis of inequality, the timing of disability onset and duration with disability is related to cumulative dis/advantage. While Elder et al. (2003) view cumulative disadvantage as a key concept within life course theory, we continue in the tradition of other life course scholars (see Dannefer, 2003; Gee et al., 2019; Lynch & Brown, 2011; O'Rand, 1996) who have better accounted for social stratification and systems of oppression such as classism, racism, and sexism to understand intracohort inequality. We extend this line of inquiry by including ableism into cumulative dis/advantage processes and integrating the timing of disability, whereas racism and sexism (and arguably classism) are *typically* associated with more static statuses such as race, ethnicity, and gender, disability is a more dynamic status – making the timing of when someone acquires a disability status an important consideration.

For those born with disability, experiences of discrimination in education and employment domains limit lifetime earnings (Stark & Noel, 2015; Zarifa et al., 2015) and contribute to high rates of poverty among disabled Americans (Maroto et al., 2019). Moreover, disabled adults with a college education face significant barriers to labor force participation that translates into lower earnings despite their high levels of educational attainment (Gillies, 2012; Zarifa et al., 2015). In fact, regardless of education and training, disabled adults are less likely to be hired (Ameri et al., 2018; Bjørnshagen & Ugreninov, 2021), more likely to be fired (Baldwin & Schumacher, 2002), less likely to receive a promotion (Maroto & Pettinicchio, 2014), more likely to receive lower pay (Schur et al., 2017), and less likely to be satisfied with their job (Brooks, 2019), relative to abled adults. The longer an individual has a work-limiting condition/impairment, the larger the impact on their career trajectory and socioeconomic standing (Shuey & Willson, 2022), and, eventually, retirement savings and income. Each missed opportunity for career advancement leads to widening inequality for people aging with disability. For those who cannot participate in the labor force, the fragmented and underfunded entitlement programs aimed at preventing poverty among disabled Americans typically fail to do so (Ball et al., 2006; She & Livermore, 2009; Stapleton et al., 2006).

Across multiple life domains, there is compelling evidence of social disadvantage among disabled Americans. Yet, instead of understanding disability as an *axis of inequality*, life course researchers have often conceptualized disability as a medical problem that is the *result of social and economic inequality* across the life course. This is an important distinction. Previous research has documented that indicators of social disadvantage (e.g., childhood conditions or belonging to historically marginalized or minoritized groups) predict disability trajectories in mid- and later life (see Bowen & González, 2010; Shuey & Willson, 2008). Although this line of inquiry highlights that cumulative disadvantage is associated with increased risk of disability, it fails to account for disability, itself, in the accumulation of dis/advantages. As Shandra (2018) notes, disability is both the cause and consequence of social disadvantage. There is a wealth of empirical data demonstrating that historically marginalized and minoritized individuals are more likely to be disabled at every stage of the life course. However, intersectional approaches have been particularly useful in understanding how disability is an axis of inequality that intersects with other systems of oppression – leading to deeply unequal life chances for disabled women, Black, Indigenous, people of color, and LGBTQ persons (see Brown & Moloney, 2019; Frederick & Shifrer, 2019; Maroto et al., 2019).

Finally, we want to highlight an area where disability studies can enhance our knowledge about the importance of timing, specifically for identity formation. Although Elder et al. (2003) briefly mention identity in relation to life transitions, we believe that more attention should be given to the subject within life course theory. Previous research underscores that the development of a disability identity (i.e., a self-concept that emphasizes disability pride) is associated with higher ratings of life satisfaction, more self-esteem, and self-efficacy among disabled people (Bogart et al., 2018; Bogart & Nario-Redmond, 2019). However, the development of a disability identity is intimately tied to age of disability onset (Darling & Heckert, 2010). Those born with disability are more likely to form a disability identity and reap the socioemotional benefits across the life course. Older adults who acquired disability in later life are much more likely to reject a disability identity and endorse the medical model of disability (Darling & Heckert, 2010). A disability identity can help resist stigma and serve as an important socioemotional resource for disabled individuals who experience nonnormative life transitions – ultimately, shaping experiences with cumulative dis/advantage and social trajectories more generally.

AGENCY, LINKED LIVES, AND LIFE-SPAN DEVELOPMENT

The Principles of Agency and Linked Lives

The Principle of Agency: Individuals construct their own life course through the choices and actions they take within the opportunities and constraints of history and social circumstance.

The Principle of Linked Lives: Lives are lived interdependently, and sociohistorical influences are expressed through this network of shared relationships. (Elder et al., 2003, pp. 11–13)

We purposefully discuss the two principles of agency and linked lives. Although this decision prevents a fuller discussion of some important topics related to linked lives, such as care partners and social supports, we think it necessary to underscore the intimate connection between the two – a tenet stressed in disability scholarship but to date not readily recognized by life course scholars. Human agency, defined as the ability to act intentionally in a way that helps determine future outcomes, is commonly conceptualized as an individual characteristic (Giddens, 1984; Sztompka, 1994). Elder's early work, as well as later work, with Hitlin takes a similar view, defining human agency as individual-level characteristics (Elder, 1994; Hitlin & Elder, 2007a, 2007b). Hitlin and Elder (2007a) adopt the view of Evans (2002) that agency can be "bounded" by social structure, meaning levels of agency are associated with levels of privilege in the social structure with individuals with less privilege having more "bounded" or lower levels of agency. Especially in light of the earlier discussion of the negative effects of policies such as forced sterilization or institutionalization (Nielsen, 2012; Trent, 1994), it is important to realize that many disabled people have experienced or continue to experience severe structural limitations on their agency that can have immediate and long-term effects on their ability to engage in agentic behavior (Landes & Settersten, 2019). In contrast, more recent public policies that increase accessibility to socioeconomic resources and fuller participation in society likely increase or augment agency in the lives of disabled people. Other research highlights how disabled individuals employ "strategies of resistance that embody individual and collective struggles for recognition" within ableist societies (Loja et al., 2013, p. 200).

Yet, it is important for life course scholars to recognize that the boundedness of human agency among disabled people is not limited to the most severe social policies such as institutionalization. Instead, more common processes such as those specified for applying for and continuing to receive support for a disability can also bound agency. As Herd and Moynihan (2019) carefully detail, many of these processes are layered with excess levels of administrative burden in the forms of bureaucracy, regulations, and endless paperwork that can further restrict agency by either delaying needed care or preventing the ability to engage in agentic decision or exercise their fundamental rights. For instance, Herd and Moynihan (2019) demonstrate that the application and approval processes required to receive disability-related benefits are often more burdensome than for nondisability-related benefits such as retirement. In instances when the disabled person and their family need sought-after supports to fully participate in their lives, the administrative burden present within the care support can delay receipt of care and reduce the agency of all involved.

Even in instances when support services are secured, the guidelines put in place regarding continued receipt of services can also bound agency. Grossman (2018) highlights how interstate differences in Medicaid programs designed to provide personal care attendant (PCA) services for physically disabled people limit cross-state moves. In essence, receipt of these services in one state does not guarantee receipt of the same services when moving to a different state. As a result, disabled individuals reliant on these services experience a form of "intrastate confinement," which reflects a severe instance of the bounding of human agency.

We think it imperative for life course scholars to carefully attend to the multiplicity of ways in which the human agency of disabled people is bound by the social structures of policies and their related administrative burden. Yet, it is also important to recognize that this is not the full extent of the barriers that exist for disabled people with regard to exercising their agency. Attention is also needed to the ways in which linked lives are intimately connected with human agency. According to Elder et al. (2003), the principle of linked lives emphasizes that all lives are interdependent within networks of interpersonal relationships. As Landes and Settersten (2019) explain, linked lives can also bind human agency. In instances where individuals are dependent on support or care from others – a characteristic of the human condition that is universal, but more obvious in the lives of many disabled people – the ability to engage in agentic activity is directly related to the quality of these relationships (Miles, 2019). Relationships that are not supportive, or in the worst instances are abusive, work to bound agency. In contrast, relationships that are supportive can help to maximize agency. In this vein, recent works by life course scholars such as Harrington Meyer and Abdul-Malak (2020) on the role of grandparents in the lives of disabled children, Mollborn et al. (2021) on the influence of parents on children's health behaviors, as well as by disability scholars such as Caldwell (2014) on how to better incorporate interdependence into research models provide insight into how to better account for the "inseparability" of agency and linked lives.

Finally, life course scholars should become more attuned to the ways in which both social structures and interpersonal relationships are often imbued with ableism. In sum, ableism is a preference for the nondisabled body and mind that is embedded within cultural values, interpersonal relationships, and social structures (Barnes, 2016; Wolbring, 2008). Similar to the argument of Mauldin and Brown (2021) regarding the need for medical sociology to recognize the influence of ableism within this field, we think it is important for life course scholars to examine the ways in which ableism bounds the agency of disabled people. While this may occur in multiple ways in the lives we study, we must also be aware that ableism can bind agency via the decisions we make regarding whom we do/do not research, how we measure social statuses such as disability, as well as whether we adequately account for critical aspects of heterogeneity within the disability experience.

The Principle of Life-Span Development

The Principle of Life-Span Development: Human development and aging are lifelong processes. (Elder et al., 2003, p. 11)

The final principle that we consider is the principle of life-span development. Elder et al. (2003) recognize that humans experience biological, psychological, and social changes throughout their lives. This principle underscores that humans adapt to changing environments and challenges at every stage of the life course. Although human development captures a wide array of human behaviors and experiences, we address this principle by examining adaptation and resilience but highlight important critiques of how these concepts have historically been applied to disability experiences (Hutcheon & Lashewicz, 2014). Drawing from Ungar's (2004) and Hutcheon and Lashewicz's (2014) work, we employ a constructivist definition of resilience. Ungar (2004) states that resilience is the result of "negotiations between individuals and their environments for the resources to define themselves as healthy amidst conditions collectively viewed as adverse" (p. 342).

Adaptation and resilience are well represented in the aging with disability literature. Most people will experience age-related declines in function (e.g., vision, hearing, mobility, and/or cognition) (Deeg, 2005). Although this deficit view of aging is often overstated and not equally weighed with considerations of psychosocial well-being in later life (Rybarczyk et al., 2012), changes to function or physical capacity are to be expected with advancing ages. Previous research documents that onset of disability in midlife often results in a temporary dip in life satisfaction, but, for most, life satisfaction returns to similar levels prior to onset after a period of adjustment (Pagán-Rodríguez, 2010). However, adapting to these changes may be more or less difficult depending on one's past experiences, individual resources, and the environments in which one lives.

Prior research reveals high levels of perceived resilience among older adults aging with disability or chronic illness (Rybarczyk et al., 2012; Silverman et al., 2017). In focus groups of older adults aging with disability, Molton and Yorkston (2017) found that many participants framed "successful aging" as being flexible and adaptable; resilience meant "an openness to selection, optimization, and compensation and to changes brought about by the disability condition" (p. 296). Flexibility and openness to doing things differently reflects a more subjective definition of resilience, which have been underscored in the disability studies literature. Equally, disability scholars have levied important critiques against applications of the concept of resilience that reaffirm positivistic and ableistic views (Hutcheon & Lashewicz, 2014). For example, Hutcheon and Lashewicz (2014) argue that psychological and ecological applications of resilience are too prescriptive with an emphasis on independence that often excludes the interdependence that is part of the lived fabric of the lives of disabled people (we would argue interdependence is part of the lives of all people; see Landes & Settersten, 2019), and they propose that resilience is best "understood as contextual, subjective, and part of a meaning-making process" (p. 1392).

Like Hutcheon and Lashewicz (2014), we argue that resilience is ordinary and, by extension, adaptation, in all its forms, is part of the human experience. However, this does not mean that the role of the environment, including physical, social, attitudinal, and policy environments, should be overlooked. To illustrate, Silverman et al. (2017) conducted focus groups with middle-aged persons with multiple sclerosis. Participants identified important barriers of resilience such as social stigma, social limitations, fatigue, and burnout (Silverman et al., 2017). Inaccessible environments restrict opportunities and exclude disabled people (Latham-Mintus & Cordon, 2021). As gerontological work highlights, environments can be too demanding (e.g., inaccessible homes, buildings, and communities), but also not demanding enough (e.g., infantilizing caregiving arrangements) (Kahana et al., 1988). If resilience is an extension of adapting to one's environments, then it is important to emphasize that there are some environments that people cannot adapt to – they are simply too inhospitable. Yet, those environments are modifiable. Because resilience is contextual, resilience is not just the product of the person but also person–environment fit (Lai & Szatmari, 2019).

Taken together, the current literature not only highlights the potential for resilience and adaptation among people aging with disability but also demonstrates the potential for past experiences, social relationships, and structural factors to limit (or enhance) experiences of resilience. This principle highlights that human development does not stop in young adulthood, which is often overlooked by researchers. However, we argue, alongside Hutcheon and Lashewicz (2014), that resilience and adaption should be viewed as normative, subjective, and contextual and also highlight the need for more supportive, accessible environments that increase person-environment fit.

DISCUSSION

As illustrated by our discussion, there is much work to do for life course scholars regarding their conceptualization and examination of disability. Although we included many starting points throughout our discussion, we want to focus attention at this point in the chapter on one specific change that we think is imperative for moving forward: measurement of disability status and timing in surveys. As Elder (1998) notes, the principles of life course theory have "empirical origins" stemming from access to longitudinal studies of children, which highlight the mutually reinforcing relationship between theory and data. Our intention here is to underscore a fundamental problem that must be addressed before life course scholarship can move forward regarding any life course principle. Accordingly, how disability is measured in national surveys influences our (lack of) understanding of the disability experience across the life course.

In large part, national surveys (e.g., American Community Survey (ACS) and National Health and Interview Survey (NHIS)) in the United States currently use disability questions based upon suggestions of the Washington Group on Disability Statistics (Centers for Disease Control, 2018). Although we agree it is beneficial to standardize disability questions across national surveys, it is important to recognize that the Washington Group questions do not sufficiently: (1) attend to the heterogeneity in cognitive disability status – the use of one cognitive disability question does not allow differentiation between very different disability statuses such as intellectual and developmental disability, traumatic brain injury (TBI), Alzheimer's disease, etc. (Havercamp et al., 2019; Krahn, 2019) or (2) include mental health disability status (Madans & Loeb, 2013).

Although problematic simply due to the inability of these questions to fully capture the breadth of disability experience, it is important to understand that these deficiencies in the survey questions are life course issues. Differentiating between varying cognitive disabilities also relates to timing, as disabilities such as intellectual and developmental disability are lifelong and diagnosed during childhood, whereas disabilities such as TBI can occur at any stage of the life course and others often occur in later life (e.g., Alzheimer's disease). Mental health disabilities also matter with regard to development across the life course as well as regarding timing of onset and effect on subsequent trajectories (Bültmann et al., 2020; Clarke et al., 2011; George, 2007). In addition, the timing of major life events and transitions and associated resource availability has been connected to mental health outcomes (Bültmann et al., 2020; Wheaton & Clarke, 2003). Inattention to these important differences severely curtails our ability to better understand variation among people with these disabilities.

Similarly, there is an important heterogeneity among those who have acquired physical disability at different stages of the life course. Based on the principle of timing, we would anticipate that someone who acquires physical disability in early midlife versus in old age would accumulate more social disadvantage. However, there is a dearth of empirical data testing this hypothesis. We believe that this lack of research, in part, stems from limitations in our nationally representative surveys of older adults. For example, the Health and Retirement Study (HRS) has measures of childhood disability and childhood conditions and multiple contemporaneous measures of disability at ages 51 and older. However, information about the timing of onset of disability between ages 19–50 is more limited. Although researchers could construct an approximate date of onset by using the year of diagnosis question for specific health conditions or first year of impairment questions (Putnam et al., 2016), this is less than ideal as it does not reflect the true complexity of disability experiences, and these measures require hefty data management. Yet, the HRS is the only nationally representative, longitudinal survey of older adults that has some information about year or age of onset for health conditions, functional limitations, and work disability (Putnam et al., 2016). We believe that with more comprehensive and readily available measures (e.g., range of disability types, asked of all respondents, no elaborate skip patterns, etc.) across popular datasets, more researchers would investigate the role of time and timing of disability experiences.

It is important to note that addressing existing problems with the measurement of disability in national surveys is a baseline remedy. While necessary, it is only a first step. We would argue that beyond the need to address foundational issues regarding the time and timing of disabilities and impairments (e.g., year of onset, age of onset, and duration), it will also be important to develop measures that better capture the rich heterogeneity of disability experiences across the life course. Though space does not permit full development of these measures, at the least, life course research would benefit from high-quality measures of disability-related discrimination, experiences with structural barriers such as administrative burden, interdependent social relationships that include but also extend beyond close family, and contextual measures.

CONCLUSION

The purpose of this chapter was to revisit the five principles of life course theory (Elder et al., 2003) while centering disability as an axis of inequality. Our goal was to highlight how disability and life course scholars could benefit from an integration of social and political dimensions of disability into life course theory.

Using the concepts of period and cohort effects, we demonstrated that disability experiences are highly contingent on sociohistorical context. We also documented how disability is related to life transitions, trajectories, and processes related to cumulative dis/advantage. We discussed the need to understand bounded agency in the context of ableism as well as linked lives. Finally, we argued that adaptation, as part of life-span development, was a lifelong process that was inherently ordinary, subjective, and contextual. Finally, we contend that, together with an underdeveloped theoretical framework, survey measurement has held back the extant literature. We hope that this chapter can provide a roadmap for life course and disability scholars by highlighting important gaps in the literature and expanding our understanding of the life course theory.

REFERENCES

Ameri, M., Schur, L., Adya, M., Bentley, F. S., McKay, P., & Kruse, D. (2018). The disability employment puzzle: A field experiment on employer hiring behavior. *ILR Review, 71*(2), 329–364. https://doi.org/10.1177/0019793917717474

Baldwin, M. L., & Schumacher, E. J. (2002). A note on job mobility among workers with disabilities. *Industrial Relations: A Journal of Economy and Society, 41*(3), 430–441.

Ball, P., Morris, M., Hartnette, J., & Blanck, P. (2006). Breaking the cycle of poverty: Asset accumulation by people with disabilities. *Disability Studies Quarterly, 26*(1). https://doi.org/10.18061/dsq.v26i1.652

Barnes, E. (2016). *The minority body: A theory of disability*. Oxford University Press.

Beller, J., & Epping, J. (2021). Disability trends in Europe by age-period-cohort analysis: Increasing disability in younger cohorts. *Disability and Health Journal, 14*(1). https://doi.org/10.1016/j.dhjo.2020.100948

Bernardi, L., Huinink, J., & Settersten, R. A., Jr. (2018). The life course cube: A tool for studying lives. *Advances in Life Course Research*. https://doi.org/10.1016/j.alcr.2018.11.004

Bjørnshagen, V., & Ugreninov, E. (2021). Disability disadvantage: Experimental evidence of hiring discrimination against wheelchair users. *European Sociological Review, 37*(5), 818–833. https://doi.org/10.1093/esr/jcab004

Bogart, K. R., & Dunn, D. S. (2019). Ableism special issue introduction. *Journal of Social Issues, 75*(3), 650–664. https://doi.org/10.1111/josi.12354

Bogart, K. R., & Nario-Redmond, M. R. (2019). An exploration of disability self-categorization, identity, and pride. In D. S. Dunn (Ed.), *Understanding the experience of disability: Perspectives from social and rehabilitation psychology* (pp. 252–267). Oxford University Press.

Bogart, K. R., Rosa, N. M., & Slepian, M. L. (2018). Born that way or became that way: Stigma toward congenital versus acquired disability. *Group Processes & Intergroup Relations, 22*(4), 594–612. https://doi.org/10.1177%2F1368430218757897

Bowen, M. E., & González, H. M. (2010). Childhood socioeconomic position and disability in later life: Results of the health and retirement study. *American Journal of Public Health, 100*(S1), S197–S203. https://doi.org/10.2105/AJPH.2009.160986

Brooks, J. D. (2019). Just a little respect: Differences in job satisfaction among individuals with and without disabilities. *Social Science Quarterly, 100*(1), 379–388. https://doi.org/10.1111/ssqu.12543

Brown, R. L., & Moloney, M. E. (2019). Intersectionality, work, and well-being: The effects of gender and disability. *Gender & Society, 33*(1), 94–122. https://doi.org/10.1177/0891243218800636

Bültmann, U., Arends, I., Veldman, K., McLeod, C. B., van Zon, S. K. R., & Amick, B. C., III. (2020). Investigating young adults' mental health and early working life trajectories from a life course perspective: The role of transitions. *Journal of Epidemiology and Community Health, 74*(2), 179. https://doi.org/10.1136/jech-2019-213245

Caldwell, K. (2014). Dyadic interviewing: A technique valuing interdependence in interviews with individuals with intellectual disabilities. *Qualitative Research, 14*(4), 488–507. https://doi.org/10.1177%2F1468794113490718

Carey, A. C. (2010). *On the margins of citizenship: Intellectual disability and civil rights in twentieth-century America.* Temple University Press.

CDC. (2020). *Disability impacts all of us.* Centers for Disease Control and Prevention. https://www.cdc.gov/ncbddd/disabilityandhealth/infographic-disability-impacts-all.html

Centers for Disease Control and Prevention (CDC). (2018). *The measurement of disability: Recommendations for the 2010 round of censuses.* https://www.cdc.gov/nchs/data/washington_group/recommendations_for_disability_measurement.pdf

Clarke, P., & Latham, K. (2014). Life course health and socioeconomic profiles of Americans aging with disability. *Disability and Health Journal, 7*(1, Suppl.), S15–S23. https://doi.org/10.1016/j.dhjo.2013.08.008

Clarke, P., Marshall, V., House, J., & Lantz, P. (2011). The social structuring of mental health over the adult life course: Advancing theory in the sociology of aging. *Social Forces, 89*(4), 1287–1313. https://doi.org/10.1093/sf/89.4.1287

Dannefer, D. (2003). Cumulative advantage/disadvantage and the life course: Cross-fertilizing age and social science theory. *The Journals of Gerontology Series B: Psychological Sciences and Social Sciences, 58*(6), S327–S337. https://doi.org/10.1093/geronb/58.6.S327

Darling, R. B., & Heckert, D. A. (2010). Orientations toward disability: Differences over the lifecourse. *International Journal of Disability, Development and Education, 57*(2), 131–143. https://doi.org/10.1080/10349121003750489

Deeg, D. J. (2005). Longitudinal characterization of course types of functional limitations. *Disability and Rehabilitation, 27*(5), 253–261. https://doi.org/10.1080/09638280400006507

Elder, G. H., Johnson, M. K., & Crosnoe, R. (2003). The emergence and development of life course theory. In J. T. Mortimer & M. J. Shanahan (Eds.), *Handbook of the life course* (pp. 3–19). Springer. https://doi.org/10.1007/978-0-306-48247-2_1

Elder, G. H., Jr. (1994). Time, human agency, and social change: Perspectives on the life course. *Social Psychology Quarterly, 57*(1), 4–15. https://doi.org/10.2307/2786971

Elder, G. H., Jr. (1998). The life course as developmental theory. *Child Development, 69*(1), 1–12. https://doi.org/10.1111/j.1467-8624.1998.tb06128.x

Engelman, M., & Jackson, H. (2019). Gradual change, homeostasis, and punctuated equilibrium: Reconsidering patterns of health in later life. *Demography, 56*(6), 2323–2347. https://doi.org/10.1007/s13524-019-00826-x

Evans, K. (2002). Taking control of their lives? Agency in young adult transitions in England and the New Germany. *Journal of Youth Studies, 5*(3), 245–269. https://doi.org/10.1080/1367626022000005965

Frederick, A., & Shifrer, D. (2019). Race and disability: From analogy to intersectionality. *Sociology of Race and Ethnicity, 5*(2), 200–214. https://doi.org/10.1177/2332649218783480

Fyson, R., & Kitson, D. (2007). Independence or protection–does it have to be a choice? Reflections on the abuse of people with learning disabilities in Cornwall. *Critical Social Policy, 27*(3), 426–436. https://doi.org/10.1177%2F0261018307078850

Gee, G. C., Hing, A., Mohammed, S., Tabor, D. C., & Williams, D. R. (2019). Racism and the life course: Taking time seriously. *American Journal of Public Health, 109*(S1), S43–S47. https://ajph.aphapublications.org/doi/abs/10.2105/AJPH.2018.304766

George, L. K. (1993). Sociological perspectives on life transitions. *Annual Review of Sociology, 19*, 353–373. https://psycnet.apa.org/doi/10.1146/annurev.so.19.080193.002033

George, L. K. (2007). Life course perspectives on social factors and mental illness. In W. R. Avison, J. D. McLeod, & B. A. Pescosolido (Eds.), *Mental health, social mirror* (pp. 191–218). Springer.

Giddens, A. (1984). *The constitution of society: Outline of the theory of structuration.* University of California Press.

Gillies, J. (2012). University graduates with a disability: The transition to the workforce. *Disability Studies Quarterly, 32*(3). https://doi.org/10.18061/dsq.v32i3.3281

Glenn, N. D. (2004). Distinguishing age, period, and cohort effects. In J. T. Mortimer & M. J. Shanahan (Eds.), *Handbook of the life course* (pp. 465–476). Springer.

Griffin, D. (2018). Public health and sterilization of the mentally disabled: Under what circumstances should it be scrutinized versus granted by court order? *Law School Student Scholarship*, *938*, 1–35.

Grossman, B. R. (2018). Disability and corporeal (im)mobility: How interstate variation in Medicaid impacts the cross-state plans and pursuits of personal care attendant service users. *Disability and Rehabilitation*, *41*(25), 1–11. https://doi.org/10.1080/09638288.2018.1483436

Havercamp, S. M., Krahn, G. L., Larson, S. A., Fujiura, G., Goode, T. D., Kornblau, B. L., & National Health Surveillance for IDD Workgroup. (2019). Identifying people with intellectual and developmental disabilities in national population surveys. *Intellectual and Developmental Disabilities*, *57*(5), 376–389. https://doi.org/10.1352/1934-9556-57.5.376

Heller, T., & Parker Harris, S. (2012). *Disability through the life course*. Sage.

Herd, P., & Moynihan, D. P. (2019). *Administrative burden: Policymaking by other means*. Russell Sage Foundation.

Hitlin, S., & Elder, G. H., Jr. (2007a). Agency: An empirical model of an abstract concept. *Advances in Life Course Research*, *11*, 33–67. https://doi.org/10.1016/S1040-2608(06)11002-3

Hitlin, S., & Elder, G. H., Jr. (2007b). Time, self, and the curiously abstract concept of agency. *Sociological Theory*, *25*(2), 170–191. https://doi.org/10.1111/j.1467-9558.2007.00303.x

Howland, C. A., & Rintala, D. H. (2001). Dating behaviors of women with physical disabilities. *Sexuality and Disability*, *19*(1), 41–70. https://doi.org/10.1023/A:1010768804747

Hutcheon, E., & Lashewicz, B. (2014). Theorizing resilience: Critiquing and unbounding a marginalizing concept. *Disability & Society*, *29*(9), 1383–1397. https://doi.org/10.1080/09687599.2014.934954

Kahana, J. S., & Kahana, E. (2017). *Disability and aging: Learning from both to empower the lives of older adults*. Lynne Rienner Publishers.

Kahana, E., Kahana, B., & Riley, K. (1988). Chapter five person-environment transactions relevant to control and helplessness in institutional settings. In *Advances in psychology* (Vol. 57, pp. 121–153). https://doi.org/10.1016/S0166-4115(08)60979-6

Krahn, G. L. (2019). Drilling deeper on the impact of the Affordable Care Act on disability-related health care access disparities. *American Journal of Public Health*, *109*(7), 956–958. https://doi.org/10.2105/ajph.2019.305114

Kristiansen, K., & Bigby, C. M. (2005). *Deinstitutionalization and people with intellectual disabilities: In and out of institutions*. Jessica Kingsley Publishers.

Lai, M. C., & Szatmari, P. (2019). Resilience in autism: Research and practice prospects. *Autism*, *23*(3), 539–541. https://doi.org/10.1177%2F1362361319842964

Landes, S. D. (2017). The association between education and mortality for adults with intellectual disability. *Journal of Health and Social Behavior*, *58*(1), 70–85. https://doi.org/10.1177%2F0022146516683227

Landes, S. D., & Lillaney, N. (2019). Trend change in the intellectual disability nursing home census from 1977 to 2004. *American Journal on Intellectual and Developmental Disabilities*, *124*(5), 427–437. https://doi.org/10.1352/1944-7558-124.5.427

Landes, S. D., McDonald, K. E., Wilmoth, J. M., & Carter Grosso, E. (2021). Evidence of continued reduction in the age-at-death disparity between adults with and without intellectual and/or developmental disabilities. *Journal of Applied Research in Intellectual Disabilities*, *34*(3), 916–920. https://doi.org/10.1111/jar.12840

Landes, S. D., & Settersten, R. A. (2019). The inseparability of human agency and linked lives. *Advances in Life Course Research*, *42*, 1–10. https://doi.org/10.1016/j.alcr.2019.100306

Latham-Mintus, K., & Cordon, S. (2021). Contextualizing disability experiences: Understanding and measuring how the environment influences disability. In *The Oxford handbook of the sociology of disability*. https://doi.org/10.1093/oxfordhb/9780190093167.013.6

Lee, J., Lau, S., Meijer, E., & Hu, P. (2020). Living longer, with or without disability? A global and longitudinal perspective. *The Journals of Gerontology: Series A*, *75*(1), 162–167. https://doi.org/10.1093/gerona/glz007

Loja, E., Costa, M. E., Hughes, B., & Menezes, I. (2013). Disability, embodiment and ableism: Stories of resistance. *Disability & Society*, *28*(2), 190–203. https://doi.org/10.1080/09687599.2012.705057

Lynch, S. M., & Brown, J. S. (2011). Stratification and inequality over the life course. In *Handbook of aging and the social sciences* (pp. 105–117). Academic Press.

MacInnes, M. D. (2011). Altar-bound? The effect of disability on the hazard of entry into a first marriage. *International Journal of Sociology, 41*(1), 87–103. https://doi.org/10.2753/IJS0020-7659410105

Madans, J. H., & Loeb, M. (2013). Methods to improve international comparability of census and survey measures of disability. *Disability and Rehabilitation, 35*(13), 1070–1073. https://doi.org/10.3109/09638288.2012.720353

Maroto, M., & Pettinicchio, D. (2014). Disability, structural inequality, and work: The influence of occupational segregation on earnings for people with different disabilities. *Research in Social Stratification and Mobility, 38,* 76–92. https://doi.org/10.1016/j.rssm.2014.08.002

Maroto, M., Pettinicchio, D., & Patterson, A. C. (2019). Hierarchies of categorical disadvantage: Economic insecurity at the intersection of disability, gender, and race. *Gender & Society, 33*(1), 64–93. https://doi.org/10.1177/0891243218794648

Mauldin, L., & Brown, R. L. (2021). Missing pieces: Engaging sociology of disability in medical sociology. *Journal of Health and Social Behavior, 62*(4), 477–492. https://doi.org/10.1177%2F00221465211019358

MeyerM. H., & Abdul-MalakY. (Eds.). (2020). *Grandparenting children with disabilities* (pp. 1–26). Springer.

Miles, A. L. (2019). "Strong Black Women": African American women with disabilities, intersecting identities, and inequality. *Gender & Society, 33*(1), 41–63. https://doi.org/10.1177/0891243218814820

Mollborn, S., Lawrence, E., & Krueger, P. M. (2021). Developing health lifestyle pathways and social inequalities across early childhood. *Population Research and Policy Review, 40*(5), 1085–1117. https://doi.org/10.1007/s11113-020-09615-6

Molton, I. R., & Yorkston, K. M. (2017). Growing older with a physical disability: A special application of the successful aging paradigm. *The Journals of Gerontology: Series B, 72*(2), 290–299. https://doi.org/10.1093/geronb/gbw122

Nagi, S. Z. (1965). Some conceptual issues in disability and rehabilitation. In M. Sussman (Ed.), *Sociology and rehabilitation* (pp. 100–113). American Sociological Association.

Nielsen, K. E. (2012). *A disability history of the United States.* Beacon Press.

O'Rand, A. M. (1996). The precious and the precocious: Understanding cumulative disadvantage and cumulative advantage over the life course. *The Gerontologist, 36*(2), 230–238. https://doi.org/10.1093/geront/36.2.230

Pagán-Rodríguez, R. (2010). Onset of disability and life satisfaction: Evidence from the German Socio-Economic Panel. *The European Journal of Health Economics, 11*(5), 471–485. https://doi.org/10.1007/s10198-009-0184-z

Pettinicchio, D. (2020). *Politics of empowerment.* Stanford University Press.

Putnam, M., Molton, I. R., Truitt, A. R., Smith, A. E., & Jensen, M. P. (2016). Measures of aging with disability in US secondary data sets: Results of a scoping review. *Disability and Health Journal, 9*(1), 5–10. https://doi.org/10.1016/j.dhjo.2015.07.002

Rosenthal, E. (2021). Residential care controversy: The promise of the UN Convention on the Rights of Persons with Disabilities to protect all children. *The International Journal of Disability and Social Justice, 1*(1), 95–117. http://doi.org/10.13169/intljofdissocjus.1.1.0095

Rowlands, S., & Amy, J.-J. (2019). Sterilization of those with intellectual disability: Evolution from non-consensual interventions to strict safeguards. *Journal of Intellectual Disabilities, 23*(2), 233–249. https://doi.org/10.1177/1744629517747162

Rybarczyk, B., Emery, E. E., Guequierre, L. L., Shamaskin, A., & Behel, J. (2012). The role of resilience in chronic illness and disability in older adults. *Annual Review of Gerontology & Geriatrics, 32*(1), 173–187. https://doi.org/10.1891/0198-8794.32.173

Schur, L., Han, K., Kim, A., Ameri, M., Blanck, P., & Kruse, D. (2017). Disability at work: A look back and forward. *Journal of Occupational Rehabilitation, 27*(4), 482–497.

Scotch, R. K. (1989). Politics and policy in the history of the disability rights movement. *The Milbank Quarterly, 67*(Suppl. 2 Pt 2), 380–400. https://doi.org/10.2307/3350150

Shakespeare, T., & Watson, N. (2010). Beyond models: Understanding the complexity of disabled people's lives. In G. Scambler & S. Scambler (Eds.), *New directions in the sociology of chronic and disabling conditions: Assaults on the lifeworld* (pp. 57–76). Palgrave Macmillan.

Shandra, C. L. (2018). Disability as inequality: Social disparities, health disparities, and participation in daily activities. *Social Forces, 97*(1), 157–192. https://doi.org/10.1093/sf/soy031

She, P., & Livermore, G. A. (2009). Long-term poverty and disability among working-age adults. *Journal of Disability Policy Studies, 19*(4), 244–256. https://doi.org/10.1177/1044207308314954

Shuey, K. M., & Willson, A. E. (2008). Cumulative disadvantage and Black-White disparities in life-course health trajectories. *Research on Aging, 30*(2), 200–225. https://doi.org/10.1177/0164027507311151

Shuey, K. M., & Willson, A. E. (2022). Cumulative disadvantage in employment: Disability over the life course and wealth inequality in later life. In R. L. Brown, M. Maroto, & D. Pettinicchio (Eds.), *The Oxford handbook of the sociology of disability* (online ed.). Oxford Academic. https://doi.org/10.1093/oxfordhb/9780190093167.013.25

Silverman, A. M., Verrall, A. M., Alschuler, K. N., Smith, A. E., & Ehde, D. M. (2017). Bouncing back again, and again: A qualitative study of resilience in people with multiple sclerosis. *Disability and Rehabilitation, 39*(1), 14–22. https://doi.org/10.3109/09638288.2016.1138556

Stapleton, D. C., O'day, B. L., Livermore, G. A., & Imparato, A. J. (2006). Dismantling the poverty trap: Disability policy for the twenty-first century. *The Milbank Quarterly, 84*(4), 701–732. https://doi.org/10.1111/j.1468-0009.2006.00465.x

Stark, P., & Noel, A. M. (2015). *Trends in high school dropout and completion rates in the United States: 1972–2012.* Compendium Report. NCES 2015-015. National Center for Education Statistics. https://eric.ed.gov/?id=ED557576

Stevens, J. D. (2019). Stuck in transition with you: Variable pathways to in(ter)dependence for emerging adult men with mobility impairments. In S. E. Green & D. R. Loseke (Eds.), *New narratives of disability (Research in social science and disability* (Vol. 11, pp. 169–184). Emerald Publishing Limited.

Sztompka, P. (1994). Evolving focus on human agency in contemporary social theory. In P. Sztompka (Ed.), *Agency and structure: Reorienting social theory* (pp. 25–60). Gordon and Breach.

Trent, J. W. (1994). *Inventing the feeble mind: A history of mental retardation in the United States.* University of California Press.

Ungar, M. (2004). A constructionist discourse on resilience: Multiple contexts, multiple realities among at-risk children and youth. *Youth & Society, 35*(3), 341–365.

Verbrugge, L. M., & Jette, A. M. (1994). The disablement process. *Social Science & Medicine, 38*(1), 1–14. https://doi.org/10.1016/0277-9536(94)90294-1

Verbrugge, L. M., Latham, K., & Clarke, P. J. (2017). Aging with disability for midlife and older adults. *Research on Aging, 39*(6), 741–777. https://doi.org/10.1177/0164027516681051

Wheaton, B., & Clarke, P. (2003). Space meets time: Integrating temporal and contextual influences on mental health in early adulthood. *American Sociological Review*, 680–706. https://doi.org/10.2307/1519758

Wolbring, G. (2008). The politics of ableism. *Development, 51*(2), 252–258. https://doi.org/10.1057/dev.2008.17

World Health Organization (WHO). (2001). *International classification of functioning, disability, and health.* World Health Organization.

Yang, Y. (2011). Aging, cohorts, and methods. In R. H. Binstock & L. G. George (Eds.), *Handbook of aging and the social sciences* (7th ed., pp. 17–30). Elsevier.

Zarifa, D., Walters, D., & Seward, B. (2015). The earnings and employment outcomes of the 2005 cohort of Canadian postsecondary graduates with disabilities. *Canadian Review of Sociology/Revue canadienne de sociologie, 52*(4), 343–376. https://doi.org/10.1111/cars.12082

MULTIPLE SCLEROSIS DIAGNOSIS PATHWAYS: AN INTERSECTIONAL FEMINIST DISABILITY LIFE COURSE PERSPECTIVE

Louise C. Palmer

AUTHOR BIOGRAPHY

Louise C. Palmer, MA, is an applied interdisciplinary mixed-methods researcher in the Virginia C. Crawford Research Institute at Shepherd Center, a rehabilitation hospital in Atlanta, Georgia, USA. Louise's research focuses on identifying the barriers to and facilitators of functional and psychosocial health and wellbeing for people with multiple sclerosis (MS). Louise incorporates a social justice and intersectional lens to center the most marginalized groups and recognize the role of oppressive systems and social determinants of health in producing health disparities. Current studies include evaluating the impact of self-management interventions for people with MS and exploring barriers to MS diagnosis and treatment for Black Americans with MS compared to White Americans. She is currently completing her PhD in Sociology at Georgia State University.

ABSTRACT

Multiple sclerosis (MS) is a chronic condition with variable physical, cognitive, and quality of life impacts. Little research has investigated how MS outcomes vary by social identity (race, gender, disability, age, sexual orientation, and nationality) and social location (place within systems of power and privilege). However, emerging evidence points to racial and ethnic group disparities in MS outcomes. This chapter integrates core concepts from the life course perspective and an intersectional feminist disability framework to interrogate the role of diagnosis pathways in determining differential MS

Disabilities and the Life Course
Research in Social Science and Disability, Volume 14, 29–47
Copyright © 2023 Louise C. Palmer
Published under exclusive licence by Emerald Publishing Limited
ISSN: 1479-3547/doi:10.1108/S1479-354720230000014003

outcomes. MS diagnosis pathways (the time from symptom onset to the point of diagnosis) are a logical place to begin this work given the varying nature of symptom onset and the importance of a quick diagnosis for optimal MS outcomes. Whereas the life course perspective provides a framework for understanding disability transitions and pathways across the life span, an intersectional feminist disability framework centers disability within an axis of overlapping social identities and locations. The combination of both frameworks provides an approach capable of examining how MS disparities and inequities emerge in different contexts over time. The chapter begins with an overview of MS and current knowledge on disparities (mainly racial) in MS prevalence, diagnosis, and outcomes. The chapter proceeds to describe the utility of key concepts of both the life course perspective and intersectional frameworks when researching health disparities. Finally, the chapter ends with a theoretical application of an intersectional feminist disability life course perspective to investigate disparities in MS diagnosis pathways.

Keywords: Multiple sclerosis; diagnosis pathways; life course perspective; intersectionality; health disparities; disability justice

In this chapter I present a theoretical application of the life course perspective combined with an intersectional feminist disability framework to understand how multiple sclerosis (MS) diagnosis pathways might unfold differentially by social identity (race, gender, disability, age, sexual orientation, and nationality), social location (a person's place within hierarchies based on overlapping identities and determined by systems of power and oppression such as racism, ableism, ageism, and sexism), and through time (both historically and in terms of stages of life).[1] I use diagnosis pathway to refer to the time from symptom onset to the point of diagnosis.

MS is the leading cause of nontraumatic disability for young and middle-aged people in the Global North with at least 730,000 people living with MS in the United States (US) alone (Wallin et al., 2019). Despite advances in understanding the pathophysiology of MS (Bjornevik et al., 2022), only a small body of research has analyzed MS disparities (differences in the presence of disease and health outcomes by social identity or social location) and inequities (unjust differences in access to or availability of modifiable factors in the physical and social environment that impact health) (Amezcua et al., 2021). Most of this research has focused on identifying binary Black–White racial disparities with some inclusion of other racial and ethnic groups (primarily Hispanic/Latino and Asian) (Gray-Roncal et al., 2021; Langer-Gould et al., 2013; Mascialino et al., 2019; Mercado et al., 2020; Romanelli et al., 2020; Wallin et al., 2019). Few studies have looked at how other drivers of health disparities and inequities (e.g., income, poverty, health insurance) intersect with race and ethnicity to inform outcomes

---

[1]This chapter focuses primarily on race and ethnicity, gender, and class at the intersection of disability due to the limited amount of research on other social identities and MS. The author recognizes this as limited in scope and encourages scholars to think holistically about the axis of identities.

(Amezcua et al., 2021), notwithstanding evidence that economic disadvantage in childhood may increase the risk of MS as an adult (Briggs et al., 2014). This chapter responds to the call to action to address these research gaps (Amezcua et al., 2021). Whereas the life course perspective provides a framework for understanding disability transitions and pathways across the lifespan, an intersectional feminist disability framework centers disability within an axis of overlapping social identities and locations (Koehn et al., 2013). The framework facilitates the level of epistemological complexity required to examine how MS disparities and inequities emerge in different contexts over time. This approach can be applied to other disability or illness diagnosis pathways and the study of health and disability disparities and inequities overall.

I focus on the diagnosis pathway for two main reasons. First, swift diagnosis and subsequent equitable access to treatment can slow disease progression and associated disability (Kingwell et al., 2010). However, MS can be difficult to diagnose; diagnosis timelines range from months to years (Mobasheri et al., 2020). Understanding if there are patterns to diagnosis pathways that help or hinder quick diagnosis could lead to interventions to reduce diagnosis delays. Second, since diagnosis delay can lead to worse MS outcomes (Kingwell et al., 2010), diagnosis pathways may shape the subsequent disability or chronic illness trajectory and corresponding functional and psychosocial outcomes.[2] However, little attention has been paid to the entry into any chronic illness trajectory (Carpentier et al., 2010) or how they vary by social identity, location, and through time.

First, I orient the reader to MS, MS diagnosis, disparities and inequities, and the gaps in knowledge on diagnosis pathways. Second, I illustrate how key principles from the life course perspective combined with an intersectional feminist disability framework can be used to research MS diagnosis pathways.

MULTIPLE SCLEROSIS

MS Disease Characteristics, Prevalence, and Disparities

An immune-mediated disease of the central nervous system, MS attacks the protective sheath (myelin) around nerve fibers in the brain and spinal cord. The resulting damage (demyelination) interrupts critical communication between

---

[2]Corbin and Strauss developed the concept of illness trajectory to understand how chronic illnesses progress through time-based phases toward increasing morbidity and eventual death (Corbin, 1998). Although most people with MS will experience disease progression, not all will, and progression does not necessarily conform to a linear trajectory. MS signs and symptoms may wax and wane with reversal from illness to apparent wellness, in which the disease while present is asymptomatic (Smeltzer, 1991). Furthermore, advances in treatment mean that MS need not lead to premature death. Thus, the illness trajectory as currently written may not align perfectly with MS. Diagnosis pathway is similar to Corbin and Strauss' stage two of the illness trajectory, "trajectory onset," in which symptoms become noticeable and are eventually diagnosed with consequences for biographical disruption (1998).

the brain and the rest of the body, producing wide-ranging physical and cognitive signs and symptoms. Demyelination presents as lesions (areas of damage from MS) on magnetic resonance imaging (MRI) scans of the brain and spinal cord. MS is complex and variable between people and across the lifespan. Physical symptoms can include severe fatigue; difficulty walking; spasticity and weakness; bowel and bladder dysfunction; visual disturbances; and pain (Frohman et al., 2011; Khan & Gray, 2010). Cognitive challenges present in at least 50% of people with MS including changes in executive functioning, speech difficulties, and behavioral and personality changes (Khan & Gray, 2010). Depression is common for people with MS (Khan & Gray, 2010; Kidd et al., 2017).

There are four types of MS with relapse-remitting MS (RRMS) the most common (85% of diagnoses), characterized by periods of relative functional and symptom stability punctuated by relapses in which new symptoms appear or existing symptoms worsen (Rejdak et al., 2010). Within 25 years of diagnosis, most people with RRMS progress to secondary progressive MS (SPMS) with more severe and permanent forms of neurologic disability (Rejdak et al., 2010). There are two additional rare types of MS associated with more severe functional limitations. Primary progressive MS (PPMS) is an initial diagnosis of severe MS among 15% of people with MS. In a small subset of people, PPMS transitions to progressive-relapsing MS (PRMS), with continued relapses and associated deterioration of symptoms (Rejdak et al., 2010).

Epidemiological studies have long indicated that MS likely results from complex gene–environment interactions whereby a genetic predisposition is triggered by exposure to environmental risks such as infections, smoking, childhood obesity, and low sun exposure (Waubant et al., 2019). In 2022, a breakthrough study confirmed a causal link between infection with Epstein–Barr virus (EBV) and MS (Bjornevik et al., 2022). However, not all people with EBV will develop MS, and more research is needed to understand the causal chain of events that results in MS. Specifically, whereas most MS studies are conducted from clinical or epidemiological standpoints, a multidisciplinary approach incorporating disciplines like sociology could aid in understanding causal mechanisms.

An interdisciplinary, intersectional approach could also help understand MS disparities. Existing US-based research (again, mostly epidemiological) is limited to analyzing MS prevalence and outcomes by the classic demographic indicators of gender, race, ethnicity, and to some extent age. Women are three times more likely to be diagnosed with RRMS than men, but men and women are equally likely to be diagnosed with PPMS (Brownlee et al., 2017). Epidemiological research points to possible genetic, hormonal, and environmental reasons for gender differences (Harbo et al., 2013). MS prevalence rates by income status have not been estimated in the United States. However, a diagnosis of MS has negative implications for future employment rates and earnings (Krause et al., 2018).

Erasing a long-held myth that MS affects mostly White people in the northern hemisphere, recent studies indicate that Black Americans with MS have the same, or higher, prevalence rates as White Americans (Langer-Gould et al., 2013, 2022;

Romanelli et al., 2020; Wallin et al., 2019).[3] This body of research typically uses the racial categories of Black or African American, White, Asian, Native American, Hawaiian/Pacific Islanders, and the ethnicity categories of Hispanic or Latino. Rather than being emergent, the high prevalence rates among Black Americans have likely always existed but been undetected (Langer-Gould et al., 2022). Additionally, Black Americans may experience higher prevalence rates of the more severe PPMS, and PRMS compared to White Americans, with corresponding higher disability burdens (Romanelli et al., 2020).

MS prevalence is lower among Asian and Hispanic and Latino racial and ethnic groups (Langer-Gould et al., 2022; Romanelli et al., 2020). However, there is speculation that MS may be an emerging disease among young Hispanics in the United States, but more studies are needed (Langer-Gould et al., 2022). Additionally, there is some indication that immigration status could play a role, with US-born Hispanics more likely to experience a younger age of onset than Hispanics who are foreign-born (Amezcua & McCauley, 2020). Our understanding of racial and ethnic disparities is hampered by the lack of a national sampling frame to use in MS prevalence studies (Langer-Gould et al., 2022).

Compared to White Americans, Black Americans with MS have consistently greater disease burden on multiple measures including cognitive processing, walking, overall disability burden, manual dexterity (Gray-Roncal et al., 2021), and greater cognitive decline (Mascialino et al., 2019). Black Americans are more likely to have severe disability at diagnosis compared to White Americans (50% vs. 14.3%, respectively), and to exhibit more severe disability at clinical visits (Mercado et al., 2020). Black Americans are more likely to experience early mortality (before age 55) compared to White Americans with MS (Amezcua et al., 2018). Finally, Black Americans with MS are 2.2 times more likely to have comorbidities (specifically obesity, type II diabetes, and hypertension) than White Americans (Chase et al., 2022). Comorbidities are associated with worse outcomes for people with MS, including decreased physical function and increased disability and hospitalizations (Chase et al., 2022). Importantly, in one study where lower-income White Americans with MS experience worse outcomes than higher-income White Americans with MS, this income gradient does not exist for Black Americans (Mascialino et al., 2019). There are limited data on MS outcomes for US-based Hispanic or Latino populations; however, preliminary data suggest there may be faster disability accumulation for Hispanics compared to White Americans with MS (Amezcua et al., 2011; Mercado et al., 2020).

The literature on MS health inequities is sparse, but suggests that there may be unequal access to diagnostic tools and treatment by racial groups (Amezcua et al., 2021). For example, Black Americans with neurological disorders (including but not exclusive to MS) are 30% less likely to see an outpatient neurologist than White Americans and more likely to be treated in the emergency

---

[3]In this chapter, I conceptualize race and ethnicity as socially constructed categories specific to the US sociohistorical context. I use the term Black American to refer to a broad racial group including people who identify as African American.

department (Saadi et al., 2017). Research in the United States has not assessed MS inequities by other social identities, such as income and gender, or at the intersection of multiple identities.

There is a broad scientific consensus that race is a social construct (Byeon et al., 2019; Fuentes et al., 2019; Tishkoff & Kidd, 2004), yet epidemiological studies continue to look for genetic-ancestral causes for racial differences in MS. A feminist intersectional disability framework could contribute to our understanding of MS disparities and inequities by investigating how they are driven by intersecting, oppressive systems that unfairly distribute or restrict wealth and power based on one's axis of identity (Collins, 2000). The entry point into living with MS – the diagnosis pathway – is a logical place to begin this work.

Diagnosis, Treatment, and Diagnostic Delay

MS is diagnosed mostly in midlife (mean age of 30 years), but early onset (early 20s) and late onset (after age 50) occur and are associated with faster progression to higher disability levels (Rejdak et al., 2010; Sanai et al., 2016). Black Americans with MS may present with MS at a later age (mean age of 38.5 years) compared to White Americans (34.6 years), Asian Americans (36.1 years), and Hispanic Americans (37.8 years) (Romanelli et al., 2020). However, contradictory research suggests Black Americans may present with MS at earlier ages (Ventura et al., 2017).

Advances in the last 20 years have improved diagnostic precision, reliability, and reduced diagnostic delays (Brownlee et al., 2017; Filippi et al., 2016; Marrie et al., 2009). Diagnosis includes clinical neurological assessments plus MRI scans of the brain and spinal cord. MS is diagnosed if additional symptoms appear through "space" (throughout the body, or at least one lesion in at least two of four areas of the brain) and "time" (more than one clinical attack, or more than one lesion separated by time) (Brownlee et al., 2017; Filippi et al., 2016). Diagnostic advances notwithstanding, the nebulous presentation of MS still poses challenges.

Symptoms vary depending on the location of the lesions and the phenotype (RRMS or PPMS) (Brownlee et al., 2017). Symptoms can be misinterpreted as natural aging such as arthritis, forgetfulness, and deterioration in vision, or doctors may dismiss symptoms as hypochondria (Courts et al., 2004; Stewart & Sullivan, 1982). Indeed, the type of symptom may predict diagnostic delay (Barin et al., 2020). In the United States, with a specialized healthcare system, this variable symptom presentation can result in a "diagnostic cascade" (Barin et al., 2020) whereby people visit a range of specialist providers before receiving a diagnosis (Brownlee et al., 2017). Thus, referral to a neurologist, the specialist who has the tools and knowledge to make swift diagnosis is critical but depends on access and referral (Mobasheri et al., 2020). As noted, Black Americans with neurological disorders are less likely to see an outpatient neurologist than White Americans and more likely to be treated in the emergency department (Saadi et al., 2017).

Diagnosis and treatment by a neurologist generally improves outcomes and slows disease progression for people with MS (Mercado et al., 2020), perhaps because of their ability to refer patients to disease modifying therapies (DMTs) (Giovannoni et al., 2016; Kavaliunas et al., 2017). DMTs, intended to slow MS progression and prevent relapses among those with RRMS only, were introduced in 1993. Prior to DMTs, clinicians could do little for MS patients other than symptom management. DMTs are lauded for increasing the life span of people with MS to within 6 and 10 years of the general population (Goodin et al., 2012; Sanai et al., 2016). There are also a range of symptomatic pharmacological treatment therapies for MS along with rehabilitation and wellness management such as physical, occupational, and speech therapy, exercise, mental health counseling, and nutrition advice (Rejdak et al., 2010). Most MS patients need referrals to these additional therapies, requiring a knowledgeable provider to not only diagnose MS, but to evaluate for specific therapy options. Research suggests that efficacy of DMTs among Black and Hispanic Americans with MS may be lower than White Americans with MS (Pérez & Lincoln, 2021), and reasons for this are unclear. Therefore, research is needed to understand what factors may influence the association between diagnosis and improved outcomes.

Given the importance of swift diagnosis, it is surprising that papers analyzing diagnostic delay are scarce. Those that exist are either international (Kingwell et al., 2010; Mobasheri et al., 2020), over 10 years old in the United States (Marrie et al., 2009), and do not analyze racial or ethnic group differences in diagnostic delays (Marrie et al., 2009). One study indicates that the mean US diagnostic delay declined from 84.3 to 22.8 months for those with symptom onset after 2000 (Marrie et al., 2009), possibly reflecting the introduction of MRIs as a diagnostic tool in 2001.

In the United States, comorbidities increase diagnostic delay (Marrie et al., 2009), an important finding since Black Americans with MS are twice as likely to have comorbidities compared to their White counterparts (Chase et al., 2022). Being married, male, and older at symptom onset may decrease diagnostic delay (Kingwell et al., 2010; Marrie et al., 2009; Mobasheri et al., 2020). These quantitative studies reveal little about the diagnosis process from the perspective of people with MS, their friends, relatives, and care partners. A few qualitative studies describe the diagnosis process as lengthy and full of anxiety, with unknowledgeable healthcare providers who misdiagnose other illnesses (Courts et al., 2004; Edwards et al., 2008; Isaksson & Ahlström, 2006; Stewart & Sullivan, 1982).

In sum, there are many unknowns about the MS diagnosis process, but given the importance of swift diagnosis for future outcomes, MS diagnosis pathways are ripe for research. MS diagnosis pathways research should analyze if and how diagnosis unfolds differentially based on social identity and social location. Both qualitative and quantitative research is needed to quantify similarities and differences and to describe underlying processes that may be driving disparities. The chapter now pivots to exploring how concepts, tools, and methods from the life course perspective combined with an intersectional feminist disability framework could complement existing MS scholarship to conduct this work.

LIFE COURSE PERSPECTIVE AND AN INTERSECTIONAL FEMINIST DISABILITY FRAMEWORK

The Life Course Perspective

The life course perspective provides a useful framework for understanding chronic illnesses that unfold through time, space, and in heterogeneous social and cultural contexts (Elder et al., 2003). The life course perspective focuses neither exclusively on the individual nor the social structural levels, but operates in the mid-range often bridging micro and macro levels of analysis (Bengtson & Allen, 1993; Heinz & Krüger, 2001). The life course perspective applies a longitudinal and holistic lens to studying social and health problems by considering the role of past and present experiences, life events, sociohistorical contexts, and relationships. Elder (1994) originally defined the following key life course perspective principles:[4] (1) *Historical time and place*: how major historical events can have long-lasting "cohort" (a characteristic that defines a subgroup, most often, the birth year) and "period" (population-wide) effects; (2) *Timing of lives*: how the social timing of life events and transitions to major life roles like marriage, parenthood, and employment can influence future outcomes; (3) *Linked lives*: the impact of interconnected lives, social networks, and relationships through time and place; and (4) *Agency*: how an individual moves through time, making decisions, engaging with others including social structures and institutions to meet their life goals.

In terms of investigating health disparities and inequities, a body of life course research has analyzed the relationship between social identity categories (mostly race, ethnicity, class, and gender) and health outcomes across the life course. For example, cumulative inequality theory suggests that wealth is an accumulated resource that can mediate health outcomes, positively and negatively, via biosocial processes of aging (Ferraro & Shippee, 2009). Pearlin et al. (2005) theorize that low-income groups, and those subject to discrimination, experience a series of structured, compounding inequalities, repeated trauma, and stress proliferation across the life course that negatively impact health. These processes may be relevant for people with MS. For example, as noted, adverse childhood socioeconomic position may increase risk for MS (Briggs et al., 2014).

At the intersection of race and gender, Warner and Brown's (2011) modeling shows that trajectories of functional limitations differ by racial group and gender. Whereas women have greater functional limitations than men over time, Black women experience "accelerated disablement" compared to other race and gender groups. The concept of accelerated disablement may have implications for MS, since studies that show Black Americans with MS present with greater disability at diagnosis and subsequent clinical visits (Mercado et al., 2020).

---

[4]Elder and colleagues later added a fifth principal "lifespan development" to acknowledge individual developmental aging processes over the life span (2003). Other life course scholars have further defined the perspective, for example, Bengtson and Allen (1993), and continue to build on its conceptual foundations.

Other life course researchers have looked at race and structural racism in determining health trajectories. For example, Gee et al. (2012) developed a conceptual model for studying how the timing of racist incidents, or repeated exposure to structural racism, can shorten the time an individual spends in "asset-building contexts" and increases time spent in disadvantaged contexts that negatively impact health. Work by Boen (2020) illustrates the physiological process by which accumulation of stress results in health disparities through the creation of biochemical pathways to illness, often referred to as "weathering." Black Americans have higher levels of both physiological biomarkers and cumulative stress burden measured by psychosocial stress variables (Boen, 2020).

Intersectional Frameworks

These prevailing life course analyses typically use race, class, or gender as a single, categorical axis of analysis to predict differences in disability outcomes. Single-axis analyses fail to capture the complexity of multiple social identities (Crenshaw, 1989), which intersect to pattern trajectories in different and dynamic ways throughout the life course. Further, a focus on single categories obscures investigation of the wider systems of oppression that generate marginalization and corresponding health disparities and inequities (Ferrer et al., 2017).

Kimberlé Crenshaw coined the term intersectionality to counter single-axis analyses of legal discrimination, in which either gender or race are prioritized as the primary form of discrimination (1989). An intersectional research approach acknowledges the multidimensionality of social identity (Crenshaw, 1989) and that identities intersect in different ways in different contexts to produce disparities and inequities (Misra et al., 2021). For example, although people with MS have higher unemployment levels than people without MS, the rate is higher for Black Americans with MS than their White counterparts, and women with MS have reduced earnings compared to men with MS (Krause et al., 2018). Therefore, a single-axis analysis of MS as disability hides both the similarities and differences experienced by people with MS based on their other overlapping identities.

Ferrer et al. (2017) merged intersectional feminism with the life course perspective to create *the intersectional life course perspective*. The intersectional life course perspective seeks to make connections between "identity categories, individual chronological life events and the impact of institutions, policies, and broader histories and systems that come to shape identities over a lifetime" (Ferrer et al., 2017, p. 10). Ferrer et al. (2017) outline four steps for undertaking intersectional life course perspective research:

Step 1: *Identify major turning points and life events, their timing, and relation to structural forces.* This step adds an intersectional lens by moving "beyond the individual level to a consideration of interlocked lives between individuals, and also with structures and institutions" and corresponding "systems of domination, and processes of differentiation" (Ferrer et al., 2017, p. 12).

Step 2: *Understand the influence of intergenerational linked lives locally and globally.* Step 2 extends the sphere of influence from immediate friends and family to ancestors, beyond national borders, and to include consideration of migration patterns.

Step 3: *Analyze how identities, categories, and processes of differentiation unfold.* This step looks at the fluidity of identities between contexts, and "extends the life course beyond historical events, timing and relationships, to be more inclusive of the structural and institutional relations that shape lived experiences and identities" (Ferrer et al., 2017, p. 13).

Step 4: *Assess individual agency and acts of resistance against systems of domination.* Step 4 enhances the life course perspective of agency by exploring how individuals actively resist oppression.

Disability is often missing from intersectional analyses (Maroto et al., 2019). An *intersectional feminist disability approach* incorporates disability as a core social identity in the marginalization process (Maroto et al., 2019) and strengthens "our understanding of how these multiple systems intertwine, redefine, and mutually constitute one another. Integrating disability clarifies how this aggregate of systems operates together, yet distinctly, to support an imaginary norm and structure the relations that grant power, privilege, and status to that norm" (Garland-Thomson, 2002, p. 4). An intersectional feminist disability framework outlines ableism as a system of oppression, which interacts with other discriminatory systems to create an axis of inequality (Maroto et al., 2019). Using the intersectional feminist disability framework, Maroto et al. (2019) demonstrate how disability intersects with gender, race, and education level to create different economic insecurity trajectories and "hierarchies of disadvantage" over time (Maroto et al., 2019).

Patricia Hill Collins distinguishes intersectionality ("forms of intersecting oppressions" (2000, p. 21)) from the matrix of domination (how oppressions are organized). Whereas an intersectional approach helps illuminate access to privilege and power based on social identity, the matrix of domination is a tool for understanding how this privilege and power is disseminated and reinforced through social institutions. To integrate disability as an axis of inequality and ableism as a system of oppression, scholars need to "read disability into" (Kafer, 2013) their research questions and analytic frameworks. This means, when interrogating disparities, asking, "Where is the ableism?" It also means "recovering the stories of disabled people or tracing histories of disability discrimination but also how notions of disability and able-mindedness/able-bodiedness have functioned in different contexts" (Kafer, 2013, p. 149).

The following section integrates elements from these intersectional frameworks with theoretical application to MS diagnosis pathways focusing on the life course perspective's principles of historical time and place, timing of lives, linked lives, and agency.

Historical Time and Place

The life course perspective analyzes human development through "multiple time clocks" (Bengtson & Allen, 1993), which are both personal and sociohistorical. Important historical advances in MS diagnosis may have period effects on diagnosis pathways (Solomon et al., 2016). Specifically, the introduction of MRI as a diagnostic tool in 2001 may have reduced the time from symptom onset to diagnosis (Marrie et al., 2009). COVID-19 may also have a period effect on both diagnosis delay and access to treatment, as people delayed doctor visits during this time and healthcare facilities temporarily restricted in-person services (Manacorda et al., 2020). Milestone legislation is often integrated into historical timelines to understand how it improves the rights and lives of people with disabilities (Jeppsson-Grassman, 2013). In the United States, landmark legislation and legal decisions for disability rights include the Americans with Disability Act (ADA) (1990) and the Olmstead Supreme Court decision (1999).[5] What impact have such policies had on MS diagnosis pathways?

An intersectional lens requires that MS researchers interrogate how social identity and social location differentiate personal and sociohistorical time clocks. While period effects create population-wide disruptions, the impact will vary by a person's positionality. For example, how did diagnosis pathways differ during the initial lockdown stages of the COVID-19 pandemic based on factors such as racial or ethnic group, insurance status, access to neurologists or telehealth technologies, or level of social support? Who delayed seeking help for symptoms during the first year of the pandemic, and who did not, and why? How did diagnosis pathways differ transnationally based on different national lockdown policies?

Timing of Lives

The life course approach distinguishes lived experience into social pathways (also called "trajectories") of education, work, family, and illness (to name a few) through time. Trajectories consist of sequences of life events and life roles shaped by social institutions and historic events (Elder, 1994). Trajectories encourage researchers to look at past sociohistoric events and how they inform the present through consideration of transitions and turning points. Transitions represent the change from one role or biographical state to another. Turning points are major life events that dramatically alter a life trajectory. Turning points and transitions offer insights into how trajectories are formed and resulting outcomes (George, 1993) and are thus important for understanding diagnosis pathways.

Often transition timings are governed by societal norms as "on time" or "off time" (George, 1993). Some illnesses are linked to specific timing, such as chicken pox in childhood or dementia in later life. By contrast, MS interrupts illness timing norms with symptom onset possible throughout the lifespan. As a chronic,

---

[5]The Olmstead decision ruled that institutionalization of people with disabilities violated the community living and integration mandate of the ADA, whereby people with disabilities have the right to services integrated in their communities.

complex, and often debilitating disease, the timing of MS onset is nonnormative. Depending on severity and perceived impact on life, each symptom onset may reflect transitions via biographical disruptions (e.g., disability-forced unemployment) (Jeppsson-Grassman, 2013). A diagnosis of MS likely represents a major turning point interrupting multiple social pathways. Using an intersectional lens, researchers could identify if transitions, biographical disruptions, and turning points along the diagnosis pathway are experienced differentially by social location, social identity, and stage of life. An intersectional lens also encourages researchers to analyze the role of social structures and institutions in determining differential pathways. For example, the absence of federal paid maternity leave and subsidized childcare can make paid labor difficult for many mothers in the United States, leaving little time for self-care (Dugan & Barnes-Farrell, 2020). Do mothers delay seeking help for MS symptoms, and are their symptoms dismissed as associated with motherhood? How might this differ for Black mothers compared to White, or uninsured women compared to insured, and why?

Pattern, sequence, and pace (Pavalko, 1997) may be useful concepts to further analyze heterogeneity in MS diagnosis pathways. Identifying patterns in MS diagnosis pathways would help us categorize MS illness trajectories into typologies (e.g., delayed vs. swift) that could predict MS outcomes across the life span. Analysis of the sequence, or order, of events leading to diagnosis might highlight differences and similarities in MS diagnosis pathways. Pace would assess the time to diagnosis from symptom onset, but it would also chart factors such as time between new symptom events, and time from symptom event to seeing a doctor. Together, sequence and pace are important concepts that could identify potential facilitators and barriers to swift diagnosis and if and why diagnosis pathways differ by social location and identity.

Linked Lives

Linked lives can reveal how social ties affect health behaviors and health outcomes across the life span and during important transitions and turning points. Some researchers focus on the partner dyad, often measured by marital status. However, a more complete and complex operationalization of linked lives considers the breadth and depth of a person's social network, the type of relationships between network individuals and the central person (for example, the person with MS), and the nature of their interactions over time. Carpentier et al.'s (2010) work of interviewing caregivers of people with Alzheimer's disease about the diagnosis pathway is instructive. By mapping the social networks of caregivers, the researchers revealed the role of social relations in the diagnosis process, including their contribution to speed of diagnosis.

A social network does not automatically produce positive outcomes. The content of social networks should be measured through the provision of social support and level of stress inherent in the relationships to determine type of influence (positive or negative) on the individual (Umberson et al., 2010). The social convoy model may be useful since it identifies social relationships in context across the life span and considers the type and quality of support given by the social network, and its social and historical context (Antonucci et al., 2019).

Using the linked lives concept, MS researchers could map social relations at intervals during the diagnosis pathway and explore the role of network members. For example, which individuals did the person with MS turn to about their symptoms? When did they approach them, and what type of interaction did they have? What impact did those interactions have on their health-seeking behavior? Which individuals remained in the network over time, and why? In addition to friends and familial social relations, social ties to institutions like faith-based groups could be investigated for their influence and provision of social support.

An intersectional lens acknowledges heterogeneity of linked lives experiences and identifies meaningful relationships and networks outside of the hegemonic institutions of marriage and the nuclear family. An intersectional approach extends social networks beyond borders and considers migration patterns and forces. There is some evidence that US-born Hispanics experience a younger age of MS onset than Hispanics who are foreign-born (Amezcua & McCauley, 2020). MS research could investigate immigration experiences and how they inform the diagnosis experience. For example, are lower MS prevalence rates among Hispanics immigrants an artifact of lack of access to health care or alternative explanations for symptoms? Research has looked at the role of spirituality and cultural beliefs about MS as ways of understanding and managing this chronic condition (Koffman et al., 2015; Obiwuru et al., 2017). An intersectional approach could examine how these illness perceptions travel through social networks and their role in the diagnosis pathway.

Agency

Life course researchers perceive the influence of agency on social pathways in different ways. For some, individual planning and decision-making are constrained by social, cultural, and economic structures and institutions (Elder et al., 2003; Ferraro & Shippee, 2009; Pearlin et al., 2005). In contrast, social construction theorists view the life course as negotiated and constructed by individuals through interaction (Holstein & Gubrium, 2007). The concept of agency is an important line of inquiry not only for MS diagnosis pathways but also for the intersectional feminist disability approach, which seeks to center people with disabilities as empowered actors while deconstructing oppressive ableist structures. Researchers might ask: at what point does a person experiencing MS symptoms interpret physical cues as troubling and seek advice? Does interpretation of symptoms differ based on social identity, social location, and life stage? For example, do people dismiss symptoms like fatigue as a sign of getting older, or for women, of menopause? Are problems with mobility interpreted with greater concern compared to memory loss prompting a quicker visit to a provider? What symptoms are more likely to prompt care-seeking?

Agency continues to be important in the diagnosis pathway in the form of self-advocacy if doctors dismiss or misdiagnose symptoms (Stewart & Sullivan, 1982). An intersectional lens would investigate the patient–provider interactions experienced along the diagnosis pathway. How were symptoms addressed (or not) by different providers and in different settings (e.g., primary care provider vs. neurology clinic), and why (e.g., what is the role of racism and sexism)? How did people self-advocate when doctors dismissed or misdiagnosed symptoms? For whom does self-advocacy work or fail, and why (e.g., what is the role of race and racism, class, language, insurance type?)

CONCLUSION

In recent years, MS disparities and inequities research has blossomed (see, for example, Amezcua et al., 2021; Chase et al., 2022; Gray-Roncal et al., 2021; Kister et al., 2021; Langer-Gould et al., 2022; Mascialino et al., 2019; Mercado et al., 2020; Onuorah et al., 2022; Pimentel Maldonado et al., 2022; Romanelli et al., 2020; Saadi et al., 2017; Ventura et al., 2017) but remains largely limited to the analysis of racial and ethnic group disparities. Many questions remain unanswered including how MS prevalence and outcomes vary by multiple social identities and social locations, and why. To contribute to this research gap, I applied the life course perspective and intersectional feminist disability frameworks to understand how MS diagnosis pathways might unfold differentially across social identities and locations. Analyzing MS diagnosis pathways could help researchers understand processes and events prior to diagnosis and how these may shape the time to diagnosis, disability burden at diagnosis, and the future illness trajectory. Since quick diagnosis and intervention can be critical to treating MS, and delays can result in increased disability, analysis of diagnosis pathways can be a starting point for researchers to understand how MS disparities and inequities manifest.

An intersectional feminist disability life course approach provides a conceptual framework to understand how and why diagnostic pathways may differ at the interstices of different social identities, locations, and oppressive systems across the life span and in connection with social networks. Applying life course concepts like pace, sequence, and pattern could help identify different diagnosis pathway typologies. In turn, diagnosis pathway typologies could provide a foundation for analyzing pathways post diagnosis, and if and in what ways the diagnosis pathway is connected to MS outcomes post diagnosis. Fundamentally, being able to describe MS diagnosis pathways and how and why they differ could facilitate the development of a variety of interventional tools to reduce disparities in time to diagnosis, critical for optimal treatment and reduction in disability.

ACKNOWLEDGMENTS

I offer deep gratitude to Georgia State University faculty for their mentorship on both the life course perspective and intersectionality including Katie L. Acosta, PhD, Cory Albertson, PhD, Elisabeth O. Burgess, PhD, Stephanie Y. Evans, PhD, Benjamin

Kail, PhD, and Veronica Newton, PhD. With special thanks to Wendy Simonds, PhD, for feedback on this manuscript and ongoing support.

REFERENCES

Americans with Disabilities Act of 1990, P.L. 101-336, 42 U.S.C. § 12101 et seq.

Amezcua, L., Lund, B., Weiner, L., & Islam, T. (2011). Multiple sclerosis in Hispanics: A study of clinical disease expression. *Multiple Sclerosis Journal, 17*(8), 1010–1016. https://doi.org/10.1177/1352458511403025

Amezcua, L., & McCauley, J. L. (2020). Race and ethnicity on MS presentation and disease course: ACTRIMS forum 2019. *Multiple Sclerosis, 26*(5), 561–567. https://doi.org/10.1177/1352458519887328

Amezcua, L., Rivas, E., Joseph, S., Zhang, J., & Liu, L. (2018). Multiple sclerosis mortality by race/ethnicity, age, sex, and time period in the United States, 1999–2015. *Neuroepidemiology, 50*(1–2), 35–40. https://doi.org/10.1159/000484213

Amezcua, L., Rivera, V. M., Vazquez, T. C., Baezconde-Garbanati, L., & Langer-Gould, A. (2021). Health disparities, inequities, and social determinants of health in multiple sclerosis and related disorders in the US: A review. *JAMA Neurology, 78*(12), 1515–1524. https://doi.org/10.1001/jamaneurol.2021.3416

Antonucci, T. C., Ajrouch, K. J., & Webster, N. J. (2019). Convoys of social relations: Cohort similarities and differences over 25 years. *Psychology and Aging, 34*(8), 1158–1169. https://doi.org/10.1037/pag0000375

Barin, L., Kamm, C. P., Salmen, A., Dressel, H., Calabrese, P., Pot, C., Schippling, S., Gobbi, C., Müller, S., Chan, A., Rodgers, S., Kaufmann, M., Ajdacic-Gross, V., Steinemann, N., Kesselring, J., Puhan, M. A., von Wyl, V., & Swiss Multiple Sclerosis Registry. (2020). How do patients enter the healthcare system after the first onset of multiple sclerosis symptoms? The influence of setting and physician specialty on speed of diagnosis. *Multiple Sclerosis, 26*(4), 489–500. https://doi.org/10.1177/1352458518823955

Bengtson, V. L., & Allen, K. R. (1993). The Life course perspective applied to families over time. In P. Boss, W. J. Doherty, R. LaRossa, W. R. Schumm, & S. K. Steinmetz (Eds.), *Sourcebook of family theories and methods* (pp. 469–504). Springer US. https://doi.org/10.1007/978-0-387-85764-0_19

Bjornevik, K., Cortese, M., Healy, B. C., Kuhle, J., Mina, M. J., Leng, Y., Elledge, S. J., Niebuhr, D. W., Scher, A. I., Munger, K. L., & Ascherio, A. (2022). Longitudinal analysis reveals high prevalence of Epstein-Barr virus associated with multiple sclerosis. *Science, 375*(6578), 296–301. https://doi.org/10.1126/science.abj8222

Boen, C. (2020). Death by a thousand cuts: Stress exposure and black–white disparities in physiological functioning in late life. *The Journals of Gerontology: Serie Bibliographique, 75*(9), 1937–1950. https://doi.org/10.1093/geronb/gbz068

Briggs, F. B. S., Acuña, B. S., Shen, L., Bellesis, K. H., Ramsay, P. P., Quach, H., Bernstein, A., Schaefer, C., & Barcellos, L. F. (2014). Adverse socioeconomic position during the life course is associated with multiple sclerosis. *Journal of Epidemiology & Community Health, 68*(7), 622–629. https://doi.org/10.1136/jech-2013-203184

Brownlee, W. J., Hardy, T. A., Fazekas, F., & Miller, D. H. (2017). Diagnosis of multiple sclerosis: Progress and challenges. *The Lancet, 389*(10076), 1336–1346. https://doi.org/10.1016/S0140-6736(16)30959-X

Byeon, Y. J. J., Sellers, S. L., & Bonham, V. L. (2019). Intersectionality and clinical decision making: The role of race. *The American Journal of Bioethics, 19*(2), 20–22. https://doi.org/10.1080/15265161.2018.1557289

Corbin, J. M. (1998). The Corbin and Strauss chronic illness trajectory model: An update. *Research and Theory for Nursing Practice, 12*(1), 33–41.

Carpentier, N., Bernard, P., Grenier, A., & Guberman, N. (2010). Using the life course perspective to study the entry into the illness trajectory: The perspective of caregivers of people with Alzheimer's disease. *Social Science & Medicine, 70*(10), 1501–1508. https://doi.org/10.1016/j.socscimed.2009.12.038

Chase, C., Connell, E., Elliott, S. N., Jones, L.-K., Larinde, O., Musachia, A. M., Smith, E. A., Cofield, S. S., & Wingo, B. C. (2022). Differences in cardiometabolic comorbidities between black and white persons living with multiple sclerosis. *Archives of Physical Medicine and Rehabilitation, 103*(2), 331–335. https://doi.org/10.1016/j.apmr.2021.10.011

Collins, P. H. (2000). *Black feminist thought: Knowledge, consciousness, and the politics of empowerment.* Routledge.

Courts, N. F., Buchanan, E. M., & Werstlein, P. O. (2004). Focus groups: The lived experience of participants with multiple sclerosis. *Journal of Neuroscience Nursing, 36*(1), 42–47.

Crenshaw, K. (1989). *Demarginalizing the intersection of race and sex: A black feminist critique of antidiscrimination doctrine, feminist theory and antiracist politics* (Vol. 8). University of Chicago Legal Forum. https://chicagounbound.uchicago.edu/uclf/vol1989/iss1/8

Dugan, A. G., & Barnes-Farrell, J. L. (2020). Working mothers' second shift, personal resources, and self-care. *Community, Work & Family, 23*(1), 62–79. https://doi.org/10.1080/13668803.2018.1449732

Edwards, R. G., Barlow, J. H., & Turner, A. P. (2008). Experiences of diagnosis and treatment among people with multiple sclerosis. *Journal of Evaluation in Clinical Practice, 14*(3), 460–464. https://doi.org/10.1111/j.1365-2753.2007.00902.x

Elder, G. H. (1994). Time, human agency, and social change: Perspectives on the life course. *Social Psychology Quarterly, 57*(1), 4–15. https://doi.org/10.2307/2786971

Elder, G. H., Johnson, M. K., & Crosnoe, R. (2003). The emergence and development of life course theory. In J. T. Mortimer & M. J. Shanahan (Eds.), *Handbook of the life course* (pp. 3–19). Springer US. https://doi.org/10.1007/978-0-306-48247-2_1

Ferraro, K. F., & Shippee, T. P. (2009). Aging and cumulative inequality: How does inequality get under the skin? *The Gerontologist, 49*(3), 333–343. https://doi.org/10.1093/geront/gnp034

Ferrer, I., Grenier, A., Brotman, S., & Koehn, S. (2017). Understanding the experiences of racialized older people through an intersectional life course perspective. *Journal of Aging Studies, 41*, 10–17. https://doi.org/10.1016/j.jaging.2017.02.001

Filippi, M., Rocca, M. A., Ciccarelli, O., De Stefano, N., Evangelou, N., Kappos, L., Rovira, A., Sastre-Garriga, J., Tintorè, M., Frederiksen, J. L., Gasperini, C., Palace, J., Reich, D. S., Banwell, B., Montalban, X., & Barkhof, F. (2016). MRI criteria for the diagnosis of multiple sclerosis: Magnims consensus guidelines. *The Lancet Neurology, 15*(3), 292–303. https://doi.org/10.1016/S1474-4422(15)00393-2

Frohman, T. C., Castro, W., Shah, A., Courtney, A., Ortstadt, J., Davis, S. L., Logan, D., Abraham, T., Abraham, J., Remington, G., Treadaway, K., Graves, D., Hart, J., Stuve, O., Lemack, G., Greenberg, B., & Frohman, E. M. (2011). Symptomatic therapy in multiple sclerosis. *Therapeutic Advances in Neurological Disorders,* 83–89. https://doi.org/10.1177/1756285611400658

Fuentes, A., Ackermann, R. R., Athreya, S., Bolnick, D., Lasisi, T., Lee, S., McLean, S., & Nelson, R. (2019). AAPA statement on race and racism. *American Journal of Physical Anthropology, 169*(3), 400–402. https://doi.org/10.1002/ajpa.23882

Garland-Thomson, R. (2002). Integrating disability, transforming feminist theory. *NWSA Journal, 14*(3), 1–32.

Gee, G. C., Walsemann, K. M., & Brondolo, E. (2012). A life course perspective on how racism may be related to health inequities. *American Journal of Public Health, 102*(5), 967–974. https://doi.org/10.2105/AJPH.2012.300666

George, L. K. (1993). Sociological perspectives on life transitions. *Annual Review of Sociology, 19*(1), 353–373. https://doi.org/10.1146/annurev.so.19.080193.002033

Giovannoni, G., Butzkueven, H., Dhib-Jalbut, S., Hobart, J., Kobelt, G., Pepper, G., Sormani, M. P., Thalheim, C., Traboulsee, A., & Vollmer, T. (2016). Brain health: Time matters in multiple sclerosis. *Multiple Sclerosis and Related Disorders, 9*, S5–S48. https://doi.org/10.1016/j.msard.2016.07.003

Goodin, D. S., Reder, A. T., Ebers, G. C., Cutter, G., Kremenchutzky, M., Oger, J., Langdon, D., Rametta, M., Beckmann, K., DeSimone, T. M., & Knappertz, V. (2012). Survival in MS: A randomized cohort study 21 years after the start of the pivotal IFNβ-1b trial. *Neurology, 78*(17), 1315–1322. https://doi.org/10.1212/WNL.0b013e3182535cf6

Gray-Roncal, K., Fitzgerald, K. C., Ryerson, L. Z., Charvet, L., Cassard, S. D., Naismith, R., Ontaneda, D., Mahajan, K., Castro-Borrero, W., & Mowry, E. M. (2021). Association of disease severity and socioeconomic status in black and white Americans with multiple sclerosis. *Neurology*, *97*(9), e881–e889. https://doi.org/10.1212/WNL.0000000000012362

Harbo, H. F., Gold, R., & Tintoré, M. (2013). Sex and gender issues in multiple sclerosis. *Therapeutic Advances in Neurological Disorders*, *6*(4), 237–248. https://doi.org/10.1177/1756285613488434

Heinz, W. R., & Krüger, H. (2001). Life course: Innovations and challenges for social research. *Current Sociology*, *49*(2), 29–45. https://doi.org/10.1177/0011392101049002004

Holstein, J. A., & Gubrium, J. F. (2007). Constructionist perspectives on the life course: Constructionist perspectives on the life course. *Sociology Compass*, *1*(1), 335–352. https://doi.org/10.1111/j.1751-9020.2007.00004.x

Isaksson, A.-K., & Ahlström, G. (2006). From symptom to diagnosis: Illness experiences of multiple sclerosis patients. *Journal of Neuroscience Nursing*, *38*(4), 229–237.

Jeppsson-Grassman, E. (2013). Time, age and the failing body. A long life with disability. In *Ageing with disability: A lifecourse perspective*. Policy Press. http://urn.kb.se/resolve?urn=urn:nbn:se:liu:diva-92381

Kafer, A. (2013). *Feminist, queer, crip*. Indiana University Press.

Kavaliunas, A., Manouchehrinia, A., Stawiarz, L., Ramanujam, R., Agholme, J., Hedström, A. K., Beiki, O., Glaser, A., & Hillert, J. (2017). Importance of early treatment initiation in the clinical course of multiple sclerosis. *Multiple Sclerosis Journal*, *23*(9), 1233–1240. https://doi.org/10.1177/1352458516675039

Khan, F., & Gray, O. (2010). Disability management and rehabilitation for persons with multiple sclerosis. *Neural Regeneration Research*, *5*(4), 301–309. https://doi.org/10.3969

Kidd, T., Carey, N., Mold, F., Westwood, S., Miklaucich, M., Konstantara, E., Sterr, A., & Cooke, D. (2017). A systematic review of the effectiveness of self-management interventions in people with multiple sclerosis at improving depression, anxiety and quality of life. *PLoS One*, *12*(10). https://doi.org/10.1371/journal.pone.0185931

Kingwell, E., Leung, A. L., Roger, E., Duquette, P., Rieckmann, P., & Tremlett, H. (2010). Factors associated with delay to medical recognition in two Canadian multiple sclerosis cohorts. *Journal of the Neurological Sciences*, *292*(1–2), 57–62. https://doi.org/10.1016/j.jns.2010.02.007

Kister, I., Bacon, T., & Cutter, G. R. (2021). How multiple sclerosis symptoms vary by age, sex, and race/ethnicity. *Neurology: Clinical Practice*, *11*(4), 335–341. https://doi.org/10.1212/CPJ.0000000000001105

Koehn, S., Neysmith, S., Kobayashi, K., & Khamisa, H. (2013). Revealing the shape of knowledge using an intersectionality lens: Results of a scoping review on the health and health care of ethnocultural minority older adults. *Ageing and Society*, *33*(3), 437–464. https://doi.org/10.1017/S0144686X12000013

Koffman, J., Goddard, C., Gao, W., Jackson, D., Shaw, P., Burman, R., Higginson, I. J., & Silber, E. (2015). Exploring meanings of illness causation among those severely affected by multiple sclerosis: A comparative qualitative study of Black Caribbean and white British people. *BMC Palliative Care*, *14*(1), 13. https://doi.org/10.1186/s12904-015-0017-z

Krause, J., Dismuke-Greer, C., Jarnecke, M., Li, C., Reed, K., & Rumrill, P. (2018). Employment and gainful earnings among those with multiple sclerosis. *Archives of Physical Medicine and Rehabilitation*, *100*. https://doi.org/10.1016/j.apmr.2018.11.005

Langer-Gould, A., Brara, S. M., Beaber, B. E., & Zhang, J. L. (2013). Incidence of multiple sclerosis in multiple racial and ethnic groups. *Neurology*, *80*(19), 1734–1739. https://doi.org/10.1212/WNL.0b013e3182918cc2

Langer-Gould, A. M., Gonzales, E. G., Smith, J. B., Li, B. H., & Nelson, L. M. (2022). Racial and ethnic disparities in multiple sclerosis prevalence. *Neurology*, *98*(18), e1818–e1827. https://doi.org/10.1212/WNL.0000000000200151

Manacorda, T., Bandiera, P., Terzuoli, F., Ponzio, M., Brichetto, G., Zaratin, P., Bezzini, D., & Battaglia, M. A. (2020). Impact of the COVID-19 pandemic on persons with multiple sclerosis: Early findings from a survey on disruptions in care and self-reported outcomes. *Journal of Health Services Research and Policy*, *26*(3), 189–197. https://doi.org/10.1177/1355819620975069

Maroto, M., Pettinicchio, D., & Patterson, A. C. (2019). Hierarchies of categorical disadvantage: Economic insecurity at the intersection of disability, gender, and race. *Gender & Society*, *33*(1), 64–93. https://doi.org/10.1177/0891243218794648

Marrie, R. A., Horwitz, R., Cutter, G., Tyry, T., Campagnolo, D., & Vollmer, T. (2009). Comorbidity delays diagnosis and increases disability at diagnosis in MS. *Neurology*, *72*(2), 117–124. https://doi.org/10.1212/01.wnl.0000333252.78173.5f

Mascialino, G., Gromisch, E. S., Zemon, V., & Foley, F. W. (2019). Potential differences in cognition by race/ethnicity among persons with multiple sclerosis in a clinical setting: A preliminary study. *NeuroRehabilitation*, *44*(3), 445–449. https://doi.org/10.3233/NRE-182654

Mercado, V., Dongarwar, D., Fisher, K., Salihu, H. M., Hutton, G. J., & Cuascut, F. X. (2020). Multiple sclerosis in a multi-ethnic population in Houston, Texas: A retrospective analysis. *Biomedicines*, *8*(12). Article 12. https://doi.org/10.3390/biomedicines8120534

Misra, J., Curington, C. V., & Green, V. M. (2021). Methods of intersectional research. *Sociological Spectrum*, *41*(1), 9–28. https://doi.org/10.1080/02732173.2020.1791772

Mobasheri, F., Jaberi, A. R., Hasanzadeh, J., & Fararouei, M. (2020). Multiple sclerosis diagnosis delay and its associated factors among Iranian patients. *Clinical Neurology and Neurosurgery*, *199*. https://doi.org/10.1016/j.clineuro.2020.106278

Obiwuru, O., Joseph, S., Liu, L., Palomeque, A., Tarlow, L., Langer-Gould, A. M., & Amezcua, L. (2017). Perceptions of multiple sclerosis in hispanic Americans: Need for targeted messaging. *International Journal of MS Care*, *19*(3), 131–139. https://doi.org/10.7224/1537-2073.2015-081

Onuorah, H.-M., Charron, O., Meltzer, E., Montague, A., Crispino, A., Largent, A., Lucas, A., & Freeman, L. (2022). Enrollment of non-white participants and reporting of race and ethnicity in phase III trials of multiple sclerosis DMTs: A systematic review. *Neurology*, *98*(9), e880–e892. https://doi.org/10.1212/WNL.0000000000013230

Pavalko, E. (1997). Beyond trajectories: Multiple concepts for analyzing long-term process. In M. A. Hardy (Ed.), *Studying aging and social change: Conceptual and methodological issues* (pp. 129–147). SAGE Publications, Inc.

Pearlin, L. I., Schieman, S., Fazio, E. M., & Meersman, S. C. (2005). Stress, health, and the life course: Some conceptual perspectives. *Journal of Health and Social Behavior*, *46*(2), 205–219. https://doi.org/10.1177/002214650504600206

Pérez, C. A., & Lincoln, J. A. (2021). Racial and ethnic disparities in treatment response and tolerability in multiple sclerosis: A comparative study. *Multiple Sclerosis and Related Disorders*, *56*. https://doi.org/10.1016/j.msard.2021.103248

Pimentel Maldonado, D. A., Eusebio, J. R., Amezcua, L., Vasileiou, E. S., Mowry, E. M., Hemond, C. C., Umeton (Pizzolato), R., Berrios Morales, I., Radu, I., Ionete, C., & Fitzgerald, K. C. (2022). The impact of socioeconomic status on mental health and health-seeking behavior across race and ethnicity in a large multiple sclerosis cohort. *Multiple Sclerosis and Related Disorders*, *58*. https://doi.org/10.1016/j.msard.2021.103451

Rejdak, K., Jackson, S., & Giovannoni, G. (2010). Multiple sclerosis: A practical overview for clinicians. *British Medical Bulletin*, *95*(1), 79–104. https://doi.org/10.1093/bmb/ldq017

Romanelli, R. J., Huang, Q., Lacy, J., Hashemi, L., Wong, A., & Smith, A. (2020). Multiple sclerosis in a multi-ethnic population from Northern California: A retrospective analysis, 2010–2016. *BMC Neurology*, *20*(1), 163. https://doi.org/10.1186/s12883-020-01749-6

Saadi, A., Himmelstein, D. U., Woolhandler, S., & Mejia, N. I. (2017). Racial disparities in neurologic health care access and utilization in the United States. *Neurology*, *88*(24), 2268–2275. https://doi.org/10.1212/WNL.0000000000004025

Sanai, S. A., Saini, V., Benedict, R. H., Zivadinov, R., Teter, B. E., Ramanathan, M., & Weinstock-Guttman, B. (2016). Aging and multiple sclerosis. *Multiple Sclerosis Journal*, *22*(6), 717–725. https://doi.org/10.1177/1352458516634871

Smeltzer, S. C. (1991). Use of the trajectory model of nursing in multiple sclerosis. *Scholarly Inquiry for Nursing Practice*, *5*(3), 219–234.

Solomon, A. J., Bourdette, D. N., Cross, A. H., Applebee, A., Skidd, P. M., Howard, D. B., Spain, R. I., Cameron, M. H., Kim, E., Mass, M. K., Yadav, V., Whitham, R. H., Longbrake, E. E., Naismith, R. T., Wu, G. F., Parks, B. J., Wingerchuk, D. M., Rabin, B. L., Toledano, M., … Weinshenker, B. G. (2016). The contemporary spectrum of multiple sclerosis misdiagnosis: A multicenter study. *Neurology*, *87*(13), 1393–1399. https://doi.org/10.1212/WNL.0000000000003152

Stewart, D. C., & Sullivan, T. J. (1982). Illness behavior and the sick role in chronic disease: The case of multiple sclerosis. *Social Science & Medicine, 16*(15), 1397–1404. https://doi.org/10.1016/0277-9536(82)90134-4

Tishkoff, S. A., & Kidd, K. K. (2004). Implications of biogeography of human populations for "race" and medicine. *Nature Genetics, 36*(S11), S21–S27. https://doi.org/10.1038/ng1438

Umberson, D., Crosnoe, R., & Reczek, C. (2010). Social relationships and health behavior across the life course. *Annual Review of Sociology, 36*(1), 139–157. https://doi.org/10.1146/annurev-soc-070308-120011

Ventura, R. E., Antezana, A. O., Bacon, T., & Kister, I. (2017). Hispanic Americans and African Americans with multiple sclerosis have more severe disease course than Caucasian Americans. *Multiple Sclerosis Journal, 23*(11), 1554–1557. https://doi.org/10.1177/1352458516679894

Wallin, M. T., Culpepper, W. J., Campbell, J. D., Nelson, L. M., Langer-Gould, A., Marrie, R. A., Cutter, G. R., Kaye, W. E., Wagner, L., Tremlett, H., Buka, S. L., Dilokthornsakul, P., Topol, B., Chen, L. H., LaRocca, N. G., & US Multiple Sclerosis Prevalence Workgroup. (2019). The prevalence of MS in the United States: A population-based estimate using health claims data. *Neurology, 92*(10), e1029–e1040. https://doi.org/10.1212/WNL.0000000000007035

Warner, D. F., & Brown, T. H. (2011). Understanding how race/ethnicity and gender define age-trajectories of disability: An intersectionality approach. *Social Science & Medicine, 72*(8), 1236–1248. https://doi.org/10.1016/j.socscimed.2011.02.034

Waubant, E., Lucas, R., Mowry, E., Graves, J., Olsson, T., Alfredsson, L., & Langer-Gould, A. (2019). Environmental and genetic risk factors for MS: An integrated review. *Annals of Clinical and Translational Neurology, 6*(9), 1905–1922. https://doi.org/10.1002/acn3.50862

DISABILITY, GENDER, OR SOMETHING ELSE? IDENTITY-BASED INTERPRETATIONS OF INEQUALITIES OVER THE LIFE COURSE IN FRANCE

Célia Bouchet and Mathéa Boudinet

AUTHOR BIOGRAPHIES

Célia Bouchet completed a PhD in Sociology at CRIS and LIEPP in 2022. Her research draws on mixed methods to investigate the measures and mechanisms of social inequalities, particularly in relation to disability and gender. Her recent publications include: Handicap et genre dans la formation des couples. Des ressorts sociologiques classiques? [Disability and gender in the forming of couples: Classical sociological drivers?] *Revue française des affaires sociales* (1), 43–68, 2021. In French. *Handicap et destinées sociales: une enquête par méthodes mixtes [Disability and social destinies: a mixed-methods study]*. PhD Dissertation in Sociology. Institut d'études politiques de paris - Sciences Po, 2022. In French Enquête Handicap et destinées sociales: entretiens (1/2) [Disability and social destinies survey: interviews (1/2)], 2022, https://doi.org/10.21410/7E4/IIQYAR, data.sciencespo, V1. In French Enquête Handicap et destinées sociales: exploitations statistiques (2/2) [Disability and social destinies survey: statistical analysis (2/2)], 2022, https://doi.org/10.21410/7E4/SY7APQ, data.sciencespo, V1. In French.

Mathéa Boudinet started her PhD in Sociology at CRIS and LIEPP in 2019. Her thesis focuses on disabled women's positions on the labor market in France, and uses both qualitative and quantitative methods. Her previous research was on sheltered workshops in France. Her recent publication include: (with Anne

Disabilities and the Life Course
Research in Social Science and Disability, Volume 14, 49–67
Copyright © 2023 Célia Bouchet and Mathéa Boudinet
Published under exclusive licence by Emerald Publishing Limited
ISSN: 1479-3547/doi:10.1108/S1479-354720230000014004

Revillard). « Politiques de l'emploi, handicap et genre [Employment policies, disability, and gender] », *Travail, genre et sociétés*, *48*(2), 71–87, 2022. In French.(with Anne Revillard) *Portraits de travailleuses handicapées [Portraits of disabled women workers]*, Québec: ESBC, 2022. In French. « Sortir d'ESAT ? Les travailleur·ses handicapé·es en milieu protégé face à l'insertion en milieu ordinaire de travail » [*Leaving the sheltered workshop? French disabled workers in sheltered employment and the question of integration in the mainstream workplace*], Formation Emploi. *154*, 137–156, 2021. In French.

ABSTRACT

This chapter draws on biographical interviews to analyze identity-based interpretations of inequalities by disabled people in France, as these understandings are formed and transformed over the course of their lives. We combined the material from two different studies to create a corpus of 65 life stories from working-age people with contrasting impairments in terms of type, degree, and onset, as well as various profiles in terms of gender, race, and class. When talking about the inequalities they face, respondents commonly made use of identity labels (gender, class, race, disability), among those available in their micro and macro environments. They usually presented these categories as separate and cumulative, and only a few upper-class disabled women developed reflections in line with an intersectional model. This fragmentation of identity categories translated into the framing of each inequality encountered through a single lens. Respondents mentioned race, class, or gender mainly when evoking topics and contexts that the public debate highlights as problematic, while their references to disability covered a variety of disadvantages. Although the interview situation might have fueled this framing, we also showed that certain earlier socialization processes led people to believe that their disability was the source of the inequalities they encountered. Lastly, we identified three turning points that encourage shifts in the interpretation of inequalities; these are the availability of a new label to qualify one's experience, a competing identity-based interpretation for a mechanism, and access to a different, intersectional model of inequality.

Keywords: Disability; reflexivity; identity; inequality; intersectionality; turning points

According to the Handicap-Santé Ménages survey carried out in France in 2008, more than a third of people with a disability officially recognized by the French administration[1] report having experienced some form of unfavorable or stigmatizing treatment in their lifetime, such as insults or denial of rights (Bouvier & Jugnot, 2013, p. 203). This proportion is more than double that of able-bodied people and 40% higher than the average for people with lasting health problems

---

[1] People with a disability officially recognized by the French administration are those who are legally entitled to employment under the disability employment quota.

or limitations. However, this result only reflects the fact that this population frequently mentions negative treatment "related to health or disability." By contrast, they declare fewer instances of negative treatment related to other causes than people without administrative recognition of a disability who share similar sociodemographic characteristics (Bouvier & Jugnot, 2013). This result suggests that interpretations of inequalities are influenced by an association with the "disability" label. However, the prompt only calls for disabled respondents to participate in an overall retrospective assessment; it does not seek to grasp how people have come to these perceptions and framings of inequalities, or the way they have reproduced or questioned them, over their life course.

Based on biographical interviews from two different studies, this chapter looks at identity-based interpretations of inequalities by disabled people in France, as they are formed and transformed over the course of their lives. We analyze how disabled people come to mention their affiliation with different social groups as explanatory factors for negative experiences, as well as the turning points that may shift their perceptions. For this purpose, we propose original connections between various fields of literature, from subjective accounts of identities and inequalities to life course actors and processes.

We will present these theoretical frameworks, and then describe the empirical protocol used to implement them. By combining two studies, we built a corpus of 65 biographical interviews with disabled people with contrasting impairments in terms of type, severity, and onset, as well as various profiles in terms of gender, race, and class. Based on the life narratives of the respondents and the reflexive analyses they provided, we show how they interpret experiences of inequality using the identity categories and analytical grids available to them in their micro- and macroenvironments. Interpretations in terms of race, class, and gender are highly dependent on the content that has been highlighted as discriminatory or injurious by public debate. Disability proves to be a more widespread and transversal angle of understanding. This assessment might have been fueled by the methods employed, notably as the advertisements used the term "disability." However, it also reflects certain socializations experienced earlier in life by respondents who were publicly labeled as disabled. Finally, we identified three types of turning points where people reshape their conception of the inequalities they encountered; these are self-identification with a new identity label, exposure to an alternative interpretation of inequality, and introduction to an intersectional model of inequalities. In all these circumstances, both macro structures and micro interactions contribute to widening the field of reflexive possibilities.

SUBJECTIVE ACCOUNTS: FROM IDENTITIES TO INEQUALITIES

Our analysis of identity-based interpretations of inequalities envisions identities as relatively stable, although context-dependent. Nevertheless, the research has yet to address peoples' own perspectives on multiple identities and engage more directly with the literature on subjective inequality.

Disability Among Salient Identities

Whether identities are circumstantial or enduring is a controversial issue in the social sciences. Some authors emphasize the fluidity of identities, showing how they are shaped in interactions (Dubar, 1992; Goffman, 1956), while others emphasize how social structures condition the way people are seen and how they see themselves. With the notion of master status, Hughes (1945) underlines that certain labels systematically override others in the eyes of observers. Building loosely on this legacy, identity scholars noticed that certain identities are more "salient" than others, meaning they are likely to affect how people present themselves and act in a variety of contexts (Stryker, 1980). We rely on a mixed conception of identities, which allows for both relative stability and forms of adjustment.

Since Goffman's (1963) seminal text, a large body of work has emphasized the importance of disability in categorizing others, if not in self-identification. Like gender and race, disability can function as a master status, operating permanently, conditioning access to other statuses, and shaping their content (Barnartt & Altman, 2016). People with visible impairments are likely to be directly stigmatized, while those with invisible impairments might be depreciated by other judgmental labels (e.g., stupidity, laziness; Engel & Munger, 2003). A few studies have noted that disability could even overshadow the categories of gender (Lorber, 2000) and race/ethnicity (Rohmer & Louvet, 2009) in labeling processes.

In contrast, self-identification of disability appears to be mixed. While pioneering research in the United States has shown the obstacles preventing disabled people from identifying themselves as a minority group (Davis, 1995; Hahn, 1988), empirical research indicates that in France, self-identification with the disability label and feelings of affiliation with a disability community vary widely (Ravaud et al., 2002). Overall, the visibility of the impairment, the timing and circumstances of its onset, and the social and legal recognition within the field of disability influence the way people qualify themselves (Barnartt & Altman, 2016; Engel & Munger, 2003).

Multiple Identities: From Interactions to Self-Perceptions

While the notions of "master status" and "identity salience" imply multiple identity labels, the links between these labels have yet to be documented. The intersectional approach is useful for this and could serve the study of self-perceptions.

The notion of intersectionality was created in North America by Black feminists, to refer to the specific disadvantages faced by Black women (Crenshaw, 1990). It was subsequently widely adopted across the social sciences, expanding into a broad agenda to study social processes for individuals and groups based on their multiple belongings (West & Fenstermaker, 1995). Historically, intersectionality has focused on the links between gender, race, and class, but recent academic work emphasizes that disability also contributes to intersectional processes (Barnartt & Altman, 2016).

Existing studies of intersectionality provide valuable insights into the dynamics that coconstruct inequalities. In contrast, individuals' own accounts of their experiences remain insufficiently studied. It seems, however, that intersectional logics are used by people unfamiliar with the theoretical concept. A rare study of subjective experiences described by members of multiple minority groups (Black gay or bisexual men) noted that many participants present their Blackness and sexual orientation as intertwined and inseparable (Bowleg, 2013). Yet a few of the interviewees felt that race predominates and generates most of the disadvantages they would encounter (Bowleg, 2013). The sources of heterogeneity in their representations are yet to be analyzed.

Connections Between Self-Identifications and Subjective Inequalities

The links between identity labels and inequalities are obvious. On the one hand, identity-based categorizations foster inequalities, given that when gender, race, or social class are salient in a social context, they are often subject to bias, ultimately resulting in social hierarchies (Ridgeway & Kricheli-Katz, 2013). On the other hand, inequalities fuel identities. Only members of disadvantaged groups must conceptualize an identity for themselves, whereas privilege, White privilege, for example, often acts as an unquestioned norm (McIntosh, 1989).

Despite these obvious connections, there has been little dialogue between studies on identity labels and studies on subjective accounts of inequality. Multiple studies have examined minority groups' views of, and responses to, adverse treatment and inequalities (e.g., Dubet et al., 2013; Lamont et al., 2016). However, these studies focus on the identification of inequalities rather than their qualification. People's interpretations of inequality drivers and their use of identity labels for this purpose are not questioned.

Taking identity categories as a starting point, we see that they are likely to play a role in the way members of disadvantaged groups interpret the inequalities they encounter. But what are these reflexive analyses, and how do people link multiple labels? To address these issues, it is important to acknowledge first that reflections develop in relation to the influence of social environments and second that they can shift over time. A life course perspective provides significant contributions in both these areas.

REFLEXIVITY THROUGH A LIFE COURSE PERSPECTIVE

The concepts of a life course approach are particularly useful when it comes to capturing the interrelationships between agency and structural influences over the lifetime, as well as in capturing the dynamics and evolutions of situations. After presenting this conceptual toolkit, we will expand on the terminology of evolutions, explaining why we focus on turning points, in contrast to the rich literature on life cycle ages and life transitions for disabled people.

Use of Agency and Structural Influences

"Agency" and "Linked Lives" are two cornerstones of the life course concept developed by Elder (1985), a pioneer in this literature. By combining these two notions, Elder surmounted a major challenge, by linking people's intentions and their capacity for action to the social circumstances imposed on them. The author also emphasized that such social circumstances operate in different domains (e.g., family, professional, organizational) and at different levels (interpersonal relationships, national institutional frameworks, etc.)

Several French studies have echoed this view. As Santelli (2019) noted, much of the existing French research on life paths ("parcours de vie") shares common ground with Elder's model, even if it does not cite it. Research on socialization also offers some related contributions, and although top-down views within this literature led Elder to abandon the concept, other work addresses the interplay of agency and structural influences over a lifetime (Dubar, 2015).

Turning Points in Disabled People's Lives

Another major advantage of the life course approach is documenting processes in a dynamic way, by reporting evolutions over time. This perspective has allowed for instructive analyses of the lives of disabled people, raising the challenges presented by life-cycle age norms (Heller, 2011; Priestley, 2003) and/or transitions to typical adult statuses (Gibson et al., 2014; Janus, 2009; Wells et al., 2003).

The temporal concept of turning points has been less used in disability research. While transitions designate the entry and exit of predetermined social statuses and roles (e.g., school, employment, conjugality), turning points cover noncodified evolutions either in material situations and/or in representations (Elder et al., 2003; Wethington et al., 1997).

However, the notion of turning points has the potential to account for a range of transformative episodes in the lives of disabled people, while avoiding a framing that would consider disability itself as a personal and tragic turning point (Barnes & Oliver, 2012). Far from reproducing a self-pitying discourse, we intend to document the conditions that encourage a sharpening of reflexivity.

METHODS

The chapter is based on 65 biographical interviews with disabled people from two different studies, respectively led by Célia and Mathéa in France. Biographical interviews were particularly useful for our investigation, as they provided both subjective narratives and life course perspectives (Caradec et al., 2012).

The two studies share some similarities (Table 1). They were both conducted in French in France, over close time periods. The two authors have similar profiles (being perceived as women, White, in their 20s, university educated, and nondisabled). The two surveys also complement each other as their target groups differ to some extent. Both focus on working-age people living in mainstream housing, but they differ in terms of gender, type and onset of the impairment, and

Table 1. Comparison of the Two Studies.

	Célia	Mathéa
Methods		
Number	37 biographical interviews	28 biographical interviews
Dates	December 2019 – June 2020	August 2020 – December 2021
Questions	"Current situation"; educational, professional, marital and parental backgrounds, other unpaid activities. Follow-up questions concerning terms such as "success," "good/bad situation" or "devaluation" to explore conceptions of inequalities and hierarchies	Free presentation; educational background, work experience, periods without work and unpaid activities, specificity of life as a disabled woman. Follow-up questions concerning events related to marital and family history and the health sphere; use of public policies.
Average length	2 h 10 min	2 h 10 min
Interview format	Face-to-face (22), videoconference (11), phone (4)	Face-to-face (1), videoconference (14), phone (13)
Recruitment	Advertisement, snowball sampling, personal network	Advertisement, personal network
Criteria		
Timing of onset	Birth, childhood, or teenage years	Unspecified
Types of impairments	Visual impairments; specific learning disorders (SLDs)	Mobility impairments; visual impairments; chronic diseases
Age	30–55 years old	25–65 years old
Characteristics of samples		
Gender identification	20 women, 15 men, and 2 nonbinary people	28 women
Education	5 years or more of higher education (4), 3 or 4 years of higher education (9), 2 years of higher education (11), high school degree (7), technical diploma (5), secondary school degree or no diploma (3)	5 years or more of higher education (13) 3 or 4 years of higher education (7), technical diploma (3), secondary school degree or no diploma (5)
Characteristics of impairments	Birth, childhood or teenagehood onset (37) Visual impairments (14), SLD (14), multiple impairments (9)	Adult onset (15), birth, childhood or teenagehood (12). Mobility impairments (12), chronic diseases (9), visual impairments (4), multiple impairments (3).
Identification with disability	24 with "disabled people," 6 "with a disability," 7 don't use the term	28 with "disabled people"
Race (declared or assigned by us)	White (31), Arab (4), Latino (1), Asian (1)	White (18), Arab (4), Black (2), unknown (4)

Source: Corpus of interviews conducted by Célia Bouchet and Mathéa Boudinet.

self-identification as disabled people. Célia targeted people with visual impairments or early onset specific learning disorders (SLDs) such as dyslexia, dyspraxia, and dyscalculia, while Mathéa focused on women with mobility impairments, visual impairments, or chronic diseases. Subsequently, the two advertisements also produced different framing effects. Célia referred to specific impairment groups and specified the timing of onset, whereas Mathéa referred to women with specific impairments. Both included the term disability, but it was not central in either case.

Both authors collected data on social class, gender, race, and the role individuals attribute to these factors in relation to their life course. Mathéa also openly asked the person to reflect on the specificity of their life course as a "disabled woman" at the end of the interview, while Célia most typically captured the episodes of inequality (and their identity-based interpretations) through follow-up questions, asking for clarification of terms such as "devaluation."

The samples include diverse profiles in terms of education, race, and (for Célia's study) gender and disability self-identification. College graduates are however slightly overrepresented, compared to the composition of the French disabled population (Vérétout, 2015).

The first analyses of the data were carried out separately by each author. They both created their own codebooks based on their research questions and treated their materials on different CAQDAS (RQDA, Atlas TI). Each author started to code deductively their material according to the themes they had selected for their interview questions. They then added inductively new thematic codes as they read the transcripts of the interviews. They shared their main results concerning intersectionality and perception of inequalities, by comparing the codes from their respective analyses. During this triangulation process, the team noticed a number of similarities in the two datasets, such as the overwhelming role of self-identification to disability in the interpretation of inequalities. They also found that their results complement each other, with Mathéa's interview featuring more perceptions of racial discrimination and Célia's interview, perceptions of discrimination due to socioeconomic background. Last, each author selected the cases from their study that illustrated best each chosen theme, and they designed together the global structure of the paper.

RESULTS

Separate Identity Labels to Describe Inequalities

Our respondents noticed inequalities in their daily lives, interpreted them, and reflected on their origins, often building on identity labels (gender, class, race, disability).[2] Overall, the identities of disadvantaged groups are more remarkable than those of privileged groups. The respondents could not always obtain official "disability" status, as this is dependent on the legal and social framework. Furthermore, most respondents framed the categories they employed as mutually exclusive: they typically aggregated them in a cumulative (e.g., "double penalization") or analogical manner (e.g., "like women"). Only a few highly educated, disabled women (3–5 years of higher education) developed reflections implicitly or explicitly rooted in intersectional theory.

---

[2] A minority of people considered that none of the categories (gender, class, race, disability) had played a role in their life paths. This group is composed of people with very heterogeneous profiles, both in terms of class, generations, types, and onset of impairments.

In their biographical accounts, people intertwined identities and inequalities, mentioning their self-identifications as they recalled the inequalities they encountered. Members of multiple minority groups, who knew they were exposed to various types of inequalities, were likely to refer to several identity labels. On the contrary, people who, apart from their disability, belonged to privileged groups (White, male, heterosexual, upper-middle class) only cited "disability" when describing their life course and the disadvantages they encountered. For instance, Jean Kieffer, a blind music teacher, presented the factors involved in hiring decisions in a binary way.[3] He distinguished his skills from prejudices about disability.

> I had a hard time getting a job! Because it doesn't depend on the skills you possess, it also depends on the openness of the different protagonists! In particular, the director of the music school, for example. Who says yes or no, depending on whether he has prejudices about disability. And that goes for any job... "Yes, the person - I'll give it a shot, I'm open, I'll give it a shot, I'll give it a shot, the person is suitable to teach." And then you have people who are closed-minded. And I've experienced that! People who tell you, "No, a blind person can't teach." So as a result, because a blind person can't teach for them, there is no openness, so there is no possibility of being hired. (Jean Kieffer, visual impairment)

As a White heterosexual man who inherited significant economic resources from his parents, Jean Kieffer did not think of any identity label other than disability that influenced the "openness" of potential employers. By extension, over the entire interview, disability was the only category of self-identification to which he referred.

Being part of a disadvantaged group is not enough to activate an identity label, self-identification is also necessary. This is strikingly evident for self-identification with disability. In Célia's sample, almost half of the respondents with an SLD never used the term "disabled person" or the term "disability." This result can partly be explained by the fact that French disability legislation has only addressed this condition since 2005, and social representations have not evolved in a corresponding manner.[4] We will expand on this result in the last section.

A second important framing effect is that most respondents treat the identity labels available to them (i.e., identities that are both disadvantaged and socially prevalent) as separate. In their view, each label represents an alternative explanation of the inequalities they experienced. The case of Karima Nadin, a woman with a mobility impairment, illustrates this. She was required to do an internship to obtain her technical certificate (French "Brevet d'études professionnelles"). She described poor working conditions, as her boss refused to give her meal vouchers and commented frequently on her inability to get work done. During the interview, she tried to determine which of her identities led her superior to treat her badly: "At first I thought, 'Because I'm an intern.' Then I thought:

---

[3]All first and last names are pseudonyms.
[4]Act No. 2005-102 of 11 February 2005 on equal rights and opportunity, the participation and integration of disabled people as fully fledged citizens.

'Well, because I'm a Rebeu [slang for Arab]'. And then I thought, 'I have no idea. Is it because I'm disabled? Actually, I don't really know, um... I know he didn't like me'." (Karima Nadin, mobility impairment). She did not think about the interconnection between labels and perceived them as distinct.

This type of reasoning follows an additive and cumulative logic. In Mathéa's study, as many as a quarter of disabled women (7 out of 28) used the term "double penalization," especially when asked to reflect on the specificity of their experience as disabled women. While Célia's study did not include the same question, a few respondents came up with metaphors based on the same idea of an accumulation "for me, it [discrimination] is like a mille feuille: dyslexia, epilepsy, non-binarity..." (Jackie Raynal, SLD).[5]

This view of identities and identity-based inequalities also favors the use of analogy: one label works "like" another, and there is little reflection on the possible connections between them. During the interviews, four White disabled respondents drew an analogy between disability and race or ethnicity, assuming similarities (community belonging) or differences (level of exposure to discrimination). Strikingly, a disabled woman even drew an analogy between disability and gender.

> Once we're in a relationship... we basically lose all our rights [reference to the method used to calculate disability welfare benefits under French law]. It's not quite that simple, but that's about it. (In an agitated tone) So... what's this bullshit? That is to say, the other partner in the couple becomes responsible for you! But why should it be so? It means that we're not a whole person... I don't know... [...] It somehow gives the other person power over you! Sort of, like before, over women who stayed at home... it's, almost the same thing, practically. (Carolina Mendoza, visual impairment)

Carolina Mendoza drew a parallel between two asymmetrical forms of economic dependence among (implicitly heterosexual) couples. On the one hand, between able-bodied men and able-bodied women who "stayed at home" in the past (based on the idea that this type of situation would no longer exist today) and on the other hand, between disabled people and their able-bodied partners. She used a "we" that placed her on the side of disabled people, without indicating the same affinity toward the group of women ("like before, the women who stayed" rather than "like before, we stayed"). She, thus, connected the two labels using an analogy.

Finally, while the vast majority of our sample shared the idea that identity mechanisms were separate and cumulative, this view was not hegemonic. A few highly educated disabled women (3–5 years of higher education) developed a rhetoric consistent with the intersectional framework, referring to a unique configuration between gender and disability. For example, Lucile Morin, a graduate with a master's degree, with both visual and hearing impairments, successively compared her income to that of her colleagues, able-bodied or disabled people, men or women. In doing so, she emphasized the uniqueness of her position as a disabled woman.

---

[5]A mille-feuille pastry is made out of layers of separate pastry sheets.

> In terms of... disabled people, disabled women, I'm in the 1%. Because first, very few disabled people work. Even fewer women. To start with, women work less than men, in terms of the employment rate. Disabled women work less than... than disabled men. And on top of that, disabled women... Well, disabled people are less qualified. With 5 years of higher education... Among the general population, people with 5 years of higher education are not the majority. And among the disabled working population, people with 5 years of higher education are even less the majority. And if they are women... you see the funnel! (Lucile Morin, visual and hearing impairments)

In this example, Lucile Morin framed her situation in an intersectional way, even though she did not actually refer to intersectional theory per se. She ended up specifically comparing herself to disabled women, as she considered that this group faced unique challenges. Relying on statistics, she presented the range of difficulties that these women face, using a "funnel" metaphor instead of an additive approach.

The fragmentation of identity labels results in most, although not all, respondents seeking to identify the mechanisms of each inequality they faced through a single lens. As we will see, the identity category they selected for their interpretation depends on the context in which the episode took place, as well as their socialization earlier in life.

Race, Class, Gender: The Social and Political Salience of Identity-Based Inequalities

Interpretations of inequality in terms of race, class, or gender are strongly shaped by the topics and contexts that public debate highlights as problematic, such as racial segregation or the gender wage gap. These framings facilitated our respondents' detection of such inequalities and their qualifications in terms of identity. In other words, the social and political focus on certain modalities of identity-based inequalities contributed to making identities salient to people in those specific circumstances.

Let us consider race first. In our samples, forced spatial division between racial groups and stereotypes tied to racial labels were both perceived as manifestations of racism. Karima Nadin, whom we mentioned earlier, described how she was shocked by the racial segmentation of workspaces when she entered one of her previous offices.

> When I entered the facility, there was a door and ..., so it's like platforms and there was... I promise you it's true, there was... they had... they had put them by color! By color! By skin color! And I promise you... No, but I promise you...[...] I turned my head to the left, there were people who were from Overseas France. So they were pretty brown. On the right, they were more white. And they had red hair. And there, next to them, they were more from the Maghreb. I promise you it's true! (Karima Nadin, mobility impairment)

A few respondents also identified stereotypical comments about them as racist. Marion Corbin, a visually impaired second-generation Asian masseuse, reported being regularly mistaken for a prostitute: "It's true that clients often ask me if I am 'that kind of masseuse'" (Marion Corbin, visual impairment).

The second form of identity-based interpretation of inequalities, through the lens of social class, was particularly invoked in the case of exclusion or bullying at school. These reflections came from people who had experienced diverse modes of schooling (mainstream or specialized). Thierry Bernat, a blind man, and Alison Todd, a woman with SLD, both had parents who were small shopkeepers. They each described being excluded by other children because of their social class in mainstream schools: "In that neighborhood, there were mostly bourgeois, upper-class people. And so it was... it was a bit complicated, this... hanging out with them. Because I didn't have their codes at all, I didn't speak like them" (Alison Todd, SLD). As they noticed a contrast between the other students' lifestyles and their own, both respondents identified it as a driver for their exclusion.

Finally, women adopted a gender perspective to interpret certain inequalities that received particular attention in the academic world and in public debate over the past few decades, for example, vertical and horizontal divisions in the labor market, wage gaps, and violence against women. Several respondents mentioned the concentration of women (whether able-bodied or disabled) in specific sectors and/or in low-level positions. Peggy Toullec combined both these aspects in her reflexive statement.

> Gender discrimination, no, I can... I can describe it, well, through the lens of the gender determinism that I experienced. Because all the [other] women in my family uh... had... no or little education. When they had some, it was in the domestic arts. [...] Above all, I have worked in professions that are very strongly gendered, with a low gender mix, and which, curiously, pay very little! (Peggy Toullec, chronic illness)

Drawing on the sociological concepts she learned during her university years, Peggy Toullec analyzed her own employment disadvantages and those of the women in her family in terms of "gender determinism." Unfavorable influences acted both vertically (obstacles to further education for women in the context of the 1970s) and horizontally (orientation toward typically female sectors that are given little market value).

Furthermore, the respondents recurrently emphasized one specific aspect of gender inequality in employment, the wage gap.

> So actually, in terms of wages, compared to women...in...in the company, I had no...I never had any problems with my disability, right. But compared to men at the same level - uh... at the same level, since I was... a supervisor and an executive - I faced a big wage gap. (She smiles) [...] Afterwards, they tried to explain to me that, no, I wasn't doing the same job as the uh... well the... the title I had in the company, and so on. I think that's pretty much what all women hear. (Martine Fabre, mobility impairment)

Martine Fabre clearly identified the gap that separates her from her male colleagues, and she was not convinced by the justifications her superiors put forward. She believed her situation mirrored a systemic problem and was "pretty much what all women heard."

Finally, many of the women in our samples reported violence in a wide variety of forms, ranging from harassment at school and in family settings during their adolescence to sexual harassment in a professional context, or the order to undress for a medical examination in a room.

A notable difference from other identity-based interpretations of inequality is that when the women we interviewed referred to such violence, they did not systematically evoke the role of gender, although their vocabulary was gender-specific. They dismissed other influences, such as disability: "[This depreciation wasn't] about my disability! It was about my appearance. [...] it bothered them that I, who... had a great figure, didn't use it to please the boys" (Audrey Rolland, SLD). The counterinterpretations were most explicit when the context might have pointed to these other factors. For instance, Mélodie Garcia, a woman with a visual and hearing impairment, immediately specified that "disability has nothing to do with it" as she finished explaining how, as a young adult, she was sexually assaulted at a vocational center for visually impaired people.

Invoking Disability: From the Interview Context to Socialization Effects

During the interviews, the respondents most often shared analyses of inequalities in terms of disability, at least among those who self-identify as disabled people. Nevertheless, we analyze some situations they interpreted as being exclusively linked to disability from an intersectional standpoint. For instance, Nathalie Petit, a woman with a mobility impairment, explained that she was "categorized [by her colleagues] as... [...] someone unstable, uh, a crazy person... and all, yes, all the clichés about disability". She believed her colleagues called her "crazy" because of her disability, stating clearly in the quote that it is a "cliché about disability." However, it can be argued that this term also originates in gender. We interpret this example as a demonstration of intersectionality; Nathalie Petit was called crazy because she was a disabled woman.

Among the interpretations expressed by respondents, the predominance of disability over other labels can be explained, in part, by the interactional context of the interviews. Both Célia and Mathéa mentioned disability in their advertisements for the survey, and while Mathéa also referred to gender, Célia did not cite any other labels. Race, class, and gender might have seemed irrelevant to some respondents, even though Célia repeatedly emphasized that she was interested in the diversity of life courses. Moreover, when people did talk about labels, the degree to which they were explicit might have depended on how they categorized Célia and Mathéa. Here, the contrast between gender and disability is explicit: it is taken for granted that as women themselves, both authors are familiar with women, but not with disability. Seven respondents (either men, women, or nonbinary people) addressed Célia using a collective "you" that includes sighted people or able-bodied people in general; and 10 respondents openly questioned her level of knowledge about disability. This asymmetry might have led people to consider it more important to detail disability-related issues, including interpretations of inequalities.

Nevertheless, these interaction dynamics do not explain all the framing effects we observe. Life course analyses also provide evidence that people categorized by others as disabled learned to prioritize the disability label over time. As this single label was repeatedly assigned to them, they ended up assimilating that it supplants any other.

Lola Joly grew up with a visible mobility impairment, which matched one of the stereotypical representations of disability (e.g., a person in a wheelchair, Engel & Munger, 2003). She explained that she has always been primarily perceived as a disabled person. Using the recent wedding of a close friend as an example, she recalled with amusement: "I asked him, 'Well, is your wedding going to be fancy or not, I'm thinking about my dress, all that stuff', And he said 'No, but who cares, anyway... it's not your dress we're going to see'. Okay... [She laughs]" (Lola Joly, mobility impairment). With his remark, her friend tactlessly informed her that her impairment would be more salient than her femininity, regardless of what she wore.

This labeling had a lasting influence on the way Lola Joly conceived her identity and, by extension, her identity-based interpretations of her experiences. This was particularly evident when she described her confusion when invited by another friend to design a conference as a woman entrepreneur.

> I said to him, "Oh, that's great, let's do it... I'll sell you a... I'll sell you a conference on disability in the workplace, etc." And he said to me, "No, no, I don't give a damn about disability, I don't give a damn about disability, uh... I want to hear you talk about... what it means to be a woman entrepreneur." [...] I said, in fact... "I'm not... I don't know what it is to be a woman. You want me to talk about... about, about... being a woman entrepreneur, but I don't know what it is to be a woman. Because I'm disabled. So... we can't... I'm not... a woman." (Lola Joly, mobility impairment)

Lola Joly's response shows that she felt legitimate to describe and reflect on her professional career as a disabled person, but not as a woman. With this, she indicated that she felt as if she had mastered the professional issues related to disability but not those related to gender. This result sheds light on how she framed her professional history throughout the interview as, in her reflective analysis, she never referred to gender and only cited the disability category.

Turning Points in Interpretations: Structural and Interpersonal Components

Although repeated labeling by others in early socializations encouraged respondents to read inequalities through the lens of disability, their interpretations did sometimes change upon secondary socializations (Berger & Luckmann, 1966). We identify three turning points in the understanding of inequalities over the life course. These are the extension of the pool of labels available to qualify one's experience, alternative identity-based interpretations for a mechanism, and the discovery of an intersectional model of inequalities. These three transformations depend on structural parameters (such as the evolution of public policies) as well as interpersonal dynamics.

The first type of turning point occurs when respondents acquired an additional label to qualify their experiences. This is particularly common among those in the sample with SLD. In France, the increasingly widespread diagnosis of this condition at the end of the twentieth century, then its connection to disability policies at the beginning of the twenty-first century, reshaped the labels disseminated in society. On a microscale, this information then reached people through significant interactions.

Four respondents were diagnosed with SLD in adulthood. All of them described their diagnosis as a major life changer. For example, when he was in his late 30s, Yacine Kasmi's wife encouraged him to consult a speech therapist. His account shows how his diagnosis led him to a serious reinterpretation of the difficulties he had encountered during his schooling. While he previously blamed his "school failure" on his "stupidity," following a meritocratic paradigm, he came to speak of legitimate "issues" linked to an "illness." Subsequently, he underwent speech therapy and decided to change profession: "It allowed me to say to myself. "But there is still time, there is still time to do things... there are still things to do, there are also other jobs, maybe"" (Yacine Kasmi, SLD).

In some cases, people self-identified as disabled after such a late diagnosis. This could also occur long after a childhood diagnosis that was not associated with the disability label at the time (typically among people who were educated before the 2005 law). In both situations, the disability label could either be a stigma that people reject, if they already had arrangements that compensate for their difficulties, or an asset to account for the disadvantages they experience. Audrey Rolland, a low-income single mother, wavered between these two views. She described how she learned that SLDs were covered by disability legislation after her son's diagnosis, three decades after her own.

> I was always told that I had SLD. I was never told that I was disabled! It was when my son was... a... when I had to ask for my son [funding for occupational therapy]. We have to ask for it, from the Caf [Caisse d'allocations familiales, the public organization that provides social benefits related to family, housing, and disability]. And there, I saw "disability benefit"! And that's when I saw that they [SLD and disability] were associated. And then... it's quite recent, you know! And... and, yes, it gave me a shock! (She laughs) Well, yeah, it was a shock. And... I think "Well, if they want." And so I said to myself, at one point (In an animated tone) "They pissed me off so much with this... that, yeah, for sure, I'll ask them! Because... because at some point, screw it!" (Audrey Rolland, SLD)

Raised in a family where she was exposed to a lot of mockery and criticism, Audrey Rolland immediately spotted the risk of stigmatization that accompanies the term disability. It is a "shock" to be "look[ed] at like that." But she also made use of this label as a tool to gain recognition of the unfair treatment she faced: people have "pissed [her] off so much." Finally, she also contemplated using the label to obtain material compensation for this prejudice.

The second turning point in the interpretation of inequalities is the replacement of one assumption of identity mechanism by another. The political and social visibility of certain modalities of inequality based on race, class, and gender (see above) provided counterpoints to disability-related interpretations. Here again, as the case of Nolwenn Dubois illustrates, interactions are an essential feature of these secondary socializations. Early in the interview, Nolwenn Dubois, a blind woman in her 30s, mentioned that people touch her on the street to help her. She immediately connected this with the fact that she is a woman and clarified that she did not think it would happen to a disabled man. When asked to explain what "in [her] personal experience" made her think this way, she elaborated:

> What made me aware, it's not so much what I experienced, it's more the discussions I had with sighted people. Men who - or women, men or women in fact who tell me, "If you were 6'3", maybe people... people would protect you less." Because I've lived it. I've done [internships], and... being the only blind person...actually most of them protect me. And then it's (she mimes someone grabbing her to guide her) "It's this way," or whatever. (Nolwenn Dubois, visual impairment)

In recent decades, there has been a growing awareness of gender stereotypes in society, including the belief that women need to be protected. This information fed the reflexivity of some of Nolwenn Dubois' intern colleagues. As they shared their perspectives with her, they broadened her understanding of the inequalities she encountered.

The third and last turning point is the following. A few women respondents changed their interpretations of inequality after acquiring an intersectional perspective, either through academic material (such as social science courses) or cultural media (podcasts, cultural programs). Exposure to these vectors of highbrow culture was selective as all the women who experienced this turning point had received a higher education.

> I think that in ten years, I will be a full-fledged woman! [...] I think that disability and... and femininity, well for me it has been... We are so infantilized with this disability that it is difficult... I didn't feel like a woman for a long time. I didn't feel equal to others. [...] And I heard a woman on the radio, her name is Rokhaya Diallo, who talked about... intersectionality. She is an intersectional feminist. I said to myself, "What is that? And in fact it's... it felt good. Because in fact, I didn't recognize myself in the feminist discourse. And they never talked about me either. And she said, "Well, you see, a Black woman is not going to experience the same discrimination as a Black man. A disabled woman will not experience the same discrimination as a non-disabled woman." And there, I recognized myself, you know. (She slaps the table to emphasize her point) I said to myself: she's awesome, this girl. (Émeline Lemaire, visual impairment)

Like Lola Joly, Émeline Lemaire grew up with the repeated experience of being labeled solely on the basis of disability, and this identity category came to trump all others in her eyes. As a law graduate, she often listened to cultural programs on the radio to "educate herself." Listening to the journalist and activist Rokhaya Diallo, introduced her to the intersectional approach to inequality, which transformed her reflective thinking. As she understood that she could experience womanhood differently to able-bodied women, she reconnected with the gender label and learned more precise labels for the inequalities she faced.

DISCUSSION

The results of this research demonstrate that the interpretation of inequalities varies according to the different kinds of social categories they relate to and are related to, throughout the life course. Being part of a disadvantaged group is not enough to activate an identity label, self-identification is also necessary. Yet self-identification with disability is not systematic among people with long-term limitations: it is shaped by the way they are perceived by others, depending on the visibility of the impairment and the criteria of what counts as a disability in various times and places.

Connecting identities with perceptions of inequalities, we show that our interviewees often followed a cumulative logic, contrary to the intersectional approach and its refusal of mathematical metaphors (West & Fenstermaker, 1995). Although the importance of intersectionality in social sciences analyses, our study shows that this kind of framework is not the main way of analysis for the disabled people we interviewed – unlike Bowleg's Black gay respondents (2013). These results complete the existing literature on intersectionality and disability (Barnartt & Altman, 2016; Iqtadar et al., 2020; Naples et al., 2019), by shedding light on how individuals come to understand inequalities.

Digging into the interpretation of inequalities, the study highlights that macrofactors such as public policies, debates, and media coverage indirectly influence perceptions at a microscale – i.e., the way our interviewees make sense of inequalities. For instance, the visibility and political significance of gendered income inequalities in France since the 1950s (Laufer, 2014; Revillard, 2016) allows some of our interviewees to interpret their situation as being an effect of gender inequality. Along the same lines, the historical model of racial segregation is a point of reference when it comes to understanding separation by skin color in the workplace. Although this has never been legal in metropolitan France, the interviewees mention it when describing their work experiences.[6] The visibility of such subjects in the public sphere enables people to critically analyze their life experiences and relate their individual inequality experiences to social structures.

In contrast with other identity-based interpretations of inequalities, our respondents invoke the role of disability in a variety of circumstances. While the context of our interviews might have encouraged this framing, we show that people who have been labeled by others as disabled over a long period encounter certain socializations that convey to them that this identity is more salient than other categories. Last, the life course approach allows us to consider reflexivity and evolutions and the role of macro and micro contexts in such dynamics. Using the concept of secondary socializations (Berger & Luckmann, 1966), we describe how people come to reinterpret the underlying causes of inequalities. Their change of perspective is influenced by their environments, both at the macro level (e.g., public policy and social framings) and in the microinteractions (e.g., links with their family and friends, occasional encounters).

CONCLUSION

This chapter contributes to understanding how people perceive inequalities in relation to their identities, how their perceptions change over their life course, and

---

[6]In Algeria, from the middle of the nineteenth century to the middle of the twentieth century, the colonial rule concerning the attribution of French nationality generated a form of apartheid.

the conditions that allow them to adopt an intersectional type of perspective. The disabled people we interviewed in France typically perceive gender, race, class, and disability as independent cumulative components. They attribute disadvantages to a single factor, which they identify based on context and their socializations earlier in life. Yet, several turning points may lead individuals to analyze their experiences in a new way. These results help gain a better understanding of disabled people's interpretations of inequalities, and the way these interpretations change (or not) over time. Future research will benefit from examining the impact of turning points, not only on people's representations but also on their practices. Moreover, an international comparison would allow for a better global understanding of the way identities – and notably disability-based identities – are constructed and function in combination with other identity labels depending on national contexts (Lamont, 1992).

FUNDING

This chapter benefits from the support provided by the ANR and the French government under the "Investissements d'Avenir" program LABEX LIEPP (ANR-11-LABX-0091, ANR-11-IDEX-0005-02) and the IdEx Université Paris Cité (ANR-18-IDEX0001).

REFERENCES

Barnartt, S. N., & Altman, B. M. (2016). *Disability and intersecting statuses*. Emerald Publishing Limited.
Barnes, C., & Oliver, M. (2012). *The new politics of disablement*. Palgrave Macmillan.
Berger, P. L., & Luckmann, T. (1966). *The social construction of reality: A treatise in the sociology of knowledge*. Penguin Books.
Bouvier, G., & Jugnot, S. (2013). Les personnes ayant des problèmes de santé ou de handicap sont plus nombreuses que les autres à faire part de comportements stigmatisants. *Economie et Statistique, 464*(1), 189–213.
Bowleg, L. (2013). "Once you've blended the cake, you can't take the parts back to the main ingredients": Black gay and bisexual men's descriptions and experiences of intersectionality. *Sex Roles, 68*(11–12), 754–767.
Caradec, V., Ertul, S., & Melchior, J. (2012). Introduction. In V. Caradec, S. Ertul, & J. Melchior (Eds.), *Les dynamiques des parcours sociaux: Temps, territoires, professions* (pp. 11–18). Presses Universitaires de Rennes.
Crenshaw, K. (1990). Mapping the margins: Intersectionality, identity politics, and violence against women of color. *Stanford Law Review, 43*, 1241–1299.
Davis, L. J. (1995). *Enforcing normalcy: Disability, deafness and the body*. Verso.
Dubar, C. (1992). Formes identitaires et socialisation professionnelle. *Revue Française de Sociologie, 33*(4), 505–529.
Dubar, C. (2015). *La socialisation* (5th ed.). Armand Colin.
Dubet, F., Macé, E., Cousin, O., & Rui, S. (2013). *Pourquoi moi? L'expérience des discriminations*. Éditions du Seuil.
Elder, G. H. (1985). *Life course dynamics: Trajectories and transitions*. Cornell University Press.
Elder, G. H., Johnson, M. K., & Crosnoe, R. (2003). The emergence and development of life course theory. In *Handbook of the life course* (pp. 3–19). Springer.

Engel, D. M., & Munger, F. W. (2003). *Rights of inclusion: Law and identity in the life stories of Americans with disabilities.* University of Chicago Press.

Gibson, B. E., Mistry, B., Smith, B., Yoshida, K. K., Abbott, D., Lindsay, S., & Hamdani, Y. (2014). Becoming men: Gender, disability, and transitioning to adulthood. *Health, 18*(1), 95–114.

Goffman, E. (1956). *The presentation of self in everyday life.* University of Edinburgh.

Goffman, E. (1963). *Stigma: Notes on the management of spoiled identity.* Prentice-Hall.

Hahn, H. (1988). The politics of physical differences: Disability and discrimination. *Journal of Social Issues, 44*(1), 39–47.

Heller, T. (2011). *Disability through the life course.* SAGE.

Hughes, E. C. (1945). Dilemmas and contradictions of status. *American Journal of Sociology, 50*(5), 353–359.

Iqtadar, S., Hern, D. I., & Ellison, S. (2020). "If it wasn't my race, it was other things like being a woman, or my disability": A qualitative research synthesis of disability research. *Disability Studies Quarterly, 40*(2).

Janus, A. L. (2009). Disability and the transition to adulthood. *Social Forces, 88*(1), 99–120.

Lamont, M. (1992). *Money, morals, and manners: The culture of the French and American upper-middle class.* University of Chicago Press.

Lamont, M., Guetzkow, J. A., Herzog, H., Silva, G. M. D. da, Mizrachi, N., Reis, E. P., & Welburn, J. S. (2016). *Getting respect: Responding to stigma and discrimination in the United States, Brazil, and Israel.* Princeton University Press.

Laufer, J. (2014). *L'égalité professionnelle entre les femmes et les hommes.* La Découverte.

Lorber, J. (2000). Gender contradictions and status dilemmas in disability. *Expanding the scope of social science research on disability* (pp. 85–103). Emerald Publishing Limited.

McIntosh, P. (1989). *White privilege: Unpacking the invisible knapsack* (pp. 10–12). Peace and Freedom Magazine.

Naples, N. A., Mauldin, L., & Dillaway, H. (2019). Gender, disability, and intersectionality (Introduction to special issue). *Gender & Society, 33*(1), 5–18.

Priestley, M. (2003). *Disability: A life course approach.* Polity Press.

Ravaud, J.-F., Letourmy, A., & Ville, I. (2002). Les méthodes de délimitation de la population handicapée: l'approche de l'enquête de l'Insee Vie quotidienne et santé. *Population, 57*(3), 541–567.

Revillard, A. (2016). *La cause des femmes dans l'État.* Presses universitaires de Grenoble.

Ridgeway, C. L., & Kricheli-Katz, T. (2013). Intersecting cultural beliefs in social relations. *Gender & Society, 27*(3), 294–318.

Rohmer, O., & Louvet, E. (2009). Describing persons with disability: Salience of disability, gender, and ethnicity. *Rehabilitation Psychology, 54*(1), 76–82.

Santelli, E. (2019). L'analyse des parcours. Saisir la multidimensionalité du social pour penser l'action sociale. *Sociologie, 10*(2), 153–171.

Stryker, S. (1980). *Symbolic interactionism: A social structural version.* Blackburn Press.

Vérétout, A. (2015). Être en situation de handicap et diplômé de l'enseignement supérieur. In J. Zaffran (Ed.), *Accessibilité et handicap: anciennes pratiques, nouvel enjeu* (pp. 249–273). Presses Universitaires de Grenoble.

Wells, T., Hogan, D. P., & Sandefur, G. D. (2003). What happens after the high school years among young persons with disabilities? *Social Forces, 82*(2), 803–832.

West, C., & Fenstermaker, S. (1995). Doing difference. *Gender & Society, 9*(1), 8–37.

Wethington, E., Cooper, H., & Holmes, C. S. (1997). Turning points in midlife. In I. H. Gotlib & B. Wheaton (Eds.), *Stress and adversity over the life course: Trajectories and turning points* (pp. 215–231). Cambridge University.

YOUNG-ADULTHOOD DEVELOPMENT IN THE LIVED EXPERIENCE OF PERSONS WITH KIDNEY FAILURE: CHALLENGES OF YOUTH, DISABILITY, AND TRANSITION

Nancy G. Kutner and Tess Bowles

AUTHOR BIOGRAPHIES

Nancy G. Kutner, PhD, Emory University, USA, is a Medical Sociologist at Emory University, Atlanta GA, USA, with appointments as Professor in the Department of Rehabilitation Medicine and as affiliated faculty in the Department of Sociology. She has previously chaired the Disability and Society Section and the Committee on Society and Persons with Disabilities of the American Sociological Association. Her publications include The sociology of disability, C. D. Bryant & D. L. Peck (Eds.), *21ˢᵗ Century Sociology: A Reference Handbook*, Vol. 2, 2006; The stigma of deviant physical function, CD Bryant (ed.), *The Handbook of Deviant Behavior*, 2011; and Disability: Sociological aspects, J. D. Wright (Ed.), *International Encyclopedia of the Social & Behavioral Sciences*, 2nd ed., Vol. 6, 2015, and she is an invited contributor on Kidney Diseases for *Behavioral and Social Science in Medicine: Principles and Practice of Biopsychosocial Care*, a first-in-class medical education textbook, 2023.

Tess Bowles, MEd, Emory University, USA, is currently a senior research specialist at Emory University School of Medicine. Her previous work experience included being a vocational counselor with the Georgia Department of Vocational Rehabilitation and Dialysis Social Worker with a major dialysis provider in the Atlanta GA metropolitan area. She has extensive experience as an interviewer and research project manager for studies focusing on young persons and adults with disabling conditions.

Disabilities and the Life Course
Research in Social Science and Disability, Volume 14, 69–87
Copyright © 2023 Nancy G. Kutner and Tess Bowles
Published under exclusive licence by Emerald Publishing Limited
ISSN: 1479-3547/doi:10.1108/S1479-354720230000014005

ABSTRACT

This study examined dimensions of young-adulthood development in lived experience reported by young persons (19 women, 18 men) with the disabling condition of kidney failure requiring chronic dialysis or kidney transplantation. In semistructured phone interviews, participants (ages 23–37) described their family/living situation, employment and community activity, current situation, and experience. Participants' qualitative responses about "the way you see things, do things, feel about things" and "how you feel about yourself" were examined to identify themes. Limited achievement of proposed "successful" dimensions of young adulthood characterized the study cohort, based on indicators included in the interview. In qualitative data, the theme of perceived stigma and spoiled identity (Goffman, 1963) was reflected in comments offered by participants regarding their self-confidence and motivation to pursue goals. A second theme in participants' qualitative responses was a sense of isolation from age peers who shared their condition, and participants expressed frustration around having an age-inappropriate condition ("why me?"). Perceived stigma and spoiled identity impact social ties and life goals and are understudied influences in the life course trajectory of young persons with kidney failure and the challenges inherent in navigating health status and developmental life course transitions.

Keywords: Young adulthood; transition; disability; stigma; lived experience; kidney failure

Life course scholars recognize that, depending on individuals' life stage, different factors and contexts become important in shaping identity and experience. Impairments and disabilities also have varied meanings and implications depending on life contexts. Thus, individuals' identity and experience of an impairment or disability in one life stage could be very different from their identity and experience at a later life stage. Within a developmental framework, in this paper, we focus on the identity and experience of young persons with the disabling condition of kidney failure, in the context of transitions/turning points associated with the life stage that has been described as "young adulthood" (Scales et al., 2016). Dimensions of young-adulthood development were examined in the experience of 37 young persons (19 women, 18 men) living with chronic kidney failure that required their reliance on dialysis or kidney transplantation. In semistructured phone interviews, study participants (ages 23–37) described their family/living situation, employment, and community activity, and participants' qualitative responses about "the way you see things, do things, feel about things" and "how you feel about yourself" were examined to identify themes. Accounts of lived experience from our study highlight how young persons with kidney failure may variably encounter their condition, including encountering perceived condition-related stigma, as they navigate life stage transitions.

BACKGROUND

Young-Adulthood Development

The constructs of "young adulthood" (Scales et al., 2016), and "youth" (e.g., Irwin, 2001; Tisdall, 2001), connote a time period in the life course that intervenes between childhood and adulthood. Transitioning to and from young adulthood is generally understood as encompassing individuals' experience of decreasing dependence on others that is characteristic of childhood years, while concurrently assuming increased independent "adult" functioning (Erickson & Macmillan, 2018; Ferris et al., 2016; Hallum, 1995; Scales et al., 2016; Tisdall, 2001). A preoccupation with the challenges of the transition from school to work dominated early transitional literature for young disabled people before a more holistic perspective evolved that posits multiple interacting types of transitions (Tisdall, 2001).

Stages of the life course are shaped in institutionally and culturally prescribed ways (Hogan & Astone, 1986; Shanahan, 2000). Balancing stability and change in relationships with family/significant others; expanding interactions with the wider community, which may include new peer groups; and entering new educational and/or employment contexts are among the generally expected aspects of the transition to and from young adulthood (e.g., Hamilton et al., 2017; Scales et al., 2016). Although suggested illustrative chronologic age periods can be found in the literature, transition to and from young adulthood is not defined by a specific chronologic age span. Irwin (2001) observed that a life course perspective draws attention to the limited value of chronological age, per se, as a sociological variable.

Research clearly identifies that young disabled people may face considerable difficulties when they leave school and its institutional support structure, especially difficulties in transitioning from school to work (Lindsay, 2019; Tisdall, 2001). Tisdall (2001) argued, however, that "successful" transition for disabled persons may not necessarily include paid employment. She noted that physical (in)dependence is also not a clear-cut goal, with advocates for independent living arguing that independence is about making one's own choices and decisions even if these involve risks. Tisdall (2001) concluded that ideally an individual's transition experience is shaped by a combination of structure and individual agency.

From a developmental psychology perspective, Scales et al. (2016) proposed that "successful dimensions of young adulthood" include physical health, psychological and emotional well-being, life skills, ethical behavior, healthy family and social relationships, educational attainment, constructive educational and occupational engagement, and civic engagement. They acknowledged that this list of goals might be criticized as merely representing examples of adjustment to dominant cultural standards of individualism and materialism. However, Scales et al. (2016) maintained that their dimensions accommodate the importance of both structure and agency in successful transition for young adults:

> ...we believe the dimensions themselves, albeit not always specific measures of them, are sufficiently general to encompass both adjustments to dominant cultural norms and carving out of developmentally agentic personal and sub-cultural paths that can also include

involvement in efforts to change those dominant culture norms through civic and political engagement. Moreover, we explicitly name several dimensions that reflect connection and concern with others (e.g., healthy relationships, ethical behavior, civic engagement), and ground other dimensions (e.g., life skills, psychological and emotional well-being) within a context of relatedness and mutual obligation that would contradict a simple evaluation of these dimensions as individualistic...[and] it is important to note that these dimensions do not denote or connote 'pure,' unattainable ideals of behavior or psychological self-perceptions. We mean these to be quite reflective of real young adults living real lives that have the ups and downs of fortune and mood, and positive and negative experiences, that are inevitable parts of life for everyone... (Scales et al., 2016, p. 158)

"Physical health" is included as a dimension of successful development by Scales et al. (2016). However, they stress that their use of this term is meant to characterize successful young adults as persons who maintain a healthy lifestyle, and it is not meant to infer that young adults are, or even should be, "risk-free." According to the authors:

Rather, they [successful young adults] have attained greater skills at managing developmentally-appropriate risks (otherwise known, less pejoratively, as explorations, adventures, or experimentations) such that they minimize harm to themselves and others...and [are] able to take steps to deal as effectively as they can with problems, disappointments, and challenges. (Scales et al., 2016, p. 158)

We suggest that this perspective on physical health is consistent with the goal of self-agency in health management. For young persons with kidney failure, the goal of self-agency is central in individuals' expected transition from a pediatric model of care to an adult model of care. The following section provides an overview of kidney failure and treatment in the United States and summarizes the challenge of transition of care for young persons with kidney disease as viewed from the perspective of the medical community (Bell, 2007, 2022; Díaz-González de Ferris et al., 2017; Icard et al., 2008).

Study Population: Young Persons With Kidney Failure

Kidney failure, also called end stage renal disease (ESRD) or end stage kidney disease, occurs when the kidneys are not able to maintain the volume, composition, and distribution of body fluids essential for well-being. Individuals with kidney failure then require a kidney transplant or maintenance dialysis therapy, and regardless of their age are entitled to coverage of their treatment under the Medicare End Stage Renal Disease (ESRD) Program that was established by federal legislation in 1972. The disability provision of Medicare is the basis for this coverage. Individuals with kidney failure were "deemed to be disabled" as the basis for this entitlement (Rettig, 1980).

Kidney transplantation is not a cure for kidney disease but is generally considered the treatment that offers increased opportunities for a normal lifestyle. Younger age is prioritized in the eligibility criteria for kidney transplant receipt. Because the number of available kidney donors is always far less than the number of persons eligible for kidney transplantation, most individuals living with kidney failure, about 70%, receive dialysis (USRDS, 2021).

Hemodialysis, in which the blood is mechanically circulated outside the body through a dialyzer, or artificial kidney, to remove toxic wastes and excess fluid and to restore the balance of essential electrolytes, is the predominant dialysis treatment in the United States (89% of dialysis users). Hemodialysis usually takes place in a dialysis center, although home hemodialysis is also possible. About 11% of dialysis users perform peritoneal dialysis, in which the person drains dialyzate fluid into the abdomen through a surgically placed catheter, or tube. This fluid comes in contact with the peritoneal membrane, a thin layer of tissue around the abdominal organs. Some of the toxins in the blood pass from blood vessels in the wall of the peritoneal membrane into the dialyzate. After about four hours, the fluid is drained out of the body through the catheter. This process, known as continuous ambulatory peritoneal dialysis, is repeated four or five times per day. An alternate form of peritoneal dialysis uses a cycling machine that changes the fluid several times each night while the person sleeps. Over time, it is common for individuals to experience changes in the type of treatment, in conjunction with medical and/or lifestyle considerations.

Age characteristics of persons who reach kidney failure, reported annually in national registry data from the United States Renal Data System (USRDS, 2021), show that the adjusted incidence of kidney failure increases dramatically as age increases. In the most recent available summary of these data, the adjusted incidence in 2019 among individuals aged 0–17 years was 12 per million population (pmp), while among individuals aged 65–74 years the incidence was 1,307 pmp and among individuals aged ≥75 years the incidence was 1,587 pmp. As Fig. 1 indicates, the incidence for individuals younger than 45 years old has changed little over recent years and is much lower than the incidence for older age

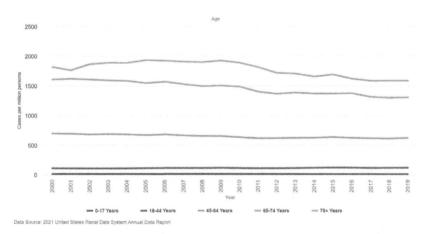

Fig. 1. US Population Kidney Failure Incidence From 2000–2018, Stratified by Age. *Source:* Figure 1.4, 2021 USRDS Annual Data Report, p. 7. US ESRD (kidney failure) patients, unknown sex and other or unknown race/ethnicity excluded. Rates are standardized to the age distribution of the 2015 US population.

categories. Children, adolescents, and young adults constitute less than 5% of the ESRD population in the United States (Ferris et al., 2016).

The value of "a combination of structure and individual agency" for successfully navigating youth to adult transition (Tisdall, 2001, p. 175) is also a strong theme in the literature on successfully living with kidney failure. In a setting of shared decision-making, individuals assume responsibility for managing their day-to-day health status, within a structure of clearly prescribed treatment and understanding of the underlying rationale for these prescriptions. Ideally, these expectations for health management shape the context of living with kidney failure regardless of the individual's particular life stage.

Young persons with kidney failure typically remain under the care of pediatric kidney specialists until age 18, and their ability to have a successful transition from a pediatric-centered to an adult-oriented care model is of major concern for medical care providers (Bell, 2007; Icard et al., 2008). The dual goals of this "so-called transition process" (Scarponi et al., 2021, p. 1) have been summarized as promoting "a sense of continuity in the development of youth, and [preparing] them to accept responsibility for and manage their own chronic kidney condition. ..." Psychosocial and developmental challenges that may impact the youth-to-adult healthcare transition process are acknowledged in the medical literature (Bell, 2022; Ferris et al., 2016; Hallum, 1995; Icard et al., 2008). However, clinics with expertise in promoting young persons' transition to an adult model of healthcare may be limited in providing resources such as peer models and access to psychosocial support. A recent assessment of evidence indicating the inclusion of "multidisciplinarity in transition pathways" concluded that "to date, transitional care is not only an objective to reach, but a process still in its developmental stages..." for young persons with kidney disease (Scarponi et al., 2021).

Perceived Condition-Related Stigma and Spoiled Identity With Kidney Disease

Stereotyped views of the treatments on which persons with kidney failure must depend may contribute to stigma. When kidney dialysis machines first became available in the United States in the 1960s, the ability of the dialysis procedure to sustain lives was viewed with awe, and dialysis users were viewed as deserving recipients of a second chance for life (Fox & Swazey, 1978). However, more recent views of dialysis emphasize patient dependence on a routinized procedure typically provided by technicians in an unappealing and sometimes marginally hygienic clinic setting, for example, an *Atlantic Magazine* article titled "God Help You, You're on Dialysis" (Fields, 2010). Receipt of a kidney transplant may be viewed more positively, a true second chance for life, although the prospect of any organ transplantation may be rejected as unnatural by some observers; see, for example, *Is It Moral to Modify Man?* (Frazier, 1973).

In a recent qualitative study of factors related to individuals' reluctance to be participants in kidney disease research, one respondent asserted that "there's kind of a stigma, unfortunately, with kidney disease." Another observed that "some people think it's communicable," or "something that you do, like drugs...I think people shut down, because who wants to get blamed...?" (Gutman et al., 2022, p. 217). Kidney failure is often a largely invisible disability, with minimal effects on outward physical appearance with the exception of possible altered body image due to medication effects for transplant recipients, or to surgical creation of an access site for use during dialysis. Thus, individuals may not be recognizably different from their age peers. But if kidney disease itself, as well as related treatments, is viewed negatively by others, a publicly shared perception of spoiled identity may be attributed to individuals with this condition. Gill (2001) described a persistent and disquieting sense of mistaken identity as a central feature of the disability experience, requiring continuing effort for people to bridge the gap between their self-views and public perceptions.

Feeling marginalized and perceived as "different" may be especially salient for young persons with a disabling condition. In this chapter, we draw on insights from conceptualizations that have been proposed for young-adulthood development (Scales et al., 2016) and for "transition to adulthood" for young disabled people (Tisdall, 2001). We examine young persons' outlooks and accounts of lived experiences in navigating transition pathways which they shared during a semistructured interview that focused on their journey with kidney failure.

METHODS

Study Cohort Recruitment

Participants in our study were young persons with kidney failure who lived throughout Georgia and had attended a series of "life and career planning" weekend workshops that comprised a program termed *Springboard* offered for young adults by the National Kidney Foundation of Georgia (NKFG). Some of these individuals had previously attended the NKFG "Camp Independence" for children, or "Club Independence" for adults, but the NKFG recognized a need to provide an opportunity for young persons to interact with age peers in a program targeted specifically to them. The *Springboard* program was developed with input from NKFG Patient Services directors (kidney transplant recipients themselves), young adults with kidney failure who had attended other NKFG programs, a dialysis nurse, a rehabilitation psychologist, and Georgia Division of Rehabilitation Services representatives with vocational services expertise. *Springboard* was initially intended specifically for individuals ages 19-26 but the upper age criterion was increased, not only because of the limited potential participant pool in the 19–26 age range in any one year in the state but also because of participation interest expressed by young adults >26 years old in response to information about the program.

Participants for this research were recruited by the second author (T.B.), using the most recent contact information available from NKFG for *Springboard* program attendees. Phone interviews, scheduled at respondents' convenience, were completed with 37 young adults (19 women, 18 men) and were audio recorded with participants' consent. The Emory University Institutional Review Board approved this research.

Interview Guide

Based on familiarity with the *Springboard* program objectives (both authors were members of the *Springboard* steering committee) and literature review, the authors developed a semistructured interview guide. Multiple sources suggest that prevalent challenges for young adulthood development are likely to include family relationship issues, employment, and community integration (e.g., Hallum, 1995; Hamilton et al., 2017; Scales et al., 2016; Tisdall, 2001). After summarizing their kidney failure treatment history and current status, study participants were asked to describe their family and living situation; school and paid work situation; and involvement in any activities, hobbies, nonpaid work, or volunteer jobs. Additionally, two open-end questions asked study participants to describe (1) "the way you see things, do things, feel about things" and (2) "how you feel about yourself."

Analysis

Summary data for participants' current age at the time of the interview, and age at the time of kidney failure onset, are described by medians and observed ranges. The sample size precluded the meaningful use of percentages as descriptive statistics, but frequency counts for the 19 women and 18 men participants provide an opportunity to view "comparison groups" embedded within a qualitative design (Lindsay, 2019).

"Transition indicators" included in our study, i.e., parental home versus independent (from parents) home, employment, and community involvement, are frequently included in the literature on young persons' transition to adulthood in the setting of disability (e.g. Hallum, 1995; Tisdall, 2001) and in literature focusing on young persons with kidney failure (e.g., Hamilton et al., 2017). Thus, for this study, indicators of "successful" young-adulthood development were categorized as:

- a family/living situation independent from parents (or parent-surrogates such as grandparents/aunts/uncles)
- regular gainful employment, defined as ongoing involvement in compensated work or being a stay-at-home parent for children (but not occasional babysitting for others' children)
- any reported community involvement, such as church activities, assistance with organized sports activities (coaching, refereeing), and/or volunteer work for general (nonkidney disease-related) organizations and for kidney disease-related organizations

After recorded interviews were transcribed, participants' responses to the two open-end questions, as well as elaborations on their responses regarding young-adulthood development indicators, were sources for thematic analysis (Glaser & Straus, 2017). In participant responses, the authors first identified a theme of perceived stigma and spoiled identity. A second theme in participant responses was feeling isolated from interaction with age peers who require treatment for kidney failure and/or feeling frustrated with having a condition that is statistically infrequent among young persons.

FINDINGS

Study Cohort Characteristics

National registry data indicate that men incur kidney failure at a younger age than women (USRDS, 2021). The median ages of women and men who were interviewed in our study, respectively, were 29 and 26. Median ages at kidney failure onset were 20 among women and 19 among men, but four men had incurred kidney failure at age 12 or younger (compared with two women) and another six participants (three women, three men) had incurred kidney failure as teenagers. More men (10) than women (four) in the study cohort had a kidney transplant at the time of the interview. Among study participants currently using dialysis, more men (5/8) than women (6/15) were currently active on a kidney transplant waiting list, and more men (5) than women (2) had experienced rejection of one or more previous kidney transplants (Table 1). The composition of the study cohort with respect to race reflected the demographics of the overall population of persons <age 45 with kidney failure in the state of Georgia, i.e., approximately 60% African American.

Indicators of Dimensions of Successful Young-Adulthood Development

Dimensions of participants' young-adulthood development, as reflected by reported independent living situations, regular employment, and community involvement, are summarized for women and men in Tables 2–5. Successful development, as measured by the three indicators, was reported with similar frequency by women and men, and the total numbers of indicators endorsed by women and men were similar.

Having a living situation independent from parents/parent surrogates was reported by fewer than half of the participants. The majority of young persons interviewed in this study continued to reside in a parental home in an extended

Table 1. Study Cohort Characteristics, by Gender: Young Persons With Kidney Failure.

	Women (*n* = 19)	Men (*n* = 18)
Age at interview, yrs		
Median	29	26
Range	23–36	23–37
Age of kidney condition onset, yrs		
Median	20	19
Range	10–29	<1–27
Current treatment status		
Transplant	4	10
In-center hemodialysis	8 (3 on transplant waitlist)	8 (5 on transplant waitlist)
Home peritoneal dialysis	7 (3 on transplant waitlist)	0

Table 2. Family/Living Situation of Study Participants, by Gender.

Independent (From Parent) Home		Parent (or Parent Surrogate) Home	
Women (*n*)	Men (*n*)	Women (*n*)	Men (*n*)
Own place; living alone: 3	Own place, living alone: 1	w/parent(s), sibling(s): 6	11
Place shared w/ roommate: 1	Place w/spouse & child(ren): 2	w/parent(s), sibling(s), and own child(ren): 3	
Place w/spouse & child(ren): 1	Place w/sibling(s): 1	w/aunt: 1	
Place w/own child(ren): 2	Place w/spouse or girlfriend: 3	w/grandfather: 1	
Place w/sibling(s): 1			
Total: 8	*Total:* 7	*Total:* 11	*Total:* 11

family situation. This living situation is consistent with cultural patterns characteristic of a southern, largely rural state; it may also reflect individual or family financial factors.

Current employment was reported by 19/37 members of the study cohort, and among the 18 study participants who were not currently employed, 12 individuals reported previously holding jobs. Both living situation and employment status reported by study participants as of their interview represent a snapshot within the fluid context of these young persons' life stage and disabling condition. Recent changes in these indicators reported by the study cohort reflected transition toward, and away from, living situations more characteristic of adulthood, as well as young persons' needs to manage their health and treatment status.

Table 3. Current Education and Employment Status of Study Participants, by Gender.

	Women (*n* = 19)	Men (*n* = 18)
Highest level of education completed		
High school or less	11	9
Post high school[a]	8	9
Further education in process or planned	5[b]	2[c]
Regular gainful employment	9	10

[a]Post high school = some college or college graduate; vocational or technical school; nursing school.

[b]Has completed some college, is thinking about returning; Formerly worked as a pharmacy assistant at CVS, wants to get pharmacy assistant degree; Maybe art school; GED in process; Formerly attended computer classes at the Urban League, wants to pursue a degree online.

[c]Currently enrolled in SAT prep classes, wants to attend 9-month pharmacy tech program; Wants to get GED.

Table 4. Community Involvement of Study Participants, by Gender.

	Women	Men
Participants who reported one or more community activities	12	10
Types of community activity reported[a]		
Church (choir, Bible School, etc.) activities	6	1
Organized sports activity contributions (coaching, refereeing, etc.)	2	5
Volunteering, general (classroom, Red Cross, Boy Scouts, Boys & Girls Club)	3	4
Volunteering, kidney disease-related (NKFG, LifeLink-GA, dialysis clinic)	5	4

Note: NKFG, National Kidney Foundation of GA. *LifeLink of Georgia*, a division of *LifeLink* Foundation, is the nonprofit Organ Procurement Organization (OPO) designated to the state *of Georgia* and two counties in South Carolina.
[a]Some participants reported more than one type of activity.

Changes in personal relationships were linked with changes in living situation, as in the case of two young men formerly living with their parents, one of whom had married five months before the interview and another who had moved out six months before the interview to live with his girlfriend. Another young man reported that he had been living "on his own" but then moved back in with his mother, sister, and niece. Changes in living situations and/or employment also reflected the need to manage treatment status. A young woman who had recently married was temporarily living with her parents and younger sister until she received an expected transplant from her father and could move to join her husband, a pilot based in another state. She had completed nursing school and worked as a nurse until recently and planned to resume work after her transplant when she expected to have more energy. A young man had recently resigned from

Table 5. Young-Adulthood Development Indicators Among Women and Men Participants: Summary for Study Cohort.

Indicators	Women (n = 19)	Men (n = 18)	Total Cohort (n = 37)
Living situation: Independent (nonparent) home	8	7	15
Regular gainful employment	9	10	19
Community involvement	12	10	22
Total # of indicators/participant			
0	3	2	5[a]
1	8	7	15
2	3	7	10
3	5	2	7[b]

[a]Additional characteristics of the five participants w/0 indicators achieved: Median age 29, range 24–31; one transplant, four dialysis; 3/5 reported perceived stigma.
[b]Additional characteristics of the seven participants w/3 indicators achieved: Median age 30, range 26–37; one transplant, six dialysis; 3/7 reported perceived stigma.

his job of several years with a commercial painting company "because of health problems related to his transplant failure."

Possible discrimination on the part of employers was noted by study participants as a suspected contributor to difficulty being hired for a job and as a source of concern about maintaining a job. A young woman on peritoneal dialysis, who had recently graduated from college with a business degree and was actively seeking employment, had been interviewed for a job with the state but said that she "thinks that she has not been hired because of her kidney disease." A young man with a kidney transplant, who had been employed for several years as a waiter, stated that his boss "knows everything he needs to know about my medical condition."

In addition, disability benefit regulations and allowed earnings limits were cited as issues that limited employment options. A young woman who had received a kidney transplant and previously worked in a retail outlet said that her monthly pay in that job sometimes exceeded the amount that she was allowed to earn while receiving disability benefits. As a result, she was now having to pay back money out of her disability check and was reluctant to pursue any new employment. Another young woman, currently on hemodialysis, had received training to work as a medical assistant but feared the loss of disability benefits if she pursued a job in that field, so she continued working in daycare instead.

Indicators of community involvement were reported by more than half of the cohort. Among the types of community activity involvement reported by young people (Table 4), women more often named church-related activities, and men more often named volunteer participation in organized sports. NKFG programs provided a community involvement opportunity for both women and men and included volunteer work in the NKFG office and assisting in various NKFG service programs. Having a job that required working long hours, having care-giving responsibilities for children, and having transportation issues were reasons cited by individuals who reported no current involvement in community activities.

Perceived Stigma/Spoiled Identity

The theme of perceived stigma and spoiled identity attributed to persons with kidney failure (Table 6) was prominent in feelings and perceptions shared by 20/ 37 members of the study cohort. This included nine individuals who were employed and 11 individuals who were not employed, suggesting that perceived spoiled identity, e.g., doubting that you can "live a normal life," can be a persistent challenge for young persons with kidney failure in their efforts to pursue and maintain employment. Both women and men recounted feelings of being viewed by others as less capable of living a "normal life," including having a job. These perceptions in turn were associated with self-doubt about life opportunity options, especially within the constraints of maintaining valued disability financial support. Doubt about their own value as persons, and a sense of change in their identity post-kidney failure, was also evident. Participants credited NKFG workshops with helping them to deal with perceived stigma

Table 6. Perceived Stigma/Spoiled Identity Expressed During Participant Interviews: By Participants' Gender and Current Employment Status.

Women		Men	
Employed (*n* = 4)	Not Employed (*n* = 7)	Employed (*n* = 5)	Not Employed (*n* = 4)
• Was "worried about what others think about me" • Had to become "more open about my kidney disease...and not to be defensive" • Had to "realize I could get a job if I wanted one" • Had to learn "...you're not as bad off as you thought"	• Have "thought I couldn't do anything" • Had to learn "that you can" • "Attitude now is 'I am who I am'. You can do things; you don't have to be shut down" • "I'm not weird, I'm Stephanie. I'm human." • "Felt like I wasn't the same person [I had been before kidney failure]" • Had to learn that "although we are sick, we can work, we can live a normal life" • Thought kidney failure was "automatically negative"	• Thought, "If you are sick you can't do, but I learned you can do the same thing. It's all in your mind." • Told himself "I can't do this; I can't do that." He heard about a program that allows you to work and still keep your money and about the 9-month trial work period. And he thought "I can do that." • Others "judge you." • Now "I don't feel so different." • "People on hemodialysis...they're not people who just sit around."	• "I thought when you get a kidney problem you couldn't do anything." • Need to learn "there's a life after renal disease" • "I'm not completely useless." • Meeting others with a transplant or on dialysis "made me feel better about myself, not outcasted. It gave me a little bit of confidence."

through, for example, learning "to be more open about my kidney disease...and not to be defensive," becoming willing to consider "that kidney failure is not automatically negative," and meeting others similar in age as well as condition who could provide reassurance that there is "a *life after renal disease.*"

Isolation From Age Peers and Questioning "Why Me?"

A second theme, isolation from age peers with kidney failure, was cited by 19/37 study participants, 10 of whom also cited perceived stigma. Individuals described feeling very age-isolated, with little or no opportunity for interaction with age peers who shared their condition, as in these illustrative quotations:

• "My centers only have one or two people my age." [Woman, 23; peritoneal dialysis]
• You need "the fellowship with others that are like you. They know how you are feeling. They take the time to get to know you. They don't judge you." [Man, 26; kidney transplant]
• [Knowing others your age] "puts you more comfortable with yourself because it lets you know 'you're not alone'." [Man, 26; kidney transplant]

- "When you get in touch with people who have been through similar things, you look at things differently" [Woman, 23; kidney transplant]

Participants who cited feeling isolated from peers also voiced a sense of unfairness that a young person must live with a condition that occurs predominantly among older persons. One young woman [age 35; hemodialysis] said that at the dialysis clinic, she only saw "old people" and all she could think was "Why me?" Another young woman [age 29; hemodialysis] said "I was in my mid-20s [when I started in-center dialysis] and there was no one to relate to at the clinic...Why me?" Kidney failure can be considered an on-time event for older persons, given a decline in normal kidney functioning with aging and the association of kidney disease with several chronic conditions whose severity increases with aging. Auer (1986, p. 204) observed that "at a stage in the life cycle when death is not uncommon in the course of nature, dialysis is considered a bonus [by elderly persons]," while "the young person, in contrast, sees the need for dialysis in terms of limitation and loss." The regular schedule of visiting the dialysis clinic may have some life-stage benefits for older persons, providing structure and purpose (Auer, 1986) and serving as a "social world" (Kutner, 1987), but seeing age peers at the dialysis clinic can be rare for young persons, as was evident in the dialysis experience of study participants.

DISCUSSION AND CONCLUSIONS

We believe that the construct of "transitions to and from young adulthood" (Scales et al., 2016) is a useful perspective for examining the experience of young persons with a disabling condition as they navigate life-stage transitions in the process of approaching youth and adulthood. *Transition* is the central theme, but the *ongoing* nature of the transition process is also central. We also suggest that it is useful to understand this process as one of *approaching*, rather than reaching, adulthood, a perspective that seems consistent with the critique of the concept of "failed" transition offered by Tisdall (2001). Tisdall appeared to resist the view that individuals either successfully transition to adulthood or they "fail" to transition, given that there are various ways to understand "adulthood." She suggested that the goal of increased independence, which is often considered a hallmark of attaining adulthood, can be positive in many ways, but that supportive interconnections among society, family, and individual agency potentially provide a stronger context for self-actualization. Similarly, Scales et al. (2016) emphasized that the dimensions of successful young adulthood that they outlined include several normative standards that reflect connection and concern with others "within a context of relatedness and mutual obligation" (Scales et al., 2016, p. 158).

The "transition indicators" included in our study, i.e., parental home versus independent (from parents) home, employment, and community involvement, are frequently included in the literature on young persons' transition to adulthood in the setting of disability (e.g., Hallum, 1995; Tisdall, 2001) and in literature focusing on young persons with kidney failure (e.g., Hamilton et al., 2017). However, we acknowledge that these indicators do not convey a holistic perspective of transition goals, such as Scales et al. (2016) provide with their reference to "healthy family and social relationships." As Tisdall (2001) emphasized, families, and other key relationships, are likely to be key mediating factors in the transitional choices and barriers for young disabled people. She observed that family negotiations and patterns may be especially salient for young persons, when one considers to what extent families limit or enhance young disabled people's self-efficacy, desire, and practice to take charge of their lives and life course decisions. *Springboard* organizers recognized that family members might discourage young persons' participation in a program that encouraged vocational success because the young person's increased earnings could jeopardize the individual's disability income which was important to the family.

It has been argued that attaining paid employment is not essential to success in transitioning to adulthood (Tisdall, 2001). At the same time, it is generally agreed that employment can be important in fostering individuals' self-esteem, and employment remains a socially valued status (Irwin, 2001). One weekend workshop in each *Springboard* series focused on "career development," with participation by Vocational Rehabilitation (VR) counselors. Social Security Administration (SSA) work incentive provisions were reviewed to help young persons better understand their options with regard to employment, insurance, and disability benefits. According to the Blue Book, a listing of disabling conditions that the SSA uses to determine an applicant's eligibility for benefits, persons undergoing dialysis that is expected to continue for at least 12 months, and who can provide supporting medical evidence are automatically approved for benefits. The SSA considers kidney transplant recipients disabled for 12 months from the date of the transplant. After that time, disability status is reassessed, based on the level of functionality after the transplant, kidney rejection episodes experienced, infections and other medical complications, and negative effects that may be related to antirejection treatment.

Gainful employment among "the maximum practical number" of persons receiving treatment for kidney failure is a specified goal in federal oversight of dialysis facilities in the kidney disease program of Medicare (Kutner et al., 2008). When Congress approved the Social Security amendment that provided coverage of kidney failure treatment costs under Medicare in 1972, the expectation was that this entitlement would be offset by individuals' expected return to work (Rettig, 1980, 2011). However, many individuals who reach kidney failure leave the labor market after initiating chronic dialysis treatment (Erickson et al., 2018; Kutner et al., 2010). In a national survey in which persons recently starting chronic dialysis therapy were interviewed, a multivariable logistic regression analysis including 564 persons who had worked in the previous year indicated that higher physical activity score and employer group health (EGH) insurance were significantly associated with continued employment after four months. Receiving disability income and hemodialysis (versus peritoneal dialysis) treatment status were significantly associated with decreased likelihood of continued employment. Age was not a significant predictor in this analysis. Two-thirds of those who continued working had EGH insurance, compared with one-third of those who did not; only 14% of those who continued working reported receiving disability income, compared with half of the individuals who left the labor force (Kutner et al., 2010). The kidney disease community acknowledges that there is a "societal perception that [persons] with ESRD are unable to work," which in turn "completes a vicious cycle of low expectations for employment" (Hallab & Wish, 2018).

Perceptions of stigma and spoiled identity with kidney disease were an ongoing influence for many young persons in this study. When persons with a disabling condition are viewed as suffering victims or as different and strange, the inference is that they are "not quite human" (Goffman, 1963, p. 6). The extension of this view is that if a person is "not quite human," with spoiled identity, it is appropriate for that person to remain outside the community of those who "should" receive just distributions of societal rewards and resources (Deutsch, 1985). Stigmatizing labels alter others' perceptions of a disabling condition and legitimize stratification (Mehan et al., 1986). As research by Shifrer (2013) showed for students who are labeled with learning disabilities, achievement expectations – among students as well as teachers – can be lowered in response to stigmatizing labels. In the experience of the young persons interviewed for this study, having the opportunity to get to know, and share experience with, similar-age peers "puts you more comfortable with yourself because it lets you know 'you're not alone'" [Man, 26; kidney transplant], as noted above. The identity-affirming role of connection with others is a shared emphasis of the life course literature (e.g., Shanahan, 2000) and the literature on disability (e.g., Zola, 1982).

As we have noted, the development and progression of kidney disease may be viewed by others as the fault of the individual (Gutman et al., 2022). Multiple studies have shown an association of younger age with nonadherence to pre-scribed treatment by persons on in-center hemodialysis (Menez & Jaar, 2018), and the medical literature has reported case studies that show disastrous conse-quences of treatment nonadherence for young persons who are dependent on dialysis or have a functioning kidney transplant (Bell, 2007). Young persons may be considered especially susceptible to risk-taking (Scales et al., 2016), and given that individuals' emotional brain development and executive functions are not considered fully mature until the mid to late 20s, young adulthood may constitute an emotionally vulnerable time period in a young person's life (Bell, 2022; Ferris et al., 2016). "Transition clinics" in the medical community, as discussed above, focus on efforts to enhance young persons' self-responsibility for their health, but they may be limited in addressing young-adulthood development issues and/or issues of perceived spoiled identity that could in turn impact self-agency learning and development.

Tisdall (2001) observed that young disabled people risk being marginalized, both theoretically and practically, for at least three reasons: because they are *young*, because they are *disabled*, and because they are in *transition*. Persons with kidney failure who are *young* are only a small proportion of the total kidney failure population and are, therefore, disadvantaged by having limited opportunities to share experiences with age-peers and to gain confidence by learning that "I'm not the only one." The salience of *disability* labeling for the lives of young persons with kidney failure is evident in the complicated work/benefits hurdles that influence employment opportunities, and in the influence on their own self-image of perceived stereotypes and stigma attributed to kidney disease and treatment. *Transition* challenges for persons with kidney failure may in turn reflect all of these factors, as well as including the need to manage condition-related complications and treatment transitions that are among the contingencies of kidney failure (Erickson & Macmillan, 2018) and which may impact life-stage contingencies of family and residence status, education, and/or work status.

We have suggested that the framework for successful young adult development provided by Scales et al. (2016) offers a valuable perspective on transition issues related to young adulthood, including issues experienced by persons with the disabling condition of kidney failure. Importantly, in the context of this framework, no young persons are considered risk-free; rather, successful development depends on young persons' attaining skills to manage risks so that potential harms are minimized (Scales et al., 2016). Persons with kidney failure are necessarily dependent on a form of kidney replacement therapy for their survival, making individuals' reported gains in self-confidence through an experience such as the *Springboard* program especially meaningful, as in young persons' assertions that "I can depend on myself to do things" (Man, 33, hemodialysis), and "...you can live by yourself; you can take care of yourself" (Woman, 34, hemodialysis).

Our objective in this chapter was not to evaluate the effectiveness of the *Springboard* program in fostering life and career skills among young persons with kidney failure, but the qualitative responses shared by study participants provide a glimpse of the functions that an initiative such as this may have (for many, but not necessarily for all, participants). We suggest also that the "transition to and from young adulthood" is a process that may be ongoing for individuals over much of a lifetime, regardless of disability status. Finally, we concur with Tisdall (2001, pp. 175–176) that the nature of the interconnections among society, family, and individual agency, and their impact on individual risks and biographies, is of central importance for youth work, youth policies, and the transitional literature on young disabled people.

ACKNOWLEDGEMENTS

A summary of the educational and vocational status of young persons after their participation in the young adult workshop series was provided, as requested, to the NKFG, but the data in this chapter have not otherwise been reported.

This research was made possible by collaboration between the Emory University Department of Rehabilitation Medicine, the NKFG, and the Division of Rehabilitation Services of the Georgia Department of Human Resources, to develop workshops for young adults with kidney disease living in Georgia (the *Springboard* program). The authors are grateful for the expertise of colleagues with instrumental roles in this collaborative program, especially Ann Koch, Chuck Brown, G. Dean Ericson (PhD), Joan Baker MSW, Sandra Payne, and Tom Tedards.

REFERENCES

Auer, J. (1986). Psychological aspects of elderly renal patients. *Aspects of Renal Care, 1*, 200–208.

Bell, L. (2007). Adolescents with renal disease in an adult world: Meeting the challenge of transition of care. *Nephrology Dialysis Transplantation, 22*, 988–991. https://doi.org/10.1093/ndt/gfl770

Bell, L. E. (2022). The transition of a pediatric kidney transplant recipient from childhood to adult care. *Clinical Journal of the American Society of Nephrology, 17*(5), 736–738. https://doi.org/10.2215/CJN.14991121

Deutsch, M. (1985). *Distributive justice.* Yale University Press.

Díaz-González de Ferris, M. E., Del Villar-Vilchis, M., Guerrero, R., Barajas-Valencia, V. M., Vander-Schaaf, E. B., de Pomposo, A., Medeiros, M., Rak, E., Cantu-Quintanilla, G., Raina, R., & lvarez-Elias, A. C. (2017). Self-management and health care transition among adolescents and young adults with chronic kidney disease: Medical and psychosocial considerations. *Advances in Chronic Kidney Disease, 24*(6), 405–409. https://doi.org/10.1053/j.ackd.2017.09.010

Erickson, G. A., & Macmillan, R. (2018). Disability and the transition to early adulthood: A life course contingency perspective. *Longitudinal and Life Course Studies, 9*(2), 188–211. http://dx.doi.org/10.14301/llcs.v912.335

Erickson, K., Zhao, B., Ho, V., & Winkelmayer, W. (2018). Employment among patients starting dialysis in the United States. *Clinical Journal of the American Society of Nephrology, 13*, 265–273. https://doi.org/10.2215/CJN.06470617

Ferris, M. E., Miles, J. A., & Seamon, M. L. (2016). Adolescents and young adults with chronic or end-stage kidney disease. *Blood Purification, 41*, 205–210. https://doi.org/10.1159/000441317

Fields, R. (2010). God help you. You're on dialysis. *Atlantic Magazine.* https://www.theatlantic.com/magazine/archive/2010/12/-god-help-you-youre-on-dialysis/308308/

Fox, R. C., & Swazey, J. P. (1978). *The courage to fail: A social view of organ transplants and dialysis* (2nd ed.). University of Chicago Press.

Frazier, C. A. (Ed.). (1973). *Is it moral to modify man?* Charles C. Thomas Publications.

Gill, C. (2001). Divided understandings: The social experience of disability. In G. L. Albrecht, K. D. Seelman, & M. Bury (Eds.), *The handbook of disability studies* (pp. 351–372). Sage.

Glaser, B. G., & Straus, A. L. (2017). *Discovery of grounded theory: Strategies for qualitative research.* Routledge.

Goffman, E. (1963). *Stigma: Notes on the management of spoiled identity.* Prentice-Hall.

Gutman, T., Kelly, A., Scholes-Robertson, N., Craig, J. C., Jesudason, S., & Tong, A. (2022). Patient and caregiver experiences and attitudes about their involvement in research in chronic kidney disease. *Clinical Journal of the American Society of Nephrology, 17*(2), 215–227. https://doi.org/10.2215/CJN.05960521

Hallab, A. l., & Wish, J. B. (2018). Employment among patients on dialysis: An unfulfilled promise. *Clinical Journal of the American Society of Nephrology, 13*, 203–204. https://doi.org/10.2215/CJN.13491217

Hallum, A. (1995). Disability and the transition to adulthood: Issues for the disabled child, the family, and the pediatrician. *Current Problems in Pediatrics, 25*(1), 12–50. https://doi.org/10.1016/s0045-9380(06)80013-7

Hamilton, A. J., Clissold, R. L., Inward, C. D., Caskey, F. J., & Ben-Shlomo, Y. (2017). Sociodemographic, psychologic health, and lifestyle outcomes in young adults on renal replacement therapy. *Clinical Journal of the American Society of Nephrology, 12*(12), 1951–1961. https://doi.org/10.2215/CJN.04760517

Hogan, D., & Astone, N. M. (1986). The transition to adulthood. *Annual Review of Sociology, 12*, 109–130. https://doi.org/10.1146/annurev.so.12.080186.000545

Icard, P. F., Hower, S. J., Kuchenreuther, A. R., Hooper, S. R., & Gipson, D. S. (2008). The transition from childhood to adulthood with ESRD: Educational and social challenges. *Clinical Nephrology*, *68*(1), 1–7. https://doi.org/10.5414/cnp69001

Irwin, S. (2001). Repositioning disability and the life course: A social claiming perspective. In M. Priestley (Ed.), *Disability and the life course: Global perspectives* (pp. 15–25). Cambridge University.

Kutner, N. G. (1987). Social worlds and identity in end-stage renal disease (ESRD). In P. Conrad & J. A. Roth (Eds.). *Research in the sociology of health care* (Vol. 6, pp. 33–71). JAI Press Inc.

Kutner, N., Bowles, T., Zhang, R., Huang, Y., & Pastan, S. (2008). Dialysis facility characteristics and variation in employment rates: A national study. *Clinical Journal of the American Society of Nephrology*, *3*, 111–116. https://doi.org/10.2215/CJN.02990707

Kutner, N. G., Zhang, R., Huang, Y., & Johansen, K. L. (2010). Depressed mood, usual activity level, and continued employment after starting dialysis. *Clinical Journal of the American Society of Nephrology*, *5*, 2040–2045. https://doi.org/10.2215/CJN.03980510

Lindsay, S. (2019). Exploring the value of qualitative comparison groups in rehabilitation research: Lessons from youth with disabilities transitioning into work. In C. M. Hayre & D. J. Muller (Eds.), *Exploring healthcare and rehabilitation: The impact of qualitative research* (pp. 33–52). Taylor & Francis Group. https://www.crcpress.com/Rehabilitation-Science-in-Practice-Series/book-series/CRCPRESERIN

Mehan, H., Hertweck, A., & Meihls, J. L. (1986). *Handicapping the handicapped: Decision making in students' educational careers.* Stanford University Press.

Menez, S., & Jaar, B. G. (2018). Missed hemodialysis treatments: A modifiable but unequal burden in the world. *American Journal of Kidney Disease*, *72*(5), 625–627. https://doi.org/10.1053/j.ajkd.2018.08.002

Rettig, R. A. (1980). *Implementing the end-stage renal disease program of Medicare.* The Rand Corporation.

Rettig, R. A. (2011). Special treatment: The story of Medicare's ESRD entitlement. *New England Journal of Medicine*, *364*, 596–598. https://doi.org/10.1056/NEJMp1014193

Scales, P. C., Benson, P. L., Oesterle, S., Hill, K. G., Hawkins, J. D., & Pashak, T. J. (2016). The dimensions of successful young adult development: A conceptual and measurement framework. *Applied Developmental Science*, *20*, 150–174. https://doi.org/10.1080/10888691.2015.1082429

Scarponi, D., Cammaroto, V., Pasini, A., La Scola, C., Mencarelli, F., Bertulli, C., Busutti, M., La Manna, G., & Pession, A. (2021). Multidisciplinarity in transition pathways for patients with kidney disease: The current state of play. *Frontiers in Pediatrics*, *9*. https://doi.org/10.3389/fped.2021

Shanahan, M. J. (2000). Pathways to adulthood in changing societies: Variability and mechanisms in life course perspective. *Annual Review of Sociology*, *26*, 667–692. https://doi.org/10.1146/annurev.soc.26.1.667

Shifrer, D. (2013). Stigma of a label: Educational expectations for high school students labeled with learning disabilities. *Journal of Health and Social Behavior*, *54*(4), 462–480. https://doi.org/10.1177/0022146513503346

Tisdall, K. (2001). Failing to make the transition? Theorising the 'transition to adulthood' for young disabled people. In M. Priestley (Ed.), *Disability and the life course: Global perspectives* (pp. 167–178). Cambridge University.

United States Renal Data System (USRDS). (2021). *2021 USRDS annual data report: Epidemiology of kidney disease in the United States.* National Institutes of Health, National Institute of Diabetes and Digestive and Kidney Diseases. https://adr.usrds.org/2021

Zola, I. K. (1982). *Missing pieces: A chronicle of living with a disability.* Temple University Press.

DOING GENDER, DOING DISABILITY: HOW DISABLED YOUNG ADULTS APPROACH GENDER IN RESPONSE TO ABLEISM

Hillary Steinberg

AUTHOR BIOGRAPHY

Hillary Steinberg, PhD, is a Survey Statistician in the Data Collection Methodology and Research Branch in the Economic Statistical Methods Division at the United States Census. She is also an affiliated research scientist at the AJ Drexel Autism Institute and works on the Social Worlds and Youth Wellbeing Study and the Health Lifestyles and the Reproduction of Inequality. She studies childhood and the transition to young adulthood, identity, disability, and gender.

ABSTRACT

Gender and disability are intimately connected as embodied experiences that young people navigate interactionally. Disabilities scholars have theorized that men and women with chronic health conditions face uniquely gendered challenges. Theories of gender and disability centered on youth continue to gain prominence as the population of children and young adults with chronic health conditions grows. This study draws on data from 22 in-depth interviews with young adults diagnosed with chronic health conditions in childhood in the United States. Women, men, and gender nonbinary individuals report that doing disability in interactions in childhood meant doing gender in expected feminine ways. Specifically, interviewees described increased empathy, a deep understanding of their own emotions, and the ability to use adversity to connect with and benefit others as expectations. Interviewees employed or resisted doing gender in ways that reflected individuals' gender locations. Women and nonbinary individuals saw feminine performance as a sign of weakness, often

Disabilities and the Life Course
Research in Social Science and Disability, Volume 14, 89–105
Copyright © 2023 Hillary Steinberg
Published under exclusive licence by Emerald Publishing Limited
ISSN: 1479-3547/doi:10.1108/S1479-354720230000014006

resisting demonstrating it in interactions. On the other hand, feminine per-
formance reportedly impacted men in the sample in positive ways. This study
takes a life course approach to illuminate how the ableist expectations
expressed to disabled children are gendered and impact how disabled young
adults negotiate an ableist world.

Keywords: Young adulthood; childhood; chronic health conditions; gender;
expectations; emphasized femininity

Disabled individuals face gendered constraints and expectations across the life
course. Disabilities scholars have theorized that men and women with chronic
health conditions face challenges that impact an individual's sense of self in
gendered ways (Charmaz, 1991; Connell, 2012; Wendell, 1996). Children with
chronic health conditions are increasingly aging into young adulthood. Theories
of gender and disability centered on youth continue to gain prominence.
Applying a life course perspective also illuminates how disabled youth take on
identities, including gender.

This study aims to understand how ableism guides gendered expectations of
disabled children within interactions and how young adults resist or accommodate femininity in response. Drawing on data from interviews with 22 young
adults who experienced the onset of serious chronic health conditions in
childhood, this chapter uses narratives to position how disabled young adults
see and enact their gender identities.[1] I find that women, men, and nonbinary
individuals report that encounters centered on ableism also included an
expectation of emphasized femininity. Specifically, interviewees described
recognizing expectations for enhanced empathy, being in touch with emotions,
and connecting with others over adversity, and often described performing in
accordance with these expectations in childhood. As adults, they examined
these expectations and their performances through participation in narrative
interviews. In their narratives, women and nonbinary individuals often framed
these expectations as negative and many told stories of resisting these expectations through gender performances in adulthood. On the other hand, men felt
they had positively integrated gendered expectations into their identities and
behavior. This study extends feminist theorizing on gender by using retrospective and current narratives of young adults to explore how gendered
expectations of disabled youth shape their sense of self as they make the
transition from childhood to young adulthood.

---

[1]A note on language: In line with Charmaz and Belgrave (2015), I refer to disability and
chronic health conditions interchangeably throughout, as the distinctions are engendered in
medicalized, Parsonian approaches to health (Charmaz & Belgrave, 2015; Mauldin &
Brown, 2021). Interviewees had differing relationships to the label of disability, as explored
in Steinberg (2020).

BACKGROUND

Traditionally, researchers have framed gender as a constant but dynamic performance produced in social settings and through interactions, in line with a "doing gender" perspective (West & Zimmerman, 1987). As such, gender is not a static performance over the life course. Specifically, children are often constrained in how they can enact gender performances because they are deeply embedded in institutions such as education and family (Meadow, 2018; Richter, 2017). In a next life course stage, young adulthoods employ gender identities and differences more flexibly but still rely on their upbringings to understand gender norms (Dalessandro, 2021). Doing gender can involve *redoing gender*, meaning because gender is an interactional process predicated on power dynamics, it can change over time to reify power (West & Zimmerman, 2009). Understanding how gender functions in everyday life is important to ground how individuals may resist or accept its constraints as a structure (Kandiyoti, 1988). Individuals, particularly women, are expected to navigate gendered norms in all interactional performances (Weitz, 2001). Responses to the constraints an individual faces in performing gender, namely resistance and accommodation, can align with emphasized femininity, or feminine performances, that legitimate unequal power structures (Kincaid et al., 2022).

Historically, disability was created as a legal category in the United States as a result of anxieties around masculine citizenship (Blum, 2020). Disabled men had to rely upon, reformulate, or reject hegemonic ideals of masculinity (Gerschick & Miller, 1995; Wenger, 2013). Norms for behaviors such as breadwinning or embodied physical performance (Gahman, 2017) can prove challenging for disabled men (Shuttleworth et al., 2012). The emphasis on men who acquired injuries or illnesses later in life reflects a normative assumption that real men become emasculated, which is problematic and reflects a narrow understanding of aging and disability (Shuttleworth et al., 2012). Similarly, applications of hegemonic masculinity in health research have been critiqued as reductive, with many works focusing on narrow conceptions of masculinity identity and performance (Matthews, 2016). Furthermore, disability can serve as a vague category for analysis and is rarely included in intersectional analyses (Egner, 2019; Naples et al., 2019). Thus, more intersectional work on gender and disabilities is needed, to move beyond narrow understandings of gendered experience across the life course.

The study of gender and disability has historically overlapped in very specific arenas, such as in the subfield of feminist theory (Cheng, 2009). The interconnected nature of disability and gender is, therefore, well theorized in some subfields (Gerschick, 2000; Lyons, 2009; Springer et al., 2012). Consequently, some previous research has highlighted how disability and gender are identities, categories, and experiences that cannot fully be separated (Brown, 2017). Feminist theorists have also been interested in gender and disability for decades. First explored in feminist scholarship in the 1980s, the "double handicap" described the added oppression women with disabilities experienced (Scotch, 1986). Feminist disabilities scholars show that inferiority is constructed in multifaceted ways, in that both femaleness and disability are seen as inherent degradation (Garland-Thomson, 2002). Because gender is constructed and performed through the body, feminist theories of disability generally focus on uncovering the cultural meaning assigned to bodies by looking at disability as a set of exclusions, looking at community and identity, revealing discrimination, using disability as a social category of analysis, and framing disability in power relations (Garland-Thomson, 2005).

Ableism is a significant constraint that disabled individuals navigate. Ableism acts as a social structure, affecting access to resources and increasing stigma and discrimination for people with disabilities. Ableism is built upon ideology that suggests there is an imagined "normal" body to deviate from (Brown, 2017). As both structure and ideology, ableism not only affects disabled people but also orients them to culture more broadly (Wolbring, 2008). In line with the social theory of disability, ableism exists because it is socially produced and reaffirmed within day-to-day interactions (Campbell, 2009). Ableism has bearing for the study of gender, especially in the context of disability, due to its similarities in being used to justify discrimination through ideas of biological deficiency (Wolbring, 2008).

The impact of ableism factors heavily into feminist and intersectional theories of disability. The history of intersectional analyses of disability also has roots in Black feminist thought. For example, Black women are under particular pressure to regulate their emotions when facing chronic illness (Beauboeuf-Lafontant, 2007; Hill, 2009; Lorde, 1997). Ableist and White supremacist ideas about work, sexuality, and inferiority work to marginalize Black people (Bailey & Mobley, 2019). Other theorists have also emphasized a queer, feminist approach in blurring the categories around disability with "crip" politics (Kafer, 2013), explicitly exploring disability as a process that queers gender and identity, as well as age and life course stage.

This study focuses on "doing gender" (West & Zimmerman, 1987), an interactional process constrained by gendered expectations learned in childhood, and doing gender with "doing disability." This interactional lens grounds our understanding of how disabled young adults respond to ableism, and how they accommodate or resist ableist ideologies through emphasized femininity. Ultimately, narratives about how disabled young adults perceive and enact gender performance in the current day are shaped in childhood as individuals learn about sexism and ableism. Although expectations for gender and disability performance change throughout the life course, the expectations formed in childhood have lasting impacts on subsequent life course stages.

METHODS

This chapter was conceived out of a larger project on health and the transition to young adulthood. Participants with "serious" health conditions in childhood, however they defined them, were invited to interview. It is difficult to define what conditions should be counted among "bonafide" chronic health conditions.

Accordingly, I chose to have interviewees identify their conditions and severity because I was purposely interested in narratives and perceptions of illness rather than "objective truth." All respondents considered their conditions to be serious, and all but one categorized their health conditions as chronic.[2] The conditions interviewees volunteered as their diagnoses ranged drastically in severity, duration, and symptom prevalence in everyday life. As explored in another piece from this project, interviewees ranged in how they spoke about disability, with some eschewing and term and others embracing it (Steinberg, 2020). All expressed commonalities by reporting medicalized experiences (Charmaz, 1991; Mattingly, 2010). Conditions included cerebral palsy, childhood cancer, diabetes, mental health conditions, injuries, and others. Age of onset varied from birth to 17 years old; thus, all experienced the onset of symptoms before turning 18 years old. More information about participants can be found in Table 1.

In total, I interviewed 22 young adults, ages 19 to 30, in 2017.[3] I recruited through my social networks to capture young adults who may have been less embedded in the medical system. This had a few advantages, specifically recruiting outside healthcare institutions and building trust with participants, who were mostly friends of friends. This method can be effective for millennials speaking about difficult topics (Dalessandro, 2021). Through these convenience and snowball sampling methods, I interviewed 13 women, seven men, and two nonbinary individuals.[4] Five respondents voluntarily defined their sexuality as queer. Most interviewees (17) were White. Pseudonyms were used to preserve confidentiality and were chosen by interviewees in most cases. Interviews were structured around a series of open-ended questions that allowed various themes and topics to emerge.

I obtained approval for this research from my university's Institutional Review Board. Every interviewee consented both in writing and verbally. Interviews took place in person and over Skype. Skype has become increasingly useful in facilitating interviews with hard-to-reach populations (Cheng, 2017), even before the COVID-19 pandemic, when these interviews took place. On average, the interviews lasted around an hour, with the shortest being 37 minutes long and the longest being nearly three hours. In-person interviews were recorded using a digital recording device, while Skype interviews were recorded through video. A third party then transcribed all interviews.

I worked inductively to code data and concentrated on narratives of gender and disability. I employed a constructivist interpretive lens, meaning I worked to find theoretical threads in the data with no specific theory in mind (Timmermans & Tavory, 2012). I began by first coding each interview broadly and then revisiting transcripts to more specifically explore the nuance of the narratives of the interviewees (Saldaña, 2013). This led to focusing on a micro-level

---

[2]As explored in my earlier work (Steinberg, 2020), differing levels of social support impacted how interviewees understood their health.

[3]See Table 1 for demographic information.

[4]All interviewees explicitly noted their genders, and I use their language to identify them throughout.

Table 1. Interviewee Demographics.

Name	Age	Gender	Condition	Education	Ethnic Identity	Age of First Diagnosis
Rick	19	Man	Adrenal Insufficiency	In College	White – Ethnically Jewish	10
Don	21	Man	Histiocytosis	In College	White	3
Jared	23	Man	Leukemia and OCD	College	White – Ethnically Jewish	7
Tommy	23	Man	Atopic Dermatitis	College	White	Birth
Tyler	23	Man	Undiagnosed Stomach Condition and Depression	Masters	White	Misdiagnosed at 20
Finn	24	Man	Depression and Anxiety	Master of Social Work	White – Ethnically Jewish	13
Brian	25	Man	Cerebral Palsy	Masters	White	Birth
Kate	20	Woman	Celiac Disease	In College	White	17
Lorelai	20	Woman	Eating Disorder and OCD and Anxiety	In College	White – Ethnically Jewish	14
Nel	20	Woman	Depression	In College	White – Ethnically Jewish	13
Aurora	21	Woman	Depression and Anxiety and Posttraumatic Stress Disorder	In College	White	21
Alexa	22	Woman	Stomach Condition and Bipolar and Eating Disorder	Less Than High School	White – Ethnically Jewish	9
Anna	22	Woman	Injury to the Back	In Graduate School	White	16
Maggie	23	Woman	Charcot-Marie-Syndrome	In Graduate School	White – Ethnically Jewish	11
Zoe	24	Woman	Diabetes and PCOS and Anxiety	College	White	4
Nadiya	25	Woman	Leukemia	College	White – Ethnically Jewish	11
Kim	26	Woman	Brain Tumor and Epilepsy, Possible Bipolar	Some College	Vietnamese and Swedish	4
Mary	26	Woman	Diabetes	Masters	White	7
Jennifer	28	Woman	Physical Arthrogryposis	Masters	White – Ethnically Jewish	Birth
Marie	30	Woman	Leukemia	High School	Latina	4
Isabelle	21	Nonbinary	Cleft Lip and Palate	In College	Filipina and White	Birth
Valerie	24	Nonbinary	Cerebral Palsy	In College	White – Ethnically Russian	Birth

Note: All information is a reflection of the definitions of the interviewee.

explanation of gendered phenomena (Jerolmack & Khan, 2017). I did not sample purposively by gender and, therefore, the findings came up organically as a pattern in narratives.

Narratives are interactional and explain how structure impacts lives (Charmaz, 2020; Frank, 1995; Irvine et al., 2019). Narratives and how the interviewees understood themselves were privileged throughout the interview process. Interviewees examined their responses to ableist expectations in childhood and speculated how this shaped their relationships to gender in the transition to young adulthood. Interviewees were often unsure about how to approach questions explicitly about gender. More specifically, the question "do you feel your condition impacted your being a girl/boy/nonbinary person in childhood and now?" elicited the most requests for clarification from interviewees. Doing gender was an everyday logic they employed subconsciously, especially in young adulthood. Consequently, their answers to other questions, such as ideas about independence and emotions, sometimes revealed deeper patterns about gender expectations and performance. Since the disability community is embedded in an inherently political social movement (Nishida, 2016; Scotch, 1988), this may have contributed to gender egalitarian views, but this was not explicitly stated by interviewees. It is also possible that interviewees held more egalitarian views on gender because of their generation and geographic location (Scarborough & Sin, 2020).

FINDINGS

Interviewees described three ways they performed emphasized femininity in response to ableist interactions in childhood. They categorized these performances as feminine. Interactions with others that indicated gendered expectations in childhood, and the subsequent need to accommodate or resist sexist and ableist expectations, impacted how interviewees thought about their relationship to gender in young adulthood. Interviewees retrospectively described responses to ableist expectations as a process that led to emphasized femininity. However, only men in the sample had the room to interpret these performances as positive, in reference to how they thought about their gender by young adulthood; as a result, men in the sample argued that they positively influenced their gender performances. Women and nonbinary individuals were more likely to resist these feminine gender expectations and did not characterize emphasized femininity as positive, even when they performed according to expectations and reaped some benefits.

Femininity as a Response to Ableism

Interviewees recounted navigating interactions stemming from structural ableism: prioritizing the comfort of strangers, being encouraged to reckon with negative emotions for the sake of others and facing (often magnified) adversity as a result. They characterized these performances as feminine. A clear and frequent example was participants' recognition that there was an expectation that they put others at ease in interactions. Brian and Jennifer were perceptibly physically disabled. Brian described interacting with strangers as emotionally taxing and characterized it as infantilizing. He said he often "made ridiculous cripple jokes" at his own expense to show strangers that he was "mentally all there." Jennifer was frustrated by expectations that she also perform similarly. She said:

> I feel like I always have to make people feel comfortable.... [Disabled people] have to be pleasant, no matter what, because if we have a bad day, we are just upset because we are disabled. We are not allowed to have feelings outside of being a person with a disability. So, yes, I have to make people feel comfortable all the time.

Individuals who were not immediately recognized as disabled were expected to make others comfortable upon disclosure. When Mary would disclose that she had type 1 diabetes, she worried about how others would feel. She said, "I don't want them to think, 'Oh, I'm sorry'. You know?...I guess I try to kind of make them feel more comfortable." The management of the emotions of others and the self is expected of women in certain circumstances (Hochschild, 2012; Jaggar, 1989), including in the context of health (Kempner, 2014). Interviewees often talked about how their conditions cultivated these stereotypically feminine responses. The above examples demonstrate the ways in which disabled young adults are frequently put into positions that encourage these performances.

Interviewees did not explicitly describe themselves as emotional in most cases. Importantly, the only interviewees who did describe themselves in this way were men. Instead, they referenced emotions, their ability to tune into them, or their struggles in the choice to become less emotional. Men, women, and nonbinary individuals told stories featuring emotional responses, but these stories varied. Men more often told stories about crying and sadness. Women and nonbinary individuals told stories about anger and frustration. Alexa, Anna, Jennifer, and Kim relayed narratives in which they responded with anger, such as healthcare providers failing to take them seriously when they tried to advocate for themselves. The narratives they told here were in line with resistance: that although deference was expected of them, their emotional responses were out of line with gender expectations.

Finn and Anna both reported that healthcare providers expected them to be emotional in gender-normative ways. Finn had severe depression and anxiety that eventually necessitated electroshock therapies at the age of 17. He found it hard to get a proper diagnosis, even after seeing a psychologist for a year. Although he described breaking down often in public, including crying frequently, the psychologist did not understand the severity of his condition as these were not typical externalizing behaviors frequent in boys. On the other hand, Anna suffered from a sports injury that doctors believed was "all in her head" (Buchbinder, 2015). When asked by providers how she felt, she described herself as feeling nothing and "empty inside." Both recounted getting back in tune with their emotions in adulthood by finding trusted providers and engaging in intensive therapy. Finn was confident this process had made him stronger emotionally. Anna worried she was perceived as weak. Both resisted gendered expectations in how their symptoms presented, with Finn's emotionality stemming from his depression and Anna's physical weakness deriving from her injury. Finn was more positive about this experience in young adulthood than Anna.

Most interviewees also described themselves as empathetic, another stereotypically feminine trait. Lorelei, who had anxiety, OCD, and anorexia, felt she could "understand the pain that people feel" and "relate to people a lot more," especially those with mental illness. Maggie also cited an ability to understand other people's disabilities. Don was proud of his ability to make friends with others with health conditions easily. Tyler told a story about seeking out a connection with a potential date with a medical condition. When discussing empathy, Brian said "everyone has their own things they're going through." However, Nadiya exemplifies resisting this feminine response despite similarly describing empathy toward others. She not only situated empathy as something she could not help but also suggested that it was not always welcome. She said:

> [N]ow I think one of my moral fibers [is] that everyone is going through something. Every single person. So as much as I might naturally and internally want to judge someone at first glance, my body just has this defense mechanism where I can't do it. Because I always think, like, that person could have lost a parent yesterday. That person could have lost a child. That person could have lost a job. So that's always where my mind wanders. I kind of stop myself from jumping to any conclusions. And just in general, I'm sympathetic, empathetic. *It's probably even worse than, it's worse than I would want it to be because like I said, I sometimes feel people's pain as it's my own. And I don't want to feel it. And I don't want to think about it.* But I do. Looking at old people, or looking at homeless people, or things like that really kind of hit me on all my emotional notes. Not even necessarily sick people; that's a whole different thing...it gets emotional. And I'm not generally a very emotional person from, like, a habitual standpoint. So, when I feel deeply concerned about something internally, it kind of resonates with everything that I do. (Author's emphasis)

Nadiya did not see increased empathy as a positive feeling, nor did she feel it bolstered her gender performance. In the quote above, she wrestled with the strength of her empathy. Finn, as a contrasting example, saw empathy more positively:

> I always was extremely empathetic to begin with. I think one of the issues I had was the fact that I was hypersensitive to other people in how I was perceiving other people's feelings. I spent a lot more time-I mean, growing up, I've always had a lot more friends who were girls than boys. I think that was just something with being more open to feeling and having really strong emotions, having those breakdowns in public where I'd cry a lot and it was visible...That I think made me a better person, just being more aware of that.

Finn equated empathy with being emotional and inferred that his feelings are gendered and feminine. He retrospectively defined himself as more comfortable emphasizing femininity and deemed this as positive for his gender performance in young adulthood and later life stages.

Many interviewees expressed a desire to help others as well. For example, several were involved in charity work, both as children and adults. Jared described attending fundraisers and learning public speaking as a child, once he was in remission from leukemia. Nadiya was very proud of a charitable organization she ran in adulthood supporting pediatric cancer research that she had started after selling rubber bracelets in childhood. Don also sold rubber bracelets to support the histiocytosis association. Although he disagrees with these fundraising activities in adulthood, he said that this fundraising in childhood "was very empowering."

Men and women talked about disclosing their experiences with medical conditions as being helpful. Brian's condition was perceptible due to mobility issues, and he was sometimes annoyed at being seen as a hero for doing everyday tasks. However, he suggested, "I wouldn't necessarily say it bothers me because I'm happy to motivate people or whatever." Many interviewees were looking to dispel stigmatized identities related to health. In adulthood this meant making others comfortable with their health conditions. For example, Jared related this to his skill of making others comfortable in conversations:

> I like to aggressively inform people of serious illnesses just for the sense of making people more comfortable with it. Because I know a lot of people, particularly my friends in college, kind of, hide their, either their prior history in something or just even when they're sick with something small now and just, like, ignore it and kind of bury it down. And I feel like the more culturally we're comfortable with talking about serious illness, the fewer problems we have.

In contrast, while women felt that social interactions with others were positive and could help to dispel stigma, they were sometimes blunt in conversation and less motivated to protect the comfort of others. Zoe said she liked to get "sassy" about her diabetes in explanations. Similarly, Alexa explained:

> I also think it's more helpful, like, I can be helpful to people. . . . If I'm more open, other people are more willing to be open with me. I definitely don't, like, try and hide or sugar coat it in any way.

A desire to dispel myths, create connections, and be honest with others was a typical response to childhood disability. Because an ableist culture causes individuals to assume that a lack of health conditions, especially in youth, is normal, disabled children are expected to manage interactions in the face of these norms. Children and young adults in this study were expected to manage the emotions of others, which some participants referred to as a feminine behavior. They felt they were doing authentic emotion work by avoiding putting others at ease, but they did not always want to be performing in this way. However, women in the study sometimes voiced resistance to gendered expectations. Alternatively, some men in the sample seemed to value this emphasized femininity and define it as positive.

Tough Women Resisting Femininity

Women did not describe feeling strongly tied to womanhood, and none described themselves as feminine. Most said they had a tomboy persona at the very least in childhood, which may be a generational narrative (Kane, 2006; Yarrow, 2018), and that they were "aggressive" or "strong" in adulthood. Most interviewees worried at some point that they might be seen as using their health conditions as an excuse (Charmaz, 1991, 2010). Women in the sample explicitly resisted seeming weak, whereas men did not share this concern. Both women and nonbinary participants tied weakness to femininity. Anna repeatedly emphasized that she was not "some damsel in distress" and explained, "I just never wanted to be associated with weakness or inability." While many interviewees wrote their college essays on their health conditions, Lorelei "did not write about it for my college essay. I thought about it, but I thought it would make me look weak." Kim rejected femininity, which she explicitly tied to appearance. She said, "Most of my life I've never cared about my appearance, as I kind of suggested there with just wearing athletic clothes and never putting on makeup." She discussed how her disability dictated an inability to accommodate this manner of emphasized femininity in childhood. She connected her gender, weakness, and presentation of self when explaining why she did not submit the college essays she drafted about her experiences with a brain tumor and epilepsy:

> [A]ll of the essays that I produced about my epilepsy and my brain tumor have been very negative and very indicative of a lot of weakness, and I think that every individual who would have read my college essay for the purpose of admission to a fancy school would have been able to recognize that "this is an unhealthy girl. She is in denial of her medical condition and she will not do well in school until she has balanced out her emotional problems."

Alexa, Kate, and Jennifer all relayed narratives that showcased annoyance that their conditions made them look like they were weak or accommodating gendered expectations or, in some cases, that they were not disabled. Jennifer told a story of an altercation with a police officer who did not believe she was disabled, despite her having a perceptible physical disability, because she was a "pretty girl." Alexa and Kate were both underweight due to stomach conditions. Alexa expressed irritation that individuals assumed she was feminine or enjoyed being sexualized because she was thin. Kate brought up how often people told her they were jealous of her weight loss:

> [A roommate] told me that she wishes she had Celiac Disease so that she could be skinny like me. Yeah. That was not once. [I was] so angry. It's things like that where I'm like, "You literally live with me. You see that I puke every night. You see that I spend my nights in the bathroom, dying, or on the balcony because I literally cannot be out of the wind." You know? I need the fresh air. And she's dense. It's not getting through her mind. There's plenty of people like that, it's not just her.

Contrarily, Tyler was also underweight due to a stomach condition. A gay man, he struggled with being coded as feminine because of this body shape. Specifically, he was suspicious of people who were attracted to him for being thin, saying, "How can someone be attracted to me, because of the physical manifestations of my struggles?" Tyler complemented this concern that embodying thinness was achieving femininity in specific ways. Tyler was an exception in comparison to other men, as achieving femininity was not a benefit to him.

Experiences with ableism in childhood were particularly complex and challenging for nonbinary individuals, because they were simultaneously dealing with oppressive gender norms. Valerie had cerebral palsy and stated their first transition was out of disability and their second was out of girlhood. "Everything is both. Everything is my gender and my disabilities." They felt constrained by the twin pressures to act like a girl and act like they were not disabled. Valerie endured years of surgeries that were explicitly to make them look "normal." Eventually, after leaving their childhood home, they began to medically transition, which put a strain on their family relationships. While many interviewees described an alienation or betrayal from their body, both nonbinary participants felt this was complicated by gender dysphoria. Isabelle was self-conscious about a scar on their face from multiple cleft palate surgeries. They felt that this impacted their gender identity and made them hyperaware of their body in interactions. Because disability and gender were highlighted simultaneously in embodied interactions, nonbinary interviewees were cognizant of the pressure they felt to accommodate both ableist and sexist expectations in childhood. This discomfort continued into young adulthood as they tried to navigate independences.

Emotional Men Accommodating Femininity

In this study, men were more likely to characterize their feminine performances as positive and claimed these made them better people or men. Rick used his medical experiences to bond with others, saying, "I think for some [event] for my fraternity we did, like, an activity where we talked about important parts of our lives or something and ... I brought that up." Rick leveraged his chronic health condition as a mechanism for showcasing vulnerability to form homosocial bonds with a group of men. Jared made jokes about the patriarchy and gushed about how his parents' egalitarian relationship, coupled with his childhood cancer experiences, had pushed him to be open about consent in sexual practices and to consider taking time off work once he had children. Finn attributed being in touch with his emotions and working with them to succeed in adulthood and manage his conditions. He also brought up self-care, a stereotypically feminine topic, at the time of interview. Finn also spoke about understanding and connecting with girls:

> Most of the treatments [I received as a child] are groups that I was involved in, and some of those were majority girls in that treatment, a lot of times at a younger age. Guys weren't as prevalent. So, I'd hear a lot more issues that the girls were going through. I mean, just even things like sexual harassment type stuff, things like that. Things I would never have even thought about being something I'd have to worry about. At a young age I kind of learned about that stuff early on through the treatments.

Men suggested that accepting feminine performances in childhood affected how they saw themselves in young adulthood. Tommy described himself as mature and effeminate as a child. Caring for his skin condition became a consistent responsibility beginning in his early childhood, and he believed that this responsibility translated into independence in adulthood. He also reiterated how much he values the deep relationships that he built with others, which included being open about his medical experiences and pain. Because of the physical manifestations of his stomach condition, Tyler said "with ... very hetero-performative ways, I'm unable to perform masculine gender." He described valuing deep friendships with women throughout his life, and explicitly credited his rejection of normative masculinity to these friendships. Women and nonbinary interviewees did not emphasize deep emotional friendships as core to their sense of self. Don was very in tune with his emotions. He broke up with an ex-girlfriend because "I just felt like I couldn't express my emotions with her."[5]

Jared mused about how performances of femininity were tied to his condition. He described how this was learned in childhood but then enacted throughout subsequent life stages:

> [P]art of what I was trying to figure out in the past couple of years is whether [managing other people's emotions] was, like, something inherent to me or something that kind of started after treatment because... I don't know. I always tell people I had my midlife crisis when I was seven. Right? Because you have to face your own mortality at seven. It's kind of weird. But that kind of, like, made me mature really fast just by necessity and I think because of that, sort of, I tend to be the resource for, kind of, emotional support or just, you know, talking to people about anything. All the way from that point until now. And, yeah, the way I've kind of concluded right now is I think that I sort of had that inherently in me, but then going under treatment sort of, like, exacerbated that in me in some ways. Or at least, like, heightened my ability to, or maybe my awareness of that, because I had to be, like, so in-tune with my emotion at that point that I sort of noticed that about other people as well.

Regardless of gender identity, and a result of ableism, participants in this study experienced similar constraints as chronically ill children. This common experience produced, or at least made them more prone to, the enactment of emphasized feminine performances. While conventional wisdom suggests that femininity is devalued, the privileges inherent in masculinity allowed for most men to take on femininity in a way that allowed them to experience personal benefit in their interactions with others. All of the interviewees that were men, with the exception of one, framed their gender performance as positive, and none used negative framing elements or questioned this in their narratives, like women and nonbinary interviewees did.

Interviewees were young adults at the time of interviews, and they often spoke about feminine expectations for gender performances retrospectively. They described the cultural expectation that they put others at ease, show increased empathy, and display heightened emotions. In adulthood, these expectations were accommodated or rejected in varying ways depending on the gender identity of the interviewee. Men saw these expectations as positively shaping their gender performance in adulthood. Women and nonbinary adults in this sample shared stories about how they resisted these expectations in interactions, and how they framed and reframed these gender expectations. The use of a life course framing, specifically to explore how young adults described socialization to cultural expectations in childhood, shed light on how ableism in those early life stages has consequences for how young adults see themselves, and those consequences lead to specific gender performances in later life stages.

---

[5]It may be the case that these men were casting themselves as more feminine in their masculinity in their interviews and were not doing so in practice. However, it is important to note that they projected this identity consistently and purposefully in interviews.

CONCLUSION

This study is informed by a life course approach and, therefore, illuminates how ableist expectations in childhood may impact gender performances across the lifespan. More specifically, interviewees' retrospective narratives about gendered expectations during interactions in childhood, in response to ableism, reportedly have an effect on how they see themselves in young adulthood. While disability scholars have increasingly attended to childhood as a life stage, they have focused on how social processes shape, and how social expectations and experiences become embedded within disabled children's sense of self and identity, and how this experience is carried across sequential life stages. This study complements that literature by focusing on how ableism is a formative structure in childhood and how it becomes a frame for how individuals also experience gender. Simultaneously, gender becomes a lens through which individuals interpret how ableism affects them in childhood and beyond. In this chapter, I focus on ableism through a "doing disability" lens, and I show how enacting ableism is an interactional process within which emphasized femininity is expected, performed, and sometimes resisted. As such, doing gender and doing disability cannot be separated as cultural expectations or in their effects on individuals' performances. Doing disability is in itself a gendered process, and vice versa.

The experience of navigating ableism affects gender identity and performance in childhood and beyond. As young adults continue to build their own identities, they make choices about doing gender in the context of their understanding of their disability; specifically, they do so by utilizing social expectations learned early on as children. As scholars build literature around disabled childhoods and young adulthoods, understanding the connections between foundational childhood socialization and how young adults understand themselves is critical. Additionally, understanding the connections between navigating disability and performing gender across the life course is essential.

Interviewees explained how responding to ableist expectations in childhood necessitated gendered behavior. The expectation was for disabled children to perform emphasized femininity regardless of gender, and participants in this sample were very conscious of this expectation. Interviewees viewed this as impactful for how they understood gender in relation to disability. Men in my sample had room to view emphasized femininity as positive, although this was slightly less so for men who could not pass as heterosexual or straight. Overall, men participants were able to accommodate gendered expectations while experiencing less tension than women and nonbinary individuals.

Women and nonbinary individuals had less luck interactionally in accommodating sexist and ableist expectations. As a result, some women employed resistance and devalued feminine performances, equating some feminine traits, such as showing emotion, with weakness. For women and nonbinary interviewees, there was little benefit to participants in accommodating the gendered expectations produced by ableism. As a result, women and nonbinary individuals in this study sometimes redefined their identities and took some control back within ableist interactions.

I could not conclude about class and race differences, which is a limitation of this study. However, my findings highlight how people do gender and do disability within the context of early life stages. Other privileges, such as financial security, racial privilege, and familial support, may have allowed men in my sample to enact more flexible feminine performances without suffering significant negative consequences. Conversely, women and nonbinary individuals were sometimes more concerned with coming off as tough and ensuring others that their disability had not left them weak. They expressed distaste for typical femininity, including the emphasized feminine performances that were expected of them in the face of ableism. They believed that their chronic conditions and disabilities required them to prove that they could be autonomous while disabled, and this often necessitated resistance to gendered expectations for behavior.

Future research on disabled young adults is needed to discern how and to what extent gender and disability performances evolve and intertwine in the early life course. Class or race may also guide much of the socialization that disabled men receive in early life stages and alter how much feminine performances can benefit them over the life course. This study demonstrates that childhood experiences with disability and gender affect how individuals will think about and perform gender or disability across the life course. In this study, it was early interactional experiences with ableism, rather than individual experiences of disability, or how perceptibly disabled an interviewee was, that dictated the recognition of gendered expectations for behavior. Thus, experience with ableism as a social structure is intertwined with, and has effects on, experiences with sexism as a social structure over time. Findings from this study are not just relevant for our understanding of how disability impacts identity in childhood and young adulthood but also our understanding of how disabled young adults feel about gender and are pressured to perform it.

REFERENCES

Bailey, M., & Mobley, I. A. (2019). Work in the intersections: A black feminist disability framework. *Gender & Society, 33*(1), 19–40. https://doi.org/10.1177/0891243218801523

Beauboeuf-Lafontant, T. (2007). You have to show strength: An exploration of gender, race, and depression. *Gender & Society, 21*(1), 28–51. https://doi.org/10.1177/0891243206294108

Blum, L. M. (2020). Gender and disability studies. In N. A. Naples (Ed.), *Companion to women's and gender studies* (1st ed., pp. 175–194). Wiley. https://doi.org/10.1002/9781119315063.ch9

Brown, L. X. (2017). Ableist shame and disruptive bodies: Survivorship at the intersection of queer, trans, and disabled existence. In *Religion, disability, and interpersonal violence* (pp. 163–178). Springer. https://doi.org/10.1007/978-3-319-56901-7_10

Buchbinder, M. (2015). *All in your head: Making sense of pediatric pain*. University of California Press.

Campbell, F. K. (2009). *Contours of ableism: The Production of disability and abledness*. Palgrave Macmillan UK. https://doi.org/10.1057/9780230245181

Charmaz, K. (1991). *Good days, bad days: The self in chronic illness and time*. Rutgers University Press.

Charmaz, K. (2010). Disclosing illness and disability in the workplace. *Journal of International Education in Business, 3*(1/2), 6–19. https://doi.org/10.1108/18363261011106858

Charmaz, K. (2020). Experiencing stigma and exclusion: The influence of neoliberal perspectives, practices, and policies on living with chronic illness and disability. *Symbolic Interaction, 43*(1), 21–45. https://doi.org/10.1002/symb.432

Charmaz, K., & Belgrave, L. (2015). Chronic illness and disability. In G. Ritzer (Ed.), *The blackwell encyclopedia of sociology.* John Wiley & Sons. https://doi.org/10.1002/9781405165518. wbeosc035.pub2

Cheng, R. P. (2009). Sociological theories of disability, gender, and sexuality: A review of the literature. *Journal of Human Behavior in the Social Environment, 19*(1), 112–122. https://doi.org/10.1080/10911350802631651

Cheng, F. K. (2017). *Using email and skype interviews with marginalized participants.* SAGE Publications Ltd.

Connell, R. W. (2012). Gender, health and theory: Conceptualizing the issue, in local and world perspective. *Social Science & Medicine, 74*(11), 1675–1683. https://doi.org/10.1016/j.socscimed.2011.06.006

Dalessandro, C. (2021). *Intimate inequalities: Millennials' romantic relationships in contemporary times.* Rutgers University Press.

Egner, J. E. (2019). "The disability rights community was never mine": Neuroqueer disidentification. *Gender & Society, 33*(1), 123–147. https://doi.org/10.1177/0891243218803284

Frank, A. W. (1995). *The wounded storyteller: Body, illness, and ethics.* University of Chicago Press.

Gahman, L. (2017). Crip theory and country boys: Masculinity, dis/ability, and place in rural Southeast Kansas. *Annals of the American Association of Geographers, 107*(3), 700–715. https://doi.org/10.1080/24694452.2016.1249726

Garland-Thomson, R. (2002). Integrating disability, transforming feminist theory. *NWSA Journal, 14*(3), 1–32. https://doi.org/10.1353/nwsa.2003.0005

Garland-Thomson, R. (2005). Feminist disability studies. *Signs: Journal of Women in Culture and Society, 30*(2), 1557–1587. https://doi.org/10.1086/423352

Gerschick, T. J. (2000). Toward a theory of disability and gender. *Signs: Journal of Women in Culture and Society, 25*(4), 1263–1268. https://doi.org/10.1086/495558

Gerschick, T. J., & Miller, A. S. (1995). Coming to terms: Masculinity and physical disability. In *Men's health and illness: Gender, power, and the body* (pp. 183–204). SAGE Publications, Inc. https://doi.org/10.4135/9781452243757.n9

Hill, S. A. (2009). Cultural images and the health of African American women. *Gender & Society, 23*(6), 733–746. https://doi.org/10.1177/0891243209346308

Hochschild, A. R. (2012). *The managed heart: Commercialization of human feeling (Updated with a new preface).* University of California Press.

Irvine, L. J., Pierce, J. L., & Zussman, R. (Eds.). (2019). *Narrative sociology.* Vanderbilt University Press.

Jaggar, A. M. (1989). Love and knowledge: Emotion in feminist epistemology. *Inquiry, 32*(2), 151–176. https://doi.org/10.1080/00201748908602185

Jerolmack, C., & Khan, S. (2017). The analytic lenses of ethnography. *Socius: Sociological Research for a Dynamic World, 3.* https://doi.org/10.1177/2378023117735256

Kafer, A. (2013). *Feminist, queer, crip.* Indiana University Press.

Kandiyoti, D. (1988). Bargaining with patriarchy. *Gender & Society, 2*(3), 274–290.

Kane, E. W. (2006). "No way my boys are going to be like that!": Parents' responses to children's gender nonconformity. *Gender & Society, 20*(2), 149–176. https://doi.org/10.1177/0891243205284276

Kempner, J. L. (2014). *Not tonight: Migraine and the politics of gender and health.* The University of Chicago Press.

Kincaid, R., Sennott, C., & Kelly, B. C. (2022). Doing and redoing emphasized femininity: How women use emotion work to manage competing expectations in college hookup culture. *Sex Roles, 86*(5–6), 305–319. https://doi.org/10.1007/s11199-022-01275-4

Lorde, A. (1997). *The cancer journals* (Special ed.). Aunt Lute Books.

Lyons, A. C. (2009). Masculinities, femininities, behaviour and health: Gender identities, health, behaviour. *Social and Personality Psychology Compass, 3*(4), 394–412. https://doi.org/10.1111/j.1751-9004.2009.00192.x

Matthews, C. R. (2016). The appropriation of hegemonic masculinity within selected research on men's health. *NORMA, 11*(1), 3–18. https://doi.org/10.1080/18902138.2015.1063761

Mattingly, C. (2010). *The paradox of hope: Journeys through a clinical borderland.* University of California Press.

Mauldin, L., & Brown, R. L. (2021). Missing pieces: Engaging sociology of disability in medical sociology. *Journal of Health and Social Behavior, 62*(4), 477–492. https://doi.org/10.1177/00221465211019358

Meadow, T. (2018). *Trans kids: Being gendered in the twenty-first century.* University of California Press.

Naples, N. A., Mauldin, L., & Dillaway, H. (2019). From the guest editors: Gender, disability, and intersectionality. *Gender & Society, 33*(1), 5–18. https://doi.org/10.1177/0891243218813309

Nishida, A. (2016). Understanding political development through an intersectionality framework: Life stories of disability activists. *Disability Studies Quarterly, 36*(2). https://doi.org/10.18061/dsq.v36i2.4449

Richter, Z. A. (2017). Melting down the family unit: A neuroqueer critique of table-readiness. In M. Rembis (Ed.), *Disabling domesticity* (pp. 335–348). Palgrave Macmillan US. https://doi.org/10.1057/978-1-137-48769-8_14

Saldaña, J. (2013). *The coding manual for qualitative researchers* (2nd ed.). SAGE.

Scarborough, W. J., & Sin, R. (2020). Gendered places: The dimensions of local gender norms across the United States. *Gender & Society, 34*(5), 705–735. https://doi.org/10.1177/0891243220948220

Scotch, R. K. (1986). Women and disability: The double handicap. *Social Forces, 65*(1), 277–278. https://doi.org/10.1093/sf/65.1.277

Scotch, R. K. (1988). Disability as the basis for a social movement: Advocacy and the politics of definition. *Journal of Social Issues, 44*(1), 159–172. https://doi.org/10.1111/j.1540-4560.1988.tb02055.x

Shuttleworth, R., Wedgwood, N., & Wilson, N. J. (2012). The dilemma of disabled masculinity. *Men and Masculinities, 15*(2), 174–194. https://doi.org/10.1177/1097184X12439879

Springer, K. W., Hankivsky, O., & Bates, L. M. (2012). Gender and health: Relational, intersectional, and biosocial approaches. *Social Science & Medicine, 74*(11), 1661–1666. https://doi.org/10.1016/j.socscimed.2012.03.001

Steinberg, H. (2020). Distance and acceptance: Identity formation in young adults with chronic health conditions. *Advances in Life Course Research, 44*, 100325. https://doi.org/10.1016/j.alcr.2020.100325

Timmermans, S., & Tavory, I. (2012). Theory construction in qualitative research: From grounded theory to abductive analysis. *Sociological Theory, 30*(3), 167–186. https://doi.org/10.1177/0735275112457914

Weitz, R. (2001). Women and their Hair: Seeking power through resistance and accommodation. *Gender & Society, 15*(5), 667–686. https://doi.org/10.1177/089124301015005003

Wendell, S. (1996). *The rejected body.* Routledge.

Wenger, L. M. (2013). Moving through illness with strong backs and soft fronts: A substantive theory of men's help-seeking during cancer. *Men and Masculinities, 16*(5), 517–539. https://doi.org/10.1177/1097184X13501177

West, C., & Zimmerman, D. H. (1987). Doing gender. *Gender & Society, 1*(2), 125–151. https://doi.org/10.1177/0891243287001002002

West, C., & Zimmerman, D. H. (2009). Accounting for doing gender. *Gender & Society, 23*(1), 112–122. https://doi.org/10.1177/0891243208326529

Wolbring, G. (2008). The politics of ableism. *Development, 51*(2), 252–258. https://doi.org/10.1057/dev.2008.17

Yarrow, A. (2018). *90s bitch: Media, culture, and the failed promise of gender equality* (1st ed.). Harper Perennial.

THE RECEPTION OF DISABILITY POLICY IN FRANCE: A QUALITATIVE LIFE COURSE PERSPECTIVE ON POLICY IMPACT

Anne Revillard

AUTHOR BIOGRAPHY

Anne Revillard, PhD, is an Associate Professor of Sociology at Sciences Po, Paris, France. She is affiliated with the Centre for Research on Social Inequalities (CRIS), and the Director of the Laboratory for Interdisciplinary Evaluation of Public Policies (LIEPP). Her research notably explores the implementation and reception of disability policies in France from a qualitative perspective. She has recently published "Realizing the Right to Access in France: Between Implementation and Activation." (*Law and Society Review*, 2019); "Disabled People Working in the Disability Sector: Occupational Segregation or Personal Fulfillment?" (*Work, Employment & Society*, 2022); "The disability employment quota, between social policy and antidiscrimination" (*Global Social Policy*, 2022). Her book, *Fragile rights: disability, public policy and social change*, was just published by Bristol University Press in 2023.

ABSTRACT

How can a qualitative life course approach inform the analysis of the impact of disability policy on individual lives? This contribution puts forward the concept of policy reception in an effort to apply the key principles of a life course perspective to the study of policy impact, a perspective which is of particular relevance in the case of disability policy. Drawing on a broader qualitative study of the reception of disability policy in France, the paper, focusing on the in-depth analysis of two life stories, makes two main contributions. The first is theoretical, putting forward the concept of policy reception to address the missing link between "the state and the life course," as pointed out by Mayer

Disabilities and the Life Course
Research in Social Science and Disability, Volume 14, 107–123
Copyright © 2023 Anne Revillard
Published under exclusive licence by Emerald Publishing Limited
ISSN: 1479-3547/doi:10.1108/S1479-354720230000014007

and Schoepflin (1989). The second is methodological, detailing how bio-graphical interviews, following this life course approach, can be used to operationalize this concept of policy reception. These contributions are illus-trated by study results focusing on the reception of disability-related educa-tional policies.

Keywords: Policy reception; biographical interviews; disability; education; life course; inclusion

Disability as a policy sector raises many challenges for policy analysis. In a similar way to gender, while it may be approached as a distinct policy domain, disability, because of its crosscutting character, indeed connects with a diversity, if not all, of other policy sectors: health, urban planning, culture, family, sports, etc. Moreover, disability policy impacts disabled people at all stages of the life course, from education and family support to employment and aging. Therefore, because it affects people "over a long stretch of lifetime" and "across life domains" (Mayer, 2009, p. 414), disability policy can be analyzed as a "life course" policy. The analysis of its impact, thus, calls for theoretical and meth-odological tools inspired by a life course approach. This is what this contribution offers to do. Beyond calling for an investigation across life domains and across the lifetime, a life course perspective also invites us to analyze policy impact as embedded in collective contexts, across cohorts, and calls for a sociological approach combining structure ("cultural frames and institutional and structural conditions") and agency ("personal characteristics and individual action") (Mayer, 2009, p. 414).

In life-course research, the study of policy impacts on the life course has mainly led to the development of quantitative, comparative, historical, or lon-gitudinal approaches (Mayer, 2009; Ulrich Mayer, 2004). This contribution puts forward an alternative, more qualitative, micro-level approach to explore the effects of public policies on the life course, through the concept of policy reception. Based on an in-depth qualitative analysis of how people relate to policies, the study of policy reception is well equipped to account for the embeddedness of both public policies and life courses in local, collective contexts, as well as how public policies may have both a constraining and an enabling effect on individuals (articulating structure and agency). Also from a life course standpoint, biographical interviews are a privileged methodological corollary of this theoretical approach, enabling the consideration of context and structure-agency interplay, as well as the comparison of cohorts.

The first part of this contribution presents the theoretical approach in terms of policy reception and how it connects to a life course approach. I then turn to the use of biographical interviews to implement this approach, drawing on life story research on the reception of disability policy in France. The fruitfulness of this qualitative life course perspective on policy impact is illustrated in the case of disability-related educational policies.

"THE STATE AND THE LIFE COURSE" REVISITED BY POLICY RECEPTION

In their seminal 1989 article on "the state and the life course," Mayer and Schoepflin (1989) commented on the emerging interest paid to the impact of the state in life course research. This impact was then envisioned at a rather macro level, focusing on the impact of the state on the structuring of the life course as a whole through the idea of "institutionalizing the life course." Attention was paid to mechanisms such as the role of state building in the emergence of the individual as a category (based on the inputs of historical sociology by Norbert Elias (2000) for example), or how the increased role of the state in society contributed to "standardizing life events" and to drawing more rigid distinctions between previously more continuous life situations, due notably to the need for clear criteria of eligibility ("one is either healthy or on sick leave") (Mayer & Schoepflin, 1989, p. 199). In this programmatic chapter, the authors raised the question: "how can one construct a conceptual framework that allows sufficiently precise inferences from state activities to the social structure of the life course?" (Mayer & Schoepflin, 1989, p. 191). Since then, even though life-course research in general includes a combination of qualitative and quantitative approaches (Giele & Elder, 2013), macro-level approaches have dominated the study of how states impact life courses, drawing mainly on comparative, historical, or longitudinal quantitative studies (Mayer, 2009; Ulrich Mayer, 2004; Verd & Andreu, 2011).

Following up on other contributions (Locke & Lloyd-Sherlock, 2011; Verd & Andreu, 2011), the concept of policy reception offers an alternative answer to the question raised by Mayer and Schoepflin (1989), drawing on a more qualitative and comprehensive perspective. I define policy reception as "the processes through which a public policy is appropriated and co-constructed by the individuals it targets, and through which it produces its effects on them" (Revillard, 2018a, p. 478). The study of policy reception is deliberately situated from the points of views of the people targeted by the public policy under study. Breaking away from a dominant institutional bias in policy analysis (Michener et al., 2022), the idea is to start the investigation with how individuals experience policies, rather than with how these policies are institutionally designed or implemented. This experience of public policies by individuals involves representations and practices. In terms of representations, one needs to account for how individuals perceive the policy under study: (what) do they know about it and what do they think of it? But policy reception also involves the study of practices: take up or non-take up, tinkering, critique, and circumventing, for example. In a similar theoretical move as that put forward by legal consciousness studies (Ewick & Silbey, 1998), the idea is to take seriously what ordinary people think about and do with/against/aside public policies, with the idea that these practices and representations contribute to the social reality of the policies under study as much as their institutional framing and implementation. Far from being a top-down perspective on policy impact, this approach pays attention to individuals' agency with regards to the policies that target them. This is precisely why an empirical investigation of policy reception is needed, since reception can never be deduced from the sole analysis of how a policy is defined and implemented. Policies never completely determine individual outcomes. This is not to say, however, that policies are not constraining on individuals. Public policies also shape, to a large extent, key aspects of individual lives, from where and how one is schooled to the built environment one evolves in, for example. In compliance with the growing tendency in general sociology to integrate structure and agency (Giddens, 1986), the study of policy reception combines an analysis of the constraining effects of public policies on individual lives with an attention to individual appropriations of these policies.

This approach in terms of policy reception may be implemented on two levels of analysis (Revillard, 2018a). The first one, which will not be addressed here, situates itself at the level of a given intervention or policy instrument: such as a training program or social benefits, for example. This approach converges with a research design which is frequent in policy evaluation, where policy reception as defined here echoes a realist approach (Pawson & Tilley, 1997). The second level of analysis aims to investigate a whole policy sector, including a variety of interventions and policy tools. Such an approach is particularly in line with the comprehensive ambition of the concept of policy reception, which strives to account as best as possible for how individuals themselves construct public policies. When the research question is already focused on a given intervention or policy tool, there is a risk of overestimating the role of the latter in individual lives. Whereas a research question pitched at the level of a whole policy sector enables us to account more openly for how individuals relate to the latter (and whether it matters at all in their lives), how they construct it, what types of interventions are more salient, etc. Moreover, an analysis at the level of the policy sector is particularly in line with the life course approach by enabling an examination of the effects of long-term changes in public policies (beyond the lifespan of a specific policy tool), through the comparison of different generations of people (Shah & Priestley, 2011).

To sum up, the study of policy reception as defined here relevantly answers the challenge of "inferring from state activities to the social structure of the life course" (Mayer & Schoepflin, 1989, p. 191). Indeed, it accounts for how policies affect individual experiences using these experiences as a starting point, thus embedding the analysis of how people relate to policies in their local and relational contexts, taking into account the structural forces at play (public policies themselves, but also structural inequalities) as well as a human agency. Biographical interviews are an appropriate method for operationalizing this theoretical perspective. The next section examines the rationale for their use and specifies how the method was implemented in this study of the reception of disability policy in France.

BIOGRAPHICAL INTERVIEWS TO STUDY POLICY RECEPTION: WHY AND HOW?

Why Rely on Biographical Interviews?

The use of life stories, including those drawing on biographical interviews, has spread in the wider context of the "narrative turn" (Rustin, 2006), but utilizing them is an old practice in the social sciences, notably since the first generation of the Chicago school (Becker, 1977). Life stories are one of the methodological tools of the life course approach (Clausen, 1998). Four common justifications for life story research also explain why life stories (here collected through biographical interviews) are relevant to the study of policy reception: giving voice to marginalized people, promoting an interpretive understanding of social action, linking micro and macro levels, and studying the interplay between structure and agency.

"Giving voice to the voiceless" is a classical rationale for the use of biographical interviews (Becker, 1977; Bourdieu, 1993; Ewick & Silbey, 1995). Within the first generation of the Chicago tradition, this method was developed to account for the lives of marginalized communities, notably poor and immigrant people and/or people involved in various deviant activities. The idea was to counterweight institutional accounts of these lives and give voice to the way people themselves experienced their lives and the activities they were involved in. Feminist research then played a leading role in the application of this analytic frame to public policy, promoting a bottom-up approach to the study of policies affecting women's lives – or, as Naples phrases it, "bringing everyday life into policy research" (Naples, 1998, p. 198). The idea is to give voice to an alternative account of policy impact, from ordinary people as opposed to the usual narrative by institutional actors. This justification of the use of life stories converges with the main theoretical choice of policy reception, using individuals rather than institutions as a starting point.

The second main rationale for the use of biographical interviews points to their use for accessing a person's subjectivity and vision of the world (Michelat, 1975), which is key to an interpretive sociology of social action (Weber, 2013). Life stories, however, are not only used to collect people's representations. Interviewees also talk about their practices but, as narrated, these practices are always connected to particular meanings. In view of a study of policy reception, biographical interviews give access to individual uses of the policy (for example, has the interviewee claimed a benefit they are entitled to?), as well as policy representations, conceptions of what the policy is, and what the policy means for the individual (i.e., is it perceived as protective, paternalistic, emancipatory, etc.?).

Thirdly, connecting the micro and macro levels, or, in Mills' terms, "biography and history" (Mills, 1959), is both an asset and a challenge of life story research. It may first seem like a challenge since there is a temptation, when working with individual life stories, to stick to the individual level. In this respect, disability research has pointed to the risk of moving away from the social model by shifting the attention back from social structures to individuals (French &

Swain, 2006). The problem, however, does not lay in life stories themselves but in the way they are produced and used. Life stories can be produced using a social model perspective: as Shah and Priestly (2011, p. 116) stress, "the empirical focus of narrative research needs to shift from the 'life experiences of disabled people' to 'experiences of disability in people's lives'." In other words, life stories are to be used for what they reveal of the social experience of disability, not only taking into account people's subjectivities and their vision of the world but also connecting this, as well as the materiality of their experiences, to broader social structures and structural effects of public policies (Beadle-Brown et al., 2018; Malhotra & Rowe, 2014). Concretely, when people narrate their individual experiences, they also refer to institutions (e.g., families, schools, workplaces, public administrations).

Finally, and in tight connection to this last dimension, biographical interviews help grasp the interplay between structure and agency. The social and sometimes very material structures that are evoked in individual narratives remind us how society and public policies shape the life course, for example, determining people's resources, life options, or social status. Rustin (2006) stresses that while it must be distanced from a celebration of individual lives, life story research should not solely focus on using biographies as a way to trace back social structures. A form of agency is also expressed in life stories, which should be taken seriously. Individual narratives tell stories of not only social structures but also stories of resistance (Ewick & Silbey, 2003). Finally, what these narratives show is the interplay between structure and agency. As stressed by Engel and Munger, "autobiographical narratives by ordinary people reflect the influence of political change, of cultural transformations – and at times, of legal innovations like the ADA. Yet the threads of individual lives also make up this fabric: through the choices and struggles people experience in their everyday lives, [. . .] events are channeled in particular directions and history is carried forward. The telling of life stories is part of this process" (Engel & Munger, 2003, p. 2).

An Implementation of the Approach in the Case of French Disability Policy

In France, as in many other countries, disability policy has undergone important transformations in the past decades, leading to a complex mix of orientations, from protection to compensation and antidiscrimination, drawing on different approaches to disability (Chauvière, 2003; Winance et al., 2007). The 2005 "law on the equal rights and opportunities, the participation and the citizenship of disabled persons" has been an important turning point, notably introducing notions of nondiscrimination, accessibility, and promoting disabled children's access to mainstream schooling. The law also extended the types of conditions legally recognized as a disability, notably including learning disabilities and chronic illnesses.

Started in 2014, the research project, "the reception of disability policy," provides an overview of how this changing policy context has impacted disabled people's lives and how they have reacted to it. To focus on the impact of policy change, two methodological choices were made in terms of the sampling frame.

First, the investigation was limited to two types of impairments (visual and mobility impairments) which had been administratively recognized for a long time, prior to the 2005 law, to account for the specific changes triggered by this law. Within the same aim, a criterion of eligibility was added regarding the onset of the impairments, which had to be at least 15 years prior to the interview.

The goal of interviewing "ordinary" disabled people then raised important questions regarding the relevant intermediaries to reach out to potential research participants. I combined a diversity of recruitment techniques, including the dissemination of a call for participants in disability-specific media as well as several nongovernmental intermediaries. Service providing NGOs proved the most efficient intermediary in reaching out to more isolated people. I made sure to obtain a diverse sample in terms of gender, social origins, education, and current occupation.

In total, 30 interviews were conducted between November 2014 and January 2016 with people aged 23–75 years of age, including 17 women and 13 men, and those with either mobility or visual impairments. Most participants lived in the Paris region at the time of interview, but five lived in other medium-sized cities in France. Their social origins are varied, as was their work status at the time of interview: students, people with a full-time job, people of working age with very punctual or no professional activity, and retired people. The extent of their impairment is also varied, although for most of them, the impairment was diagnosed at an early age.

Based on the conception of disability policy as a life course policy (i.e., affecting all domains and all stages of life), I adopted a very open, biographical interview format, asking people to tell their life stories following the different stages of the life course, with the idea of asking further questions when interventions or public administrations in charge of disability policy would be mentioned in the interviews.

This approach, however, raised the question of how the research would be presented in the call to potential participants. Being too explicit about the policy focus of the research in the call risked inducing a selection bias against people who would not feel competent to answer questions about policy. Conversely, not mentioning it raised ethical issues. The compromise adopted as a solution consisted of referring to possible policy implications of the research on the post, and then explaining more clearly to prospective participants the type of research at hand in the conversation prior to scheduling the interview. Potential participants were then told how the interview included both general questions regarding their life stories, and more specific policy-related questions.

While the interview outline included both types of questions, an effort was made to avoid asking policy questions before the corresponding interventions or policy tools were mentioned by the interviewee, in order not to bias their accounts. Hence, most of the interview outline consisted of general questions about the person's life story: family context, diagnosis of the impairment, schooling, housing, personal life, professional life, other activities, and description of the current daily life (i.e., housing, mobility, etc.). A series of questions were also prepared to address the person's contact with the administrations in charge of disability as well as other questions regarding disability policy (notably its evolution) and politics (perception of and/or belonging to disability organizations).

The analysis combined portrait analysis (Rodríguez-Dorans & Jacobs, 2020), focusing on each individual life story, with cross-cutting thematic content analysis using Atlas-Ti, and in-depth analyses of selected excerpts (Revillard, 2017). In what follows, an example is given based on the results of portrait analysis, specifically analyzing the effects of policy change while comparing different generations of disabled people.

The results presented here focus on the reception of disability-related educational policies. This is only one aspect of the four facets of disability policy explored in the broader project: education, employment, social rights, and accessibility (all interviews covered these four dimensions). The conclusions regarding the reception of employment policies, social rights, and accessibility provisions have been developed in other publications (Revillard, 2018b, 2019, 2022, 2023), but I have chosen to focus on education in this contribution because of the particular importance of this analysis within the context of a life course lens. The experience of schooling played an important role in shaping the array of employment opportunities reported by interviewees as well as a certain number of fundamental representations regarding self and inclusion.

THE RECEPTION OF DISABILITY-RELATED EDUCATIONAL POLICIES

Education is one of the historic pillars of disability policy. In France, as in many other countries, interventions initially took the form of the development of specialized institutions, starting with educational institutions for deaf and blind children as of the eighteenth century, then with special classes and special schools developed for children with other types of impairments, notably intellectual, at the end of the nineteenth century and throughout the twentieth century. These latter changes occurred within the context of the broader generalization of access to education. While the education of disabled children had historically been considered as a "favor" (Buton, 2009), the first major blueprint law in the field of disability policy in France, the 1975 law, promotes a "right to special education" for disabled children. According to this law, education is to be provided as "either a mainstream education or, failing that, a special education determined according to the special needs of each child [. . .]" (Loi n°75-534, article 4). Following the broader shift from special to inclusive education at the international level (Peters, 2007), the notion of "school integration" (*intégration scolaire*), referring to the schooling of disabled children within mainstream schools, started being more actively promoted in the 1980s. Many NGOs then developed accommodations to support disabled children educated in mainstream schools, and the profession of school educational assistant was developed. The 1989 Framework Act on education recognized school integration as a "national priority" and formalized the role of the NGO-led medico-social sector in accommodating disabled children in

mainstream schools. Finally, while maintaining the possibility of special education, the 2005 law "on the equal rights and opportunities, the participation and
the citizenship of disabled persons" proclaimed more firmly the state's responsibility in school inclusion, asserting that "[within] its field of competence, the
State provides the financial and human resources needed for children, teenagers,
and adults with disabilities to be educated in mainstream institutions" (Loi n°
2005-102, article 19). In practice, this policy of "school integration" favors the
schooling of disabled children and teenagers in mainstream schools, and provides
them with some individual accommodations, but seldom questions existing
mainstream teaching formats and practices to make them more readily inclusive,
which would correspond to the idea of inclusive education in its strongest sense
(favoring a readily accessible mainstream educational environment to limit the
need for individual accommodation) (Peters, 2007).

How does this gradual shift in policies from special to mainstream education
reflect in the experiences of different generations of people? What effects did it
have on their actual modes of schooling, and on their value judgments regarding
the different options? Two portraits of interviewees with mobility impairments,
Maryse Cloutier born in 1942 and Victor Jaucourt born in 1985, will be developed and then compared to answer these questions. The discussion will situate
these two participants within our broader corpus, to qualify the conclusions that
may be drawn from their comparison.

Maryse Cloutier

Maryse Cloutier was born in 1942 in a village in the mountains. Her father was a
soldier, and her mother ran the home. Her early years were dominated by medical
interventions related to her poliomyelitis, diagnosed when she was 18 months old.
She describes how, in the first local hospital where her parents took her, her
illness was little known ("They talked about infant paralysis. The word polio did
not mean much to them. So, I saw a whole procession of doctors who'd say,
'What's the matter with her? What can we do?', but they did not really know").
So the family moved to a large city, where she was hospitalized until the age of
five and a half, suffering ill treatment at the hands of the nuns who ran the
hospital ("They would beat us. The food was bad. They made us eat food again if
we had not managed to [keep it down]. It was really awful treatment."). She
describes how her mother's daily visits gave her some measure of protection
("Luckily [my mother came every day] because in that hospital the worst treatment was reserved for children who did not have visits").

Between the ages of five and seven, Maryse returned to her village, where she
was educated at the local state school. She did not have a wheelchair at that time,
so had to be carried, but does not seem to have found this to be too much of a
constraint ("Everybody carried me. I was not heavy"). She was also not the only
one in her family in that situation; several of her cousins also contracted polio.
She has happy memories of that time ("The teacher was very nice. She taught me
to play the piano with two fingers"). When she was seven, her parents moved to
Paris so that she could become a boarder at Garches, a school that specialized in

educating children with polio. She continued her schooling there until she was 18. Her memory of Garches is very positive, although overshadowed by her regular hospitalizations in the Parisian hospital where, between the ages of 7 and 11, she underwent a series of major operations that she describes as "more like experiments." These surgeries all had the aim to "get people walking" at all costs. She explained, "In the old days, the idea was always to get people walking, to get them upright, by doing operations that were often experimental. I was terrified of the operations. It was one after another."

Each operation meant a long period in hospital during which Maryse could not go to school, sometimes for as long as 10 months. She was once again ill-treated by nuns, as she had been when she was very young. As soon as she could express her own opinion, Maryse said that she did not want any more operations, and her mother listened: "As time passed, I said I did not want anyone to touch me anymore, because I was sick of it. And my mother listened. [. . .] I'm more independent in a wheelchair than on my feet, there's no doubt about that."

During Maryse's long periods in hospital, away from school, Maryse's mother taught her to read. When she returned to Garches on a more permanent basis, she benefited from the support of a teacher who gave her intensive coaching. She managed to catch up on her missed education and continued her studies up to the *baccalauréat* (the exam at the end of high school). She is very happy with the education she received at Garches: "[It was] a real school with real teachers. [. . .] The classes were small, and people liked working [there], so it worked well [. . .] The level [of education] was good." She also describes a lively social life alongside her studies during this period:

> It was extremely well organized. At the high school, for example, we would go out every Thursday to the theater or the Pleyel concert hall for the youth concerts. It was a dream, really. And then as well as that there were young people who lived locally who'd come over, and we'd go out a lot. I do not think I've ever gone out as much as I did then. (Maryse Cloutier, motor impaired, 72, November 2014)

Her depiction of the school is a far cry from the image of a repressive, inward-looking "total" institution (Goffman, 1961). She describes it as "paradise" compared to her experiences of hospitalization. Her perception of being schooled in a special institution is influenced by this previous and much more negative institutional experience of continual hospitalizations, which corresponds to the image of the total institution for her. In comparison, the educational institution she attends seems much more freeing. She attained her *baccalauréat* at Garches and continued her studies in Paris.

At the end of the interview, I asked Maryse to sum up what had helped her most in her educational development, and the first thing she mentioned was Garches ("What helped me, I can tell you, was ending up at Garches"). She nevertheless felt the need to justify this perception within the current context of placing high value on school integration: "I have not even got one bad memory of it, it's funny [. . .] it was not this integration thing [referring to the more recent policy emphasis on school integration], but it did not matter, it was still organized in a very interesting way."

Victor Jaucourt

Victor Jaucourt, the son of two engineers, was born in 1985 in the Paris region. At eight months old he was diagnosed with a genetic illness that caused muscular atrophy. He attended nursery school in a town a few kilometers away from his parents' home. It was a mainstream school with an integrated health center where there was capacity for between 10 and 15 children with disabilities. He changed schools at the beginning of elementary school. Indeed, at elementary level the first school he attended only accepted children with disabilities. However, his parents wanted him to be "with nondisabled children too," so they made an ad hoc arrangement with the mayor to have an educational assistant for him in the local primary school: "The mayor acted through positive discrimination, employing someone who'd been working for the mayor's office to be my permanent assistant in class. It was a very good thing for me, but it was a case of special treatment." He was very happy with his experience at this second school: "I really liked primary school because I was surrounded by nondisabled children, because I could take the tests and get the same marks as the other children. I was not bad [at academics], so it was very rewarding."

Victor had to attend *collège* (as of age 10–11) in another town, however, because the buildings at the local school were not accessible. He was very much affected by his departure from the local primary school ("It felt to me like a punishment"). The new school provided several different arrangements, with classes "just for students with disabilities" as well as mainstream classes that included a few individual students with disabilities (around 15 children spread over all of the classes). Victor, who was in one of these classes, describes the poor relationships both among the children and between children and staff:

> The situation quickly became absolutely awful, both with the staff and with the other students. With the other students it was just because we were teenagers, and it's an age when everyone's nasty to everyone else. And with the staff I had problems because I've always wanted to do lots of things. (Victor Jaucourt, motor impaired, 30, January 2015)

His desire to "do lots of things" was, in fact, a straightforward demand for equal treatment (that is, to have access to the same opportunities as nondisabled children). This aspiration was thwarted by discrimination. For example, he was excluded from a school trip organized in the first year of *college* ("They did not even invite me to go"). He put his name down for a theater class the following year but he was not invited to take part. When he protested to the headmaster, he learned that "The teacher of the theater class did not want [me] in his class. [. . .] The headmaster told me: 'That's the way it is. It's my decision'."

His *lycée* (high school) years were better. He was able to go back to the town where his parents lived and, in the late 1990s, integrate into a newly built mainstream *lycée* that was wheelchair-accessible and already had several students in wheelchairs studying in a vocational track. He was, therefore, not the first person to be integrated and had an assistant. He worked from photocopies and took exams by dictation. His relationships with teachers and classmates were good. He felt that attending a *lycée* close to home made all the difference: "When you go home in the evening and you live near your classmates, it changes everything: you all spend time with the same people." He obtained good results and chose a scientific *baccalauréat*, known as a "bac S," against the advice of the school:

> As I was good at math, I chose S because it had more prestige. The *lycée* would have preferred me to take ES [in economics and social science], even though, for nondisabled students, if they were good at math there was no problem if they wanted to do S. It was difficult for them [the *lycée*] to arrange for me to do physics because of the practicals. I said to them: 'I've got the grades I need; you cannot stop me'. And I did S. (Victor Jaucourt, motor impaired, 30, January 2015)

DISCUSSION

Taken together, the stories of Maryse and Victor cover a wide range of modes of disability-related education: from the total absence of schooling due to hospitalization to mainstream schooling with the necessary accommodations to schooling in a specialized institution or in special classes within mainstream schools. The comparison of Maryse's and Victor's trajectories, in line with several other examples among research participants, reveals the material and symbolic impact of the policy shift from special to mainstream education (this impact being a first aspect of policy reception). Unlike Maryse who did most of her schooling in a specialized institution, Victor was schooled in a diversity of mainstream institutions. This difference illustrates a broad shift from special to mainstream education: generally speaking, the experience of having been educated entirely as a boarder in a specialized institution is more frequent among older people, while younger interviewees have more commonly had experiences of integration into mainstream schools. This result, however, must be qualified in several respects.

Firstly, as illustrated by Maryse's first years of schooling, special education was not the only option for disabled people of her generation. She herself was schooled for several years at the local state school. For Maryse's generation, mainstream public schools may be retrospectively analyzed as objectively discriminatory because of their lack of accessibility and accommodation, but access to mainstream schools, in the sense of being able to enroll at the school and attend it, was not necessarily a problem. In the case of Maryse, it also corresponds to a time when mobility impairment was rather commonplace (e.g., several of her cousins also had polio). The fact that mainstream schools were relatively open to enrollment by disabled children – access was not necessarily denied – is confirmed by the experiences of several other research participants of the same generation who attended such schools. The decision to attend a special school is, thus, influenced less by the impossibility of enrolling at a mainstream school than by the lack of accommodations at such schools, and by the constraints of social class which mean that families might not have the resources to compensate for this lack of accommodation. A counterexample in our sample is Jean-Marc Sernin who, as a blind child, managed to remain in a mainstream school in the 1960s thanks to the support of his parents who paid for Braille and typing lessons at home to compensate for the lack of accommodation within the school.

Secondly, mainstream schooling is far from guaranteed among young people, and is not synonymous with successful inclusion. To be sure, 40 or 50 years after Maryse went to school, this kind of linear progression whereby (almost) all of a person's education takes place in a specialized institution is rarer for children and teens with mobility or visual impairments. Mainstream schooling, however, is far from being a given in more recent decades, even with policy changes. Victor's experience, in this respect, stands out as an exception among our other interviewees with quadriplegia, as this latter group of participants completed at least part, if not all, of their education in specialized institutions – which is not necessarily the case of people with lighter forms of mobility impairments. In this respect, Victor's story reflects the importance of social class and parental support in creating access to mainstream schooling. But his trajectory, made possible by the support of his parents, also relevantly illustrates the extent to which mainstream schooling is not a given and has to be fought for. The inaccessibility or lack of inclusion of several establishments required frequent school changes, including far from the family home. Within a given school, Victor faced several forms of discrimination on the part of teachers, refusing to include him in some activities, or trying to channel him to a track that would require fewer accommodations by the school. Despite being more exposed to mainstream schooling than others in our study, Victor's story reflects the general reports of piecemeal educational trajectories very common among younger generations, as opposed to more linear and often institutionalized educational trajectories among older generations.

In terms of perceptions regarding the different schooling options, the comparison of the two narratives reflects the strong value placed on mainstream schooling within cultural and policy discourse. Unlike the way it is often portrayed by promoters of inclusive education, however, Maryse had a positive experience of being schooled in a specialized institution (Shah, 2007). She has very good memories of her experiences at Garches, both in terms of academic success and relationships with friends and teachers. Her account also reminds us of the need to avoid any generalized depictions of experiences of special education. For her, boarding at Garches was liberating compared to her other experiences of being confined to another institution, the hospital, which was synonymous with ill-treatment, isolation, and a complete lack of schooling. Maryse uses a defensive tone at times while giving her positive account of attending a special school, because of the high cultural value placed on school integration.

This contemporary norm of school integration, as promoted by educational policy in France, is especially marked among young people in our sample, as illustrated by the case of Victor, even though fully integrated education often fails to become a reality for them. Parents play an important role in the promotion of this norm: Victor's parents refuse to let him be schooled in a class or school with only disabled children, and they argue for him in front of the mayor to obtain an educational assistant in the mainstream school. The opportunity for mainstream schooling then creates expectations for inclusion and equal access: unlike disabled children who can only compare themselves to other disabled children in specialized institutions, Victor sees and is shocked by instances of differential treatment in mainstream schooling. The material effect of educational policy change and a push for mainstreamed education, thus, creates the conditions for his agency: similar to several other interviewees of his generation, Victor protests his exclusion and insists on having the same opportunities in terms of orientation as his fellow students.

The case of education, thus, illustrates the usefulness of biographical interviews to operationalize the study of policy reception. This method reveals how public policies (here educational reforms) shape key aspects of the research participants' experiences and perceptions: where they are schooled (with special education being more present in Maryse's life and mainstream schooling being the norm in spite of difficulties of access and accommodation for Victor), and how they perceive the respective worth of special and mainstream education (Maryse valuing this option while Victor rejects it). Yet biographical interviews also provide insight into individual agency and the tactics and adaptations individuals develop facing these structural constraints. In the case of educational reforms, these strongly rely on the parents' initiatives (for example, Maryse's mother taught her how to read to compensate for the lack of schooling; Victor's parents lobbied the mayor to obtain better support for him in mainstream education).

CONCLUSION

A life course perspective calls for a contextualized analysis of individual experiences, in all domains, across the life course, taking into account both structure and agency (Mayer, 2009). The study of policy reception as defined here enables a connection between "the state and the life course" (Mayer & Schoepflin, 1989), or, more specifically, between public policies and one's life course. This approach takes the individuals targeted and affected by a given policy as the starting point and explores how these individuals experience the policy at hand: how it affects them both objectively and subjectively (how the policy frames their life circumstances and their visions of the world), and what they think about or do with this policy. Biographical interviews are an appropriate tool to use when investigating policy reception, encompassing the life course and enabling an analysis of the interplay between policy effects and policy appropriations in people's lives.

The comparison of two generations of people in a study of the reception of disability policy in France also demonstrates the fruitfulness of a life course lens, here illustrated by two individuals who experienced educational institutions in two very different policy moments. In terms of policy impact, our analysis reveals a broad contrast in modes of schooling, as well as strikingly different perceptions of the legitimacy of special education and expectations for mainstream schooling. The life stories also reveal how agentic people (and their parents) might be in the reception of educational reforms, pressing for inclusion and negotiating the needed accommodations. Maryse's and Victor's reception of policy for integrated education generally reflects the still very imperfect fulfillment of the promise of inclusion.

Beyond this chapter's focus on the immediate reception of disability-related educational policies as such, the broader research project confirms the influence of this moment of the life course (and the formative nature of primary and secondary educational experiences) in participants' later reception of other types of disability policy, such as policy guiding employment, human rights, and accessibility for people with disabilities. Ultimately, individuals in our study who were schooled in mainstream settings have higher expectations of inclusion and equality (Revillard, 2023).

While this contribution has stressed the input of a qualitative method (biographical interviews) to the study of policy reception, other methodological approaches should be utilized as well. Quantitative methods can be usefully integrated in the study of policy reception, for example, to give a broader and more systematic view of the objective effect of a given policy. In further research, mixed methods research designs are, thus, likely to provide a fuller picture of policy reception.

ACKNOWLEDGEMENTS

This research was supported by the French National Research Agency (ANR) as part of the "Investissements d'Avenir" program LIEPP (ANR-11-LABX-0091, ANR-11-IDEX-0005-02) and the Université Paris Cité IdEx (ANR-18-IDEX-0001).

REFERENCES

Beadle-Brown, J., Biggeri, J. M., Halvorsen, R., Hvinden, B., Tossebro, J., & Waldschmidt, A. (Eds.). (2018). *Lived experiences of persons with disabilities: Active citizenship and disability in Europe* (Vol. 2). Routledge.

Becker, H. S. (1977). The life history and the scientific mosaic. In *Sociological work* (pp. 63–73). Transaction.

Bourdieu, P. (1993). *La misère du monde*. Seuil.

Buton, F. (2009). *L'administration des faveurs: L'État, les sourds et les aveugles (1789-1885)*. Presses Universitaires de Rennes.

Chauvière, M. (2003). Handicap et discriminations. Genèse et ambiguïtés d'une inflexion de l'action publique. In D. Borrillo (Ed.), *Lutter contre les discriminations* (pp. 100–122). La Découverte.

Clausen, J. A. (1998). Life reviews and life stories. In *Methods of life course research: Qualitative and quantitative approaches* (pp. 189–212). SAGE Publications, Inc.

Elias, N. (2000). *The civilizing process*. Blackwell.

Engel, D. M., & Munger, F. W. (2003). *Rights of inclusion. Law and identity in the life stories of Americans with disabilities*. University of Chicago Press.

Ewick, P., & Silbey, S. (1995). Subversive stories and hegemonic tales: Toward a sociology of narrative. *Law & Society Review, 29*(2), 197–226.

Ewick, P., & Silbey, S. S. (1998). *The common place of law: Stories from everyday life*. University of Chicago Press.

Ewick, P., & Silbey, S. S. (2003). Narrating social structure: Stories of resistance to legal authority. *American Journal of Sociology, 108*(6), 1328–1372.

French, S., & Swain, J. (2006). Telling stories for a politics of hope. *Disability & Society, 21*(5), 383–396.

Giddens, A. (1986). *The constitution of society: Outline of the theory of structuration*. University of California Press.

Giele, J., & Elder, G. (2013). *Methods of life course research: Qualitative and quantitative approaches*. SAGE.

Goffman, E. (1961). *Asylums: Essays on the social situation of mental patients and other inmates*. Anchor Books.

Locke, C., & Lloyd-Sherlock, P. (2011). Qualitative life course methodologies: Critical reflections from development studies. *Development and Change, 42*(5), 1131–1152.

Malhotra, R., & Rowe, M. (2014). *Exploring disability identity and disability rights through narratives. Finding a voice of their own*. Routledge.

Mayer, K. U. (2009). New directions in life course research. *Annual Review of Sociology, 35*(1), 413–433.

Mayer, K. U., & Schoepflin, U. (1989). The state and the life course. *Annual Review of Sociology, 15*(1), 187–209.

Michelat, G. (1975). Sur l'utilisation de l'entretien non-directif en sociologie. *Revue Française de Sociologie, 16*(2), 229–247. https://doi.org/10.2307/3321036

Michener, Sorelle, M., & Thurston, C. (2022). From the margins to the center: A bottom-up approach to welfare state scholarship. *Perspectives on Politics, 20*(1), 154–169. https://doi.org/10.1017/S153759272000359X

Mills, C. W. (1959). *The sociological imagination*. Oxford University Press.

Naples, N. A. (1998). Bringing everyday life to policy analysis: The case of white rural women negotiating college and welfare. *Journal of Poverty, 2*(1), 23–53.

Pawson, R., & Tilley, N. (1997). *Realistic evaluation*. Sage.

Peters, S. J. (2007). 'Education for all?': A historical analysis of international inclusive education policy and individuals with disabilities. *Journal of Disability Policy Studies, 18*(2), 98–108.

Revillard, A. (2017). Analyzing the reception of disability policies: The contribution of biographical interviews. *Revue Française de Sociologie, 58*(1), 71–95.

Revillard, A. (2018a). Understanding policy consequences from the perspective of its targeted beneficiaries: The reception of public policy. *Revue Française de Science Politique, 68*(3), 469–491.

Revillard, A. (2018b). Vulnerable rights: The incomplete realization of disability social rights in France. *Social Sciences (Basel), 7*(6), 88. https://doi.org/10.3390/socsci7060088

Revillard, A. (2019). Realizing the right to access in France: Between implementation and activation. *Law & Society Review, 53*(4), 950–982.

Revillard, A. (2022). Disabled people working in the disability sector: Occupational segregation or personal fulfilment? *Work, Employment & Society, 36*(5), 875–892. https://doi.org/10.1177/09500170221080401

Revillard, A. (2023). *Fragile rights: Disability, public policy and social change*. Bristol University Press.

Rodríguez-Dorans, E., & Jacobs, P. (2020). Making narrative portraits: A methodological approach to analysing qualitative data. *International Journal of Social Research Methodology, 23*(6), 611–623. https://doi.org/10.1080/13645579.2020.1719609

Rustin, M. (2006). Réflexions sur le tournant biographique dans les sciences sociales. In I. Astier & N. Duvoux (Eds.), *La société biographique: une injonction à vivre dignement* (pp. 33–53). L'Harmattan/Logiques sociales.

Shah, S. (2007). Special or mainstream? The views of disabled students. *Research Papers in Education, 22*(4), 425–442.

Shah, S., & Priestley, M. (2011). *Disability and social change. Private lives and public policies*. Policy Press.

Ulrich Mayer, K. (2004). « Whose lives? How history, societies, and institutions define and shape life courses ». *Research in Human Development*, *1*(3), 161–187. https://doi.org/10.1207/s15427617rhd0103_3

Verd, J. M., & Andreu, M. L. (2011). The rewards of a qualitative approach to life-course research. The example of the effects of social protection policies on career paths. *Forum, Qualitative Sozialforschung [Forum: Qualitative Social Research]*, *12*(3). https://doi.org/10.1080/13645579.2020.1719609

Weber, M. (2013). *Economy and society*. University of California Press.

Winance, M., Ville, I., & Ravaud, J. (2007). Disability policies in France: Changes and tensions between the category-based, universalist and personalized approaches. *Scandinavian Journal of Disability Research*, *9*(3–4), 160–181.

STATUTES REFERENCED

Loi n8 2005-102 du 11 fevrier 2005 pour l'egalite des droits et des chances, la participation et la citoyennete des personnes handicapees [Law on the Equal Rights and Opportunities, the Participation and the Citizenship of Disabled Persons] (2005, February 11).

Loi n8 75-534 du 30 juin 1975 d'orientation en faveur des personnes handicapees [Framework Law in Favor of Disabled Persons] (1975, June 30).

COLLEGE COMPLETION AMONG YOUNG ADULTS WITH A DISABLED SIBLING

Anna Penner

AUTHOR BIOGRAPHY

Anna Penner, PhD, is an Assistant Professor of Sociology at Pepperdine University in the United States. Anna's research examines disability and the family as well as health and disability among emerging adults.

ABSTRACT

Twelve percent of families in the United States have a child with a disability, yet little is known about the long-term consequences of growing up with a disabled sibling. This study builds on previous research regarding disability effects on families and offers an additional view on the linked lives of families and, in particular, siblings. Using secondary data from the National Longitudinal Survey of Youth 1979 Children and Young Adults, this study examines the odds of college completion among young adults with a disabled sibling during childhood. Specifically, I examine the gender differences among those who had a sibling with a disability. Women are more than 35% less likely to complete college if they had a disabled sibling during childhood; there is no significant difference by sibling disability status for boys. To understand whether children in low-resourced families are particularly penalized by having a disabled sibling, I examine whether various family resources attenuate the low graduation odds among those who had a disabled sibling. I find that having stably married parents during childhood largely eliminates the college completion gap between those with and without a disabled sibling. However, increases in mothers' education or family income do not attenuate the college completion gap. By identifying this gender disadvantage in college completion, this study shows that disabilities have consequences not just for disabled

Disabilities and the Life Course
Research in Social Science and Disability, Volume 14, 125–144
Copyright © 2023 Anna Penner
Published under exclusive licence by Emerald Publishing Limited
ISSN: 1479-3547/doi:10.1108/S1479-354720230000014008

individuals but for their siblings as well, shining a light on a hidden cost of disability on families.

Keywords: Siblings; disability; education; gender; life course; family

More than one in eight American families has a disabled child (National Center for Education Statistics, 2017), affecting both disabled individuals and their families (Priestley, 2001).[1] Parental stress increases (Baker et al., 2011) and marriages dissolve earlier when raising a disabled child (Hogan, 2012). While disability is prevalent in American society, it is underrepresented in sociological literature (Shandra, 2018). Furthermore, despite a wide range of research on sibling effects more generally (Brody et al., 2003), sociological research rarely examines the life course influences of having a disabled sibling.

This study draws on life course theory to address this lacuna, investigating how growing up with a disabled sibling relates to educational attainment, specifically college completion. This chapter makes three main contributions. First, I examine this common – but often overlooked – experience of having a disabled sibling, using nationally representative data to document whether college completion rates differ between young adults whose siblings were and were not disabled. Second, I address the gendered nature of how disability and family intersect to shape the college outcomes of the brothers and sisters of disabled children differently. Third, I investigate the role family resources play in the college completion rates among those with a disabled sibling. I show that sisters, but not brothers, of disabled siblings have lower college completion rates and that having a stably married mother during childhood buffers against the academic disadvantage of having a disabled sibling. This study uses a life course approach to examine impacts from childhood on life course trajectories in adulthood and demonstrate the salience of a life course perspective on the linked lives of disabled children and their siblings.

The linked lives perspective explains that people are impacted both by the people in their lives and the society and institutions in which they are embedded (Elder, 1994; George, 2012). These individual and institutional components influence the trajectories of the life course and are notable in the family context (Cherlin et al., 2013) as sociologists examine how significant others impact those around them (Settersten, 2017). Individual-level research in the life course perspective examines historical contexts as well as the impact of events early in childhood on outcomes in adulthood (George, 1993). As such, considering the impact of disability on families can further life course research more generally.

---

[1] I use identity-first language (e.g., disabled person) over person-first language (e.g., person with a disability). Within the disability community, using person-first language is viewed as erasing disability as an identifying feature (Kenny et al., 2016). In addition, research suggests that person-first language stigmatizes disability (Gernsbacher, 2017), and the American Psychological Association recommended identity-first language (Dunn & Andrews, 2015).

While disability certainly impacts the life course trajectory of a disabled individual (Brault, 2012), nuclear family members of disabled people also face additional stressors due to the disability (Houser et al., 2010). The social model of disability argues that what causes disability is not primarily an impairment but rather the ableism and inaccessibility of the social world in a particular historical context. Furthermore, according to the social model of disability, physical barriers and stigmas keep disabled people from getting the access they deserve (Oliver, 1983). As such, while disability is solely experienced by disabled individuals, other members of their families also incur additional stressors (Brown & Ciciurkaite, 2021). The ableism present in society that inhibits support for disabled individuals also affects family members as they seek out complex social supports such as an Individualized Education Program (Kurth et al., 2020). This is not to say that family members are also disabled by society or encounter stigmatization in the same way as their disabled family member, but as the linked lives perspective would suggest they experience stress that is not encountered by people whose family members are not disabled.

FAMILIES OF DISABLED CHILDREN

While there is no definitive number of how many children or young adults have a disabled sibling in the United States, 13% of school-age children have a disability (National Center for Education Statistics, 2017), affecting families across all demographics. Consistent with the life course concept of linked lives, disability affects the disabled individual as well as their family unit. This mutuality of relationships influences the psychological health of partners (Brown & Ciciurkaite, 2021) and the marriage and work status of parents (Hogan, 2012), as well as adult siblings of disabled children (Hodapp et al., 2010; Wolfe et al., 2014).

Family disability research points to distinct challenges with implications for siblings and their educational achievement. Studies investigate how having a disabled sibling is associated with high school completion and college enrollment (e.g., Hogan, 2012). However, few studies examine college completion (see Wolfe et al., 2014), which is of particular importance in the transition to adulthood (Crosnoe & Johnson, 2011) and the ability to enter the skilled labor force competitively (Bureau of Labor Statistics, 2021). Adolescents with a disabled sibling are 16% less likely to believe they will complete college and 31% less likely to enroll in college (Hogan, 2012).

Studies point to circumstances that reduce parental health (Ekas & Whitman, 2011), household stability (Hogan, 2012), and economic resources (Mitra et al., 2009), resulting in increased economic and time demands for families of disabled children. These demands are linked to higher maternal stress and depression (Baker et al., 2011; Ekas & Whitman, 2011), and stress more generally due to the additional supervision required for a disabled child (Dupont, 1980). Without the proper social support, caring for family members with severe illnesses or disabilities is often linked to burnout (Ybema et al., 2002) and depression (Covinsky et al., 2003). Once again, the concept of linked lives is evidenced as mothers' mental health is correlated with secure attachment among young children (Martins & Gaffan, 2000). And, relevant to this study, among mothers without higher education, depression is associated with a decrease in their child's educational achievement (Augustine & Crosnoe, 2010).

Higher rates of early divorce impact resources in families with a disabled child compared to families where children are not disabled (Hogan, 2012). While there is significant variation when divorces tend to occur by type of disability, the divorce rates across the life course are similar between couples who do and do not have a disabled child (Hartley et al., 2010). In general, children who live in a stressful or divorced household have lower educational attainment than those whose families remain intact (Amato, 2005). When faced with increased marital conflict, fathers often disengage from their children, which can have deleterious effects on their educational attainment (Harris et al., 1998). In addition, it may be difficult for parents with a disabled child to stay engaged with their nondisabled children, in part due to the considerable time and emotional energy their disabled child takes (Crowe, 1993; Siegal & Silverstein, 2007).

Conversely, parents may engage with their nondisabled child by sharing concerns that are inappropriate given the child's age (Burton, 2007). Furthermore, when adolescents are satisfied with their relationship with their parents, they are more academically engaged and complete more education (Hair et al., 2005). Children with a disabled sibling, however, may have fewer positive experiences of closeness to parents than their peers, particularly given the link between maternal depression and insecure attachment earlier in childhood (Martins & Gaffan, 2000). Returning to the life course perspective, the stress present in these families and the higher rates of early divorce may yield lower odds of college completion among those with a disabled sibling.

Parental time and supervision are also positively associated with educational attainment (Lareau, 2003). However, parents with a disabled child are apt to reduce their time with nondisabled children to care for their disabled child and expect their nondisabled child to help with care and chores (Siegal & Silverstein, 2007). In addition, parents with a disabled child also tend to display traditional gender roles – mothers are more likely to be full-time homemakers than work outside the home. Fathers often work longer hours, add a second job, or work past retirement age to provide for their family (Hogan, 2012). Unsurprisingly, apart from disability specifically, a child's health concerns have a much more significant impact on mothers' paid work than fathers' paid work (Noonan et al., 2005).

Parental division of labor may encourage gendered behavior of their children into adulthood (Cunningham, 2001). While we do not know about the sibling care provided in childhood, women are more often caretakers for their disabled siblings as adults (Krauss et al., 1996; Seltzer et al., 2005). This is not surprising as gendered care work is seen across families even where disability is absent. During childhood, girls provide, on average, eight more hours of care per week for younger siblings than boys (Aronson et al., 1996). This discrepancy is exacerbated in low-income families where children, particularly girls, are counted on for household chores and care work, and consequently, these girls spend less time engaging in educational activities (Dodson & Dickert, 2004). It is plausible that girls who have a disabled sibling spend more time in care work as children than their peers whose siblings are not disabled resulting in lower educational attainment.

Gender is an essential consideration in understanding resource allocation in families with a disabled child. In families with a disabled child, every part of life can take a little longer due to the increased need for primary childcare, not just supervisory care. For example, additional dietary constraints increase time in food production, leading to direct care (e.g., supervision and feeding) or indirect care (e.g., laundry and cleaning) being assumed by daughters, along with the role of a confidant for an overwhelmed parent (Burton, 2007). Such adultification occurs when children are exposed to problems typically handled by adults. They thus begin to assume adult roles as children. As a result, they know more about their family's affairs than their peers do or assume the role of an adult in the family, even becoming a sounding board for their parents or assuming care roles that are usually left to adults.

ECONOMICS OF DISABILITY

The life course perspective focuses on how significant others impact the life course trajectories of loved ones. The life course perspective also examines the impact of the institutions and social context people live in (George, 2012). Given how expensive disability can be (Mitra et al., 2009) and the difficulty of navigating the health insurance system in the United States (Sofaer, 2009), it is not surprising that there is a link between poverty and disability, though the causal direction is unclear. Hogan et al. (1997) showed that children in impoverished homes are 40% more likely to be disabled. Other studies suggest that 16% of children without disabilities and 28% of children with a disability live below the poverty line (Fujiura & Yamaki, 2000).

Whatever the family income, having a disabled child increases child-rearing expenses, such as therapies or specialized equipment (Kuhlthau et al., 2005). Healthcare expenses alone can cost up to four times more for a disabled person than for a nondisabled individual (Mitra et al., 2009). These higher care costs may have further bearing on family income if they necessitate a parent forgoing paid work to care for the disabled child (Hogan, 2012) and point to another way social and economic support would relieve family stress.

To the extent that living in poverty is detrimental to educational development and outcomes (Brooks-Gunn & Duncan, 1997), the lower economic resources, along with the necessary resource reallocation among disabled and nondisabled children, could depress the educational achievement of children with a disabled sibling. As socioeconomic status is positively correlated with educational outcomes, families from low socioeconomic backgrounds who have a disabled child may have additional stress that is negatively correlated with the educational completion of siblings than families with higher socioeconomic statuses.

DISABILITY IMPACT ON SIBLINGS AND CHALLENGES OF DISABLED SIBLING RESEARCH

Disability literature has only briefly examined impacts on the family's nondisabled children, notably overlooking the life course implications of having a disabled sibling during childhood for outcomes in adulthood. This dearth is understandable given the challenges of research on disabled siblings. First, samples tend to be small and nonrepresentative. Qualitative studies show increased behavioral problems during childhood for siblings of disabled children (Meyer et al., 2011). Having a disabled sibling in early childhood is linked to several negative behavioral outcomes (Eisenberg et al., 1998). However, there are also benefits such as better sibling relationships (Zaidman-Zait et al., 2020), increased altruism (Siegal & Silverstein, 2007), and cognitive empathy (Rum et al., 2022) that stem from having a disabled sibling.

A second challenge is the heterogeneity in disability that makes generalization difficult. For example, studies typically examine only one or two types of disabilities (e.g., Hodapp & Urbano, 2007). While readily defensible in terms of the unique needs and circumstances of different disabilities, the disability-specific design across the literature makes it difficult to generalize mixed findings to disability writ large. These issues of sample size and generalizability also apply to qualitative studies that offer some of the richest insights into the lives of families with a disabled child (e.g., Cuskelly & Gunn, 2006).

Finally, many studies are cross-sectional, losing the ability to investigate outcomes across the life course (Seltzer et al., 2005). Studies on sibling disability that examine the care provided by adult siblings find that young adults play a significant role in caring for their disabled siblings. In particular, sisters are more likely than brothers to care for their disabled siblings and expect to coreside with their disabled siblings as adults (Krauss et al., 1996; Seltzer et al., 2005). Even ambitious studies with large samples are limited by the cross-sectional nature of the data (e.g., Hodapp & Urbano, 2007; Kuhlthau et al., 2005).

Two studies stand out as exemplars in longitudinal research on sibling outcomes. First, Hogan's (2012) work on the families of disabled children examines the siblings' outcomes across the early life course. Using the National Longitudinal Survey of Youth 1997, Hogan found that adolescents with a disabled sibling are as likely to graduate from high school as their peers whose siblings are not disabled (I found the same in supplemental analyses which are available upon request), but are three times less likely to enroll in college. Hogan, however, does not report gender differences in these outcomes. Furthermore, while Hogan examines college enrollment, he does not examine college completion, which is a notable marker for entry into adulthood (Crosnoe & Johnson, 2011), and sets life course trajectories in a way that completing high school does not (Bureau of Labor Statistics, 2021). Finally, this project expands on Hogan's work by following adults for another decade, allowing a new birth cohort (including not just Millennials but also Generation Z) to reach early adulthood, providing information about current young adults in the United States today.

A second notable study uses the Wisconsin Longitudinal Survey (WLS) to address the educational, labor force, and family formation outcomes of having a sibling with a developmental disability or mental illness (Wolfe et al., 2014). The WLS surveyed over 10,000 1957 Wisconsin high school graduates. The children of those graduates are the focus of the disability study and were, on average, 37 years old in 2004 when the education, labor force, and marriage outcomes were measured. Respondents whose siblings were developmentally delayed experienced lower marriage rates and higher divorce rates but did not have significantly different educational and labor force outcomes compared to their counterparts whose siblings were not disabled. The current study extends this work by using data that are broadly representative of the United States (though Wolfe et al. note the lack of racial minorities in the WLS as a limitation) as well as using a sample of current young adults as mentioned above. It also extends the analysis to the differences in gender in college completion rates.

Because the implication of having a disabled sibling is still relatively under-researched, these challenges discussed above are not surprising. Ideally, data on families with disabled children would be large and nationally representative. Additionally, data would be longitudinal to capture change over time both for the measurement of disability itself and the family context. Furthermore, longitudinal data would allow greater insight into the life course trajectories surrounding disability. Following children into adulthood (as the WLS did) facilitates understanding of the long-term effects of disability on the family.

RESEARCH QUESTIONS AND HYPOTHESES

Drawing on the literature documenting the challenges facing families with a disabled child, I expect that:

H1. Young adults who had a disabled sibling during childhood will have lower odds of completing college than young adults whose siblings were not disabled.

While Buchmann and DiPrete (2006) show that girls outperform boys in disadvantaged families, I expect a different outcome among families with a disabled child. Since sisters typically provide more care work than brothers and expect to do so as adults, I posit that:

H2. The negative association of having a disabled sibling with college completion will be stronger for sisters than brothers.

Finally, because families with a disabled child likely allocate more resources to their disabled child than their nondisabled children, I expect resources are a factor in the negative association between having a disabled sibling and college completion.

H3. A more resourced family will buffer the negative relationship between having a disabled sibling and college completion.

DATA AND METHODS
Data

Given the data and design challenges discussed above, the limitations of studies on individuals with disabled siblings are understandable. Examining variation in college completion by sibling disability status requires a few key elements from a dataset. This study used the National Longitudinal Survey of Youth 1979 (NLSY79) and the accompanying Children and Young Adults surveys (CNLSY) administered by the Bureau of Labor Statistics. The NLSY79 provides information about the mothers of the CNLSY respondents, such as their mothers' educational attainment and income. The NLSY79 surveyed 14- to 22-year-olds in 1979 annually until 1994, at which time they conducted surveys biennially. In 1986, the CNLSY began biennial surveys of all children born to the NLSY79 women (Bureau of Labor Statistics, 2011).

The NLSY79 and CNLSY together overcome many limitations of prior research. First, it is longitudinal (I used data from biennial waves from 1986 to 2014) and nationally representative, even oversampling minorities to ensure sufficient samples for reliable estimates (National Longitudinal Surveys, n.d.). The CNLSY addresses the call for large sample sizes and nationally representative data for the study of disability (Seltzer et al., 2005).

Furthermore, instead of relying on just one focal respondent, it collects information on the mother and all her biological children, providing both family context and information about multiple children in the family. This enabled me to identify sibling sets and examine educational outcomes for all of a mother's biological children. Finally, the respondents' ages ranged from 24 to 44 (the average age was 29) in the last wave of data. Because many groundbreaking studies of families with disabled children reference earlier cohorts, the CNLSY is invaluable as a source of information about today's young adults.

Dependent Variables
College completion was dichotomous (1 = completed at least a bachelor's degree, 0 = did not complete a bachelor's degree) and self-reported by respondents who are 24 years old and older. I measured college completion in the last wave of respondents' report.

Independent Variables
The key independent variable of *sibling disability* during childhood was dichotomous (had a disabled sibling = 1, else = 0), which came from information on the mother- and self-reported disabilities. Mothers completed disability information for their children under 15 as well as for children with disabilities who could not complete the survey after the age of 15 due to their disability. Any respondent who ever had a reported disability during childhood was excluded from my analysis – both from the focal group and the comparison group.

The Americans with Disabilities Act of 1990 (ADA) defines disability as "a physical or mental impairment that substantially limits one or more major life activities; a record of such an impairment; or being regarded as having such an impairment" (Americans with Disabilities Act, 2009). Disabilities range from sensory (e.g., blindness) and physical disabilities (e.g., wheelchair user) to cognitive disabilities (e.g., learning disability) and include individuals with multiple disabilities. Therefore, I classified a CNLSY respondent as having a disability if a report indicated the child being affected by one or more of the following between 1986 and 2014: autism, chronic nervous disorder, crippled or orthopedic handicap, difficulty seeing or blindness, emotional disturbance, epilepsy/seizures, hearing difficulty or deafness, learning disability, mental retardation, minimal brain dysfunction, or speech impairment. Also included in the disability measurement was answering affirmatively to having a condition that limits play activities, school attendance, or schoolwork, or requires a doctor, use of medication, or special equipment. This measurement was wide-ranging but was consistent with the formal ADA definition in its attention to conditions linked to activity limitations.

If a respondent under 19 years old with a disability had a never-disabled sibling during childhood in the wave the disability is first reported, that sibling was coded as having a disabled sibling. Disabled children were never included in the sample, even if the disability was not reported again. Because the interest was in formative childhood influences, a respondent was coded as having a disabled sibling if both the focal respondent and the disabled sibling were 18 or younger when both children were likely to live at home together.

In short, the disabled sibling measure was a dichotomous variable for whether the respondent had a disabled sibling for multiple waves during childhood. As disability status is often dynamic over time (Mann & Honeycutt, 2016), only individuals with multiple reports of disability were counted as disabled. Although the stricter measure yielded fewer respondents with a disabled sibling, it is arguably a more reliable measure and captured respondents with longer, and likely more consequential, exposure to a disabled sibling.

In the CNLSY, 5,314 respondents were never disabled, at least 24 years old, and had at least one biological sibling. Nearly 1,800 (33.8%) respondents had a disabled sibling during childhood for at least one wave, and almost 700 (13.1%) had a disabled sibling for at least two waves. In my analytic sample of 2,625, 22% had a disabled sibling for more than one wave. Due to dropping respondents with missing data, the percentage of respondents with a disabled sibling in my data was higher than the CNLSY dataset more broadly. See the methods section for how missing data were handled.

Gender (female = 0, male = 1) captured the main effect to control for any differences between brothers and sisters of disabled children in their college completion rates. Additionally, gender was interacted with disabled sibling status to investigate whether the implications of having a disabled sibling differ for brothers and sisters.

Resources

Other variables of interest included the resource measures of family income, mothers' education, mothers' marital status, and household cognitive stimulation.

The NLSY79 provides *family income* as well as *poverty status*. The poverty measure takes account of family size following the United States Department of Health and Human Services guidelines. Poverty (ever in poverty during childhood = 1, never in poverty = 0) was used for direct comparisons as it is dichotomous, while logged family income (averaged across childhood) was used in logistic regression analyses.

As reported in the latest wave, *mothers' education* measured whether the mother completed college (completed college = 1, did not complete college = 0).

Mothers' marital status (married for the entirety of the focal respondent's childhood = 1, else = 0) was measured before the focal child was 19 years old.

A *household cognitive stimulation scale* captured resources of the home environment that promoted academic success. Interviewer observations and mother self-reports covered such items as the number of books a child had; whether the child received lessons or belonged to a sport, music, art, dance, or drama organization; and whether the mother provided toys to her child. These scales were created separately for children aged 0–2, 3–5, 6–9, and 10–14, as items vary in appropriateness by age. The subscales are normed by the NLSY, and for the purposes of this study respondents' percentiles were averaged across reports.

Control Variables

Additional control variables accounted for individual characteristics and were measured in the latest wave. Given that individual characteristics such as respondents' birth order (Härkönen, 2014; Hauser & Sewell, 1985) and race (Ryan & Bauman, 2016) are linked to educational outcomes, both were included as controls. Age (24 and older) and birth order (1–11) are continuous variables. Race was controlled using dummy variables. The NLSY race categories are Black, Hispanic, or non-Black and non-Hispanic. The latter was the omitted reference category in multivariate analyses.

ANALYSIS

To identify differences in college completion between those with and without a disabled sibling, I used STATA version 16 to analyze logistic regression models examining the odds of college graduation and test each of my hypotheses. Gender and disabled sibling status were interacted to examine differences in disabled sibling status for men and women. Logistic regression tests were also used to measure the impact of various resource variables.

Regression models relied on cluster-robust standard errors to account for the clustering of multiple respondents within families. Listwise deletion (Allison, 2014) restricted the sample to include only respondents who answered with information on all variables. To test robustness of the results, I used both multiple imputation and dummy variable adjustments to set all missing data to zero and flag the cases with missing data using dummy variables. These robustness checks yielded similar results. Weights for each wave, as provided by the CNLSY, adjusted for the higher attrition of disadvantaged respondents and accounted for the oversampling of minorities. These weights were used in all analyses.

RESULTS

Twenty-two percent (576 of 2,625) of respondents had a disabled sibling during childhood. *T*-tests reveal that respondents with a disabled sibling were less likely than others to have completed college, though this difference was only marginally significant ($p < 0.10$). Families with a disabled child, on average, had 0.8 more children ($p < 0.001$). Over 50% of respondents with a disabled sibling experienced poverty during childhood, compared to 44% of respondents without a disabled sibling ($p < 0.05$). Respondents with a disabled sibling were also significantly disadvantaged in terms of cognitive stimulation at home ($p < 0.001$). Respondents with a disabled sibling tended to be younger siblings ($p < 0.001$). On average, respondents with a disabled sibling were slightly younger than those without a disabled sibling, though this was only marginally significant ($p < 0.10$). Respondents with a disabled sibling were more likely to be girls – likely because of the higher rates of disability reported for boys, though this was also only marginally significant ($p < 0.09$). Young people with and without a disabled sibling were not significantly different on mother's education, average family income, or racial composition (Table 1).

To test *H1*, Table 2 shows logistic regression models of college graduation. Model 1 indicates a statistically nonsignificant result in the bivariate relationship between disabled sibling status and college completion. Model 1 failed to support *H1*'s expectation of sibling disability negatively influencing college completion.

As men in the United States are less likely than women to complete college, Model 2 controlled for gender differences in college completion and introduces the interaction of a disabled sibling with male. With these gender controls, the negative disabled sibling coefficient became stronger and statistically significant ($p < 0.05$). The marginally significant ($p < 0.08$) interaction suggests a stronger gendered component of college completion that favors men with a disabled sibling over women with a disabled sibling, thus failing to reject *H2*.

Models 3–6 added each family resource variable separately to test whether socioeconomic resources condition educational outcomes. Not surprisingly, higher family income was significantly ($p < 0.001$) associated with higher odds of completing college (Model 3). Controlling for family income resulted in a slightly smaller estimate of having a disabled sibling, but yielded a larger estimate of the negative association between male and the interaction, which remained marginally statistically significant ($p < 0.06$). Net of family income, having a disabled sibling, had negative implications for women's college graduation (-0.470) but

Table 1. Weighted Descriptive Statistics by Sibling Disability Status: Child Respondents, 24 and Older, With at Least One Sibling.

	Respondents *without* a Sibling with a Disability		Respondents *with* a Sibling with a Disability	
	Mean or %	Standard Error	Mean or %	Standard Error
Education				
Graduated from college (%)	30.37		25.64†	
Family characteristics				
Number of children (mean)	2.91	0.025	3.68	0.075***
Mother's years of education (mean)	13.34	0.064	13.30	0.125
Mother graduated from college (%)	19.42		20.29	
Family income (mean)	10.25	0.022	10.21	0.038
In poverty (%)	44.44		50.61*	
Always married mothers (%)	48.82		44.77	
Home cognitive stimulation (mean)	51.94	0.488	47.54	0.938***
Respondent characteristics				
Birth order (mean)	1.83	0.023	2.06	0.052***
Age (mean)	29.87	0.109	29.46	0.194†
Male (%)	55.18		48.04*	
Black (%)	24.42		25.15	
Hispanic (%)	11.72		13.00	
Non-hispanic, non-Black (%)	63.86		61.85	
Number	2,049		576	

Note: Mean and percent difference significance ***$p < 0.001$, **$p < 0.01$, *$p < 0.05$, †$p < 0.10$.

carried no particular disadvantage for men's ($-0.470 + 0.531 = 0.061$). Model 3 failed to support *H3*, which argued that controlling for resources would weaken the association between disabled sibling status and college completion.

Mother's education (Model 4) also had a strong positive association with college completion ($p < 0.001$). As with family income, controlling for maternal education pointed to the negative and significant ($p < 0.05$) main effect of disabled sibling status and the significant ($p < 0.05$) disabled sibling by gender interaction. (0.628) offset the disabled sibling coefficient (-0.590), indicating that while there was a negative association between having a disabled sibling and graduating from college for women, such an association does not exist for men when controlling for mother's education. As the disabled sibling coefficient is higher in Model 4 than in Model 2, the association between having a disabled sibling and college completion was not attributable to the mothers' education. Like Model 3, Model 4 failed to support *H3*.

Having a married mother throughout childhood (Model 5) also significantly contributed to college completion. Controlling for mothers' marital status, the disabled sibling coefficient was only marginally significant ($p < 0.07$), and its interaction with gender was not statistically significant. Similarly, controlling for

Table 2. Logistic Regression of Odds of Graduating From College on Having a Sibling With a Disability for Multiple Waves During Childhood.

	Model 1	Model 2	Model 3	Model 4	Model 5	Model 6	Model 7
Sibling with a disability	−0.211	−0.480*	−0.470*	−0.590*	−0.399†	−0.323	−0.450*
	(0.164)	(0.209)	(0.208)	(0.216)	(0.208)	(0.202)	(0.214)
Male		−0.437***	−0.535***	−0.506***	−0.485***	−0.395**	−0.532***
		(0.121)	(0.128)	(0.127)	(0.125)	(0.125)	(0.132)
Sibling with a disability × male		0.497†	0.531†	0.628*	0.377	0.414	0.486†
		(0.278)	(0.282)	(0.279)	(0.279)	(0.276)	(0.282)
Resources							
Average family income (logged)			1.089***				0.461***
			(0.122)				(0.132)
Mother's education				0.305***			0.210***
				(0.030)			(0.032)
Married mother					1.129***		0.690***
					(0.130)		(0.146)
Home cognitive stimulation						0.038***	0.022***
						(0.003)	(0.004)
Respondent characteristics							
Age	−0.092***	−0.093***	−0.028	−0.052**	−0.082***	−0.102***	−0.035†
	(0.012)	(0.017)	(0.018)	(0.018)	(0.017)	(0.018)	(0.019)
Birth order	−0.341***	−0.340***	−0.267**	−0.264***	−0.328***	−0.194*	−0.167*
	(0.075)	(0.075)	(0.077)	(0.079)	(0.074)	(0.077)	(0.077)
Race (ref. = white)							
Black	−0.782***	−0.807***	−0.136	−0.842***	−0.393**	−0.209	0.058
	(0.132)	(0.134)	(0.147)	(0.140)	(0.139)	(0.143)	(0.157)
Hispanic	−0.971***	−0.991***	−0.382***	−0.760***	−0.889***	−0.429**	−0.300†
	(0.153)	(0.153)	(0.159)	(0.162)	(0.157)	(0.163)	(0.170)
Constant	−0.830	3.040	−10.462	−2.441	1.985	0.721	−8.456
Psuedo R-squared	0.0016	0.0693	0.1420	0.1431	0.1121	0.1398	0.2104
N	2,625	2,625	2,625	2,625	2,625	2,625	2,625

***$p < 0.001$, **$p < 0.01$, *$p < 0.05$, †$p < 0.10$ two-tailed test.
Note: Numbers in parentheses are standard errors. All models restricted to respondents age 24 or greater and compare respondents with disabled siblings to respondents with siblings.
Weights included.

cognitive stimulation during childhood (Model 6) yielded nonsignificant disabled sibling status and disabled sibling status by gender interaction coefficients. This suggests that much of the impact of having a disabled sibling is borne by mothers' marital status and the cognitive stimulation of young children. Thus, Models 5 and 6 failed to reject *H3*.

In short, mothers' marriage and cognitive stimulation were resources that seem to offer a partial explanation for the association between college completion and disabled sibling and the disabled sibling by male interaction. On their own, family income (Model 3) and maternal education (Model 4) did not. Model 7 includes all four resource indicators, which are all statistically significant ($p <$ 0.001). Once again, having a disabled sibling was linked to lower college completion odds, particularly for girls as the disabled sibling by male interaction offset the disabled sibling coefficient (0.486–0.450), though the interaction was only marginally significant ($p < 0.09$). This reinforces the conclusion that having a disabled sibling and gender are linked to educational disadvantage, such that there is likely no disabled sibling hindrance for brothers while there is for sisters, failing to support *H3*. Taken together, this shows that unmarried mothers and lower home cognitive stimulation are strongly associated with the negative college completion outcomes of women with a disabled sibling. In the full model, having a disabled sibling remained a barrier to college completion, particularly for girls, which fails to reject *H2*.

The mixed support for *H3* in Models 3–6 invites a closer analysis. According to supplemental analyses, the predicted probability of completing college did not vary by disabled sibling status across family income, mother's education, and

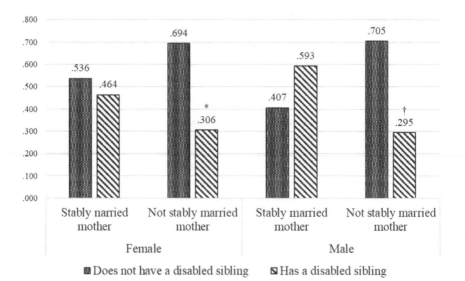

Fig. 1.   Predicted Probabilities of Graduating from College by Disabled Sibling Status.

cognitive stimulation measures, so further analyses focused on the mothers' marital status. Fig. 1 shows the predicted probability of college completion between having and not having a disabled sibling by gender and mothers' marital status.

Among respondents whose mothers were not continuously married during their childhood, women and men with a disabled sibling had lower predicted probabilities of completing college than their counterparts who did not have a disabled sibling. Among this subset, women with a disabled sibling had a predicted probability of 0.31 of completing college, only half that of other women respondents (0.70), a difference which is statistically significant ($p < 0.05$). Men with a disabled sibling had a similar predicted probability as women, though their difference in college completion was only marginally statistically significant ($p < 0.09$). There was no consistent significant difference by disabled sibling status among those whose mothers were stably married. This indicates that marital stability buffers against not completing college for young adults with a disabled sibling.

DISCUSSION

Inspired by life course theory and previous research showing that disability affects families, I examined the impact of having a disabled sibling during childhood on college completion among young adults. Using the CNLSY, and controlling for family and individual characteristics, I found that having a disabled sibling was not significantly associated with differences in college completion. However, this is because, on average, brothers who grew up with a disabled sibling had similar odds of completing college as other men. In contrast, sisters who had a disabled sibling were significantly less likely to complete college than other women. In addition, having a continuously married mother buffered against any negative link between having a disabled sibling and college completion for both boys and girls.

This study's findings extend the life course literature by examining disability within both the family context and an inherently ableist society. Furthermore, these findings call attention to the gendered ways that disabilities affect families as ableist institutions impact not just the disabled person but also increase stress for the entire family and may lead siblings, particularly young women, to forgo educational achievements. While Wolfe et al. (2014) did not find differences in educational attainment among young adults with a developmentally disabled sibling, this broader definition of disability coupled with the examination of gender differences show a different story. Sisters of disabled individuals are less likely to complete college than women who did not have a disabled sibling. As roughly 30% of mothers with a disabled child decrease their working hours or no longer work outside the home (Williams, 2010), these gender dynamics may lead sisters of disabled children to follow similar trajectories.

Furthermore, as children with more severe disabilities are typically able to attend public school until age 21, college-age sisters may face greater caregiving requirements as adults than they did as children. Given the literature that finds that sisters are much more likely to care for their disabled siblings as adults (e.g., Seltzer et al., 2005), women may see fewer benefits in completing college. Future research should investigate the mechanisms for the gender gap as well as whether older or younger siblings' education is differently influenced by having a disabled sibling.

These findings also indicate that economic resources such as family income or education do not buffer the association between having a disabled sibling and college completion as we might expect (e.g., Brooks-Gunn & Duncan, 1997). Building on Hogan's (2012) work that shows higher rates of early divorce among parents with a disabled child, this study reveals that children who have a disabled sibling and do not have a stably married mother see a significant drop in the predicted probability of completing college as we would expect (Amato, 2005). This suggests that it is not just about the resources available to a family but the ability of the family to distribute the resources. Unmarried mothers may have fewer economic resources, but it appears that the lack of a stable partner to share the childcare carries the negative association between having a disabled sibling and low college completion odds for their nondisabled children. These findings suggest that it is not the lack of economic resources that are detrimental for siblings, but more likely that the time and energy are negatively impacted by single parenthood.

This study is limited in a few ways. First, it is limited in its ability to investigate whether the siblings who are identified as nondisabled have less severe or unreported disabilities. Less pronounced and thus unreported disabilities could account for any deficit in the educational attainment of young people with disabled siblings compared to their peers since disability may cluster in families. However, if this were the case, there would be no reason to expect a gender disadvantage in education as unobserved disabilities would affect both brothers and sisters. There is no reason to think a shared genetic disposition or family environment, much less an underreporting of disabilities within families, explains the disabled sibling educational relationship.

Additionally, this study could not examine differences in the severity of the disability among disabled siblings, which would add nuances about possible care expectations that cannot be investigated using the CNLSY. Finally, I could not directly model the impact of family stress due to the lack of stress measures. Future studies should examine specific disabilities and differences by the severity of disability on a national and longitudinal level while also considering more specifically the timing of the disability's onset and the duration of the disability in keeping with the life course perspective.

This research addressed an understudied topic using data on contemporary young adults across the United States. By identifying an unrecognized and consequential type of gender disadvantage in the sisters of a disabled child, this study showed that disabilities have consequences not just for the individuals with disabilities but for their families as well. While previous research focused on parents, my results showed that they have significant and substantial effects on siblings, particularly sisters and children of unmarried parents. Prior research has revealed both positive and negative socioemotional (Eisenberg et al., 1998; Rum et al., 2022) and socioeconomic (Wolfe et al., 2014) outcomes linked to having a disabled sibling, and this research builds on that by illuminating a previously hidden cost of disability on society.

REFERENCES

Allison, P. (2014). Listwise deletion: It's NOT evil. *Statistical Horizons.* https://statisticalhorizons.com/listwise-deletion-its-not-evil

Amato, P. R. (2005). The impact of family formation change on the cognitive, social, and emotional well-being of the next generation. *Future of Children, 15*(2), 75–96. https://doi.org/10.1353/foc.2005.0012

Americans with Disabilities Act. (2009). *The public health and welfare.* U.S. Department of Justice Civil Rights Division. https://www.ada.gov/pubs/adastatute08.htm

Aronson, P. J., Mortimer, J. T., Zierman, C., & Hacker, M. (1996). Generational differences in early work experiences and evaluations. In J. T. Mortimer & M. D. Finch (Eds.), *Adolescents, work, and family: An intergenerational development analysis* (pp. 25–62). Sage Publications.

Augustine, J. M., & Crosnoe, R. (2010). Mothers' depression and educational attainment and their children's academic trajectories. *Journal of Health and Social Behavior, 51*(3), 274–290. https://doi.org/10.1177/0022146510377757

Baker, J. K., Seltzer, M. M., & Greenberg, J. S. (2011). Longitudinal effects of adaptability on behavior problems and maternal depression in families of adolescents with autism. *Journal of Family Psychology, 25*(4), 601–609. https://doi.org/10.1037/a0024409

Brault, M. W. (2012). *Americans with disabilities: 2010.* US department of commerce, economics and statistics administration. US Census Bureau.

Brody, G. H., Kim, S., Murry, V. M., & Brown, A. (2003). Longitudinal direct and indirect pathways linking older sibling competence to the development of younger sibling competence. *Developmental Psychology, 39*(3), 618–628. https://doi.org/10.1037/0012-1649.39.3.618

Brooks-Gunn, J., & Duncan, G. (1997). The effects of poverty on children. *Future of Children, 7*(2), 55–71. https://doi.org/10.2307/1602387

Brown, R. L., & Ciciurkaite, G. (2021). The "own" and the "wise" revisited: Physical disability, stigma, and mental health among couples. *Journal of Health and Social Behavior, 62*(2), 170–182. https://doi.org/10.1177/0022146521998343

Buchmann, C., & DiPrete, T. A. (2006). The growing female advantage in college completion: The role of family background and academic achievement. *American Sociological Review, 71*(4), 515–541. https://doi.org/10.1177/000312240607100401

Bureau of Labor Statistics. (2011). *NLSY79 children and young adults.* National Longitudinal Surveys. https://www.bls.gov/nls/nlsy79-children.htm

Bureau of Labor Statistics. (2021). Education pays. *Career Outlook.* https://www.bls.gov/careeroutlook/2022/data-on-display/education-pays.htm

Burton, L. (2007). Childhood adultification in economically disadvantaged families: A conceptual model. *Family Relations, 56*(4), 329–345. https://doi.org/10.1111/j.1741-3729.2007.00463.x

Cherlin, A. J., Cumberworth, E., Morgan, S. P., & Wimer, C. (2013). The effects of the great recession on family structure and fertility. *The Annals of the American Academy of Political and Social Science, 650*(1), 214–231. https://doi.org/10.1177/0002716213500643

Covinsky, K. E., Newcomer, R., Fox, P., Wood, J., Sands, L., Dane, K., & Yaffe, K. (2003). Patient and caregiver characteristics associated with depression in caregivers of patients with dementia. *Journal of General Internal Medicine, 18*(12), 1006–1014. https://doi.org/10.1111/j.1525-1497.2003.30103.x

Crosnoe, R., & Johnson, M. K. (2011). Research on adolescence in the twenty-first century. *Annual Review of Sociology, 37*(1), 439–460. https://doi.org/10.1146/annurev-soc-081309-150008

Crowe, T. K. (1993). Time use of mothers with young children: The impact of a child's disability. *Developmental Medicine and Child Neurology, 35*(7), 621–630. https://doi.org/10.1111/j.1469-8749.1993.tb11700.x

Cunningham, M. (2001). The influence of parental attitudes and behaviors on children's attitudes toward gender and household labor in early adulthood. *Journal of Marriage and Family, 63*(1), 111–122. https://doi.org/10.1111/j.1741-3737.2001.00111.x

Cuskelly, M., & Gunn, P. (2006). Adjustment of children who have a sibling with down syndrome: Perspectives of mothers, fathers and children. *Journal of Intellectual Disability Research, 50*(12), 917–925. https://doi.org/10.1111/j.1365-2788.2006.00922.x

Dodson, L., & Dickert, J. (2004). Girls' family labor in low-income households: A decade of qualitative research. *Journal of Marriage and Family, 66*(2), 318–332. https://doi.org/10.1111/j.1741-3737.2004.00023.x

Dunn, D., & Andrews, E. E. (2015). Person-first and identity-first language: Developing psychologists' cultural competence using disability language. *American Psychologist, 70*(3), 255–264. https://doi.org/10.1037/a0038636

Dupont, A. (1980). A study concerning the time-related and other burdens when severely handicapped children are reared at home. *Acta Psychiatrica Sandinavica, 62*(S285), 249–257. https://doi.org/10.1111/j.1600-0447.1980.tb07697.x

Eisenberg, L., Baker, B., & Blacher, J. (1998). Siblings of children with mental retardation living at home or in residential placement. *Journal of Child Psychology and Psychiatry, 39*(3), 355–363. https://doi.org/10.1111/1469-7610.00331

Ekas, N. V., & Whitman, T. L. (2011). Adaptation to daily stress among mothers of children with an autism spectrum disorder: The role of daily positive affect. *Journal of Autism and Developmental Disorders, 41*(9), 1202–1213. https://doi.org/10.1007/s10803-010-1142-4

Elder, G. H. (1994). Time, human agency, and social change: Perspectives and the life course. *Social Psychology Quarterly, 57*(1), 4–15. https://doi.org/10.2307/2786971

Fujiura, G. T., & Yamaki, K. (2000). Trends in demography of childhood poverty and disability. *Exceptional Children, 66*(2), 187–199. https://doi.org/10.1177/001440290006600204

George, L. K. (1993). Sociological perspectives of life transitions. *Annual Review of Sociology, 19*, 353–373. https://doi.org/10.1146/annurev.so.19.080193.002033

George, L. K. (2012). Life-course perspectives on mental health. In C. Aneshensel, J. Phelan, & A. Bierman (Eds.), *Handbook of the sociology of mental health* (pp. 585–602). Springer.

Gernsbacher, M. A. (2017). Editorial perspective: The use of person-first language in scholarly writing may accentuate stigma. *Journal of Child Psychology and Psychiatry, 58*(7), 859–861. https://doi.org/10.0.4.87/jcpp.12706

Hair, E. C., Moore, K. A., Garrett, S. B., Kinukawa, A., Lippman, L. H., & Michelson, E. (2005). The parent-adolescent relationship scale. In K. A. Moore & L. H. Lippman (Eds.), *What do children need to flourish? Conceptualizing and measuring indicators of positive development* (pp. 183–202). Springer.

Härkönen, J. (2014). Birth order effects on educational attainment and educational transitions in West Germany. *European Sociological Review, 30*(2), 166–179. https://doi.org/10.1093/esr/jct027

Harris, K. M., Furstenberg, F. F., & Marmer, J. K. (1998). Paternal involvement with adolescents in intact families: The influence of fathers over the life course. *Demography, 35*(2), 201–216. https://doi.org/10.2307/3004052

Hartley, S. L., Barker, E. T., Seltzer, M. M., Floyd, F., Greenberg, J. S., Orsmond, G. I., & Bolt, D. (2010). The relative risk and timing of divorce in families of children with an autism spectrum disorder. *Journal of Family Psychology, 24*(4), 449–457. https://doi.org/10.1037/a0019847

Hauser, R. M., & Sewell, W. H. (1985). Birth order and educational attainment in full sibships. *American Educational Research Journal, 22*(1), 1–23. https://doi.org/10.3102/00028312022001001

Hodapp, R. M., & Urbano, R. C. (2007). Adult siblings of individuals with down syndrome versus with autism: Findings from a large-scale US survey. *Journal of Intellectual Disability Research, 51*(12), 1018–1029. https://doi.org/10.1111/j.1365-2788.2007.00994.x

Hodapp, R. M., Urbano, R. C., & Burke, M. M. (2010). Adult female and male siblings of persons with disabilities: Findings from a national survey. *Intellectual and Developmental Disabilities, 48*(1), 52–62. https://doi.org/10.1352/1934-9556-48.1.52

Hogan, D. (2012). *Exceptional children, challenged families: Raising children with disabilities.* Russell Sage Foundation Press.

Hogan, D., Msall, M. E., Rogers, M. L., & Avery, R. C. (1997). Improved disability population estimates of functional limitation among American children aged 5–17. *Maternal and Child Health Journal, 1*(4), 203–216. https://doi.org/10.1023/A:1022354126797

Houser, A., Gibson, M. J., & Redfoot, D. L. (2010). *Trends in family caregiving and paid home care for older people with disabilities in the community: Data from the national long-term care survey.* AARP Public Policy Institute.

Kenny, L., Hattersley, C., Molins, B., Buckley, C., Povey, C., & Pellicano, E. (2016). Which terms should be used to describe autism? Perspectives from the UK autism community. *Autism, 20*(4), 442–462. https://doi.org/10.1177/1362361315588200

Krauss, M. W., Seltzer, M. M., Gordon, R., & Friedman, D. H. (1996). Binding ties: The roles of adult siblings of persons with mental retardation. *Mental Retardation, 34*(2), 83–93.

Kuhlthau, K., Hill, K. S., Yucel, R., & Perrin, J. M. (2005). Financial burden for families of children with special health care needs. *Maternal and Child Health Journal, 9*(2), 207–218. https://doi.org/10.1007/s10995-005-4870-x

Kurth, J. A., Love, H., & Pirtle, J. (2020). Parent perspectives of their involvement in IEP development for children with autism. *Focus on Autism and Other Developmental Disabilities, 35*(1), 36–46. https://doi.org/10.1177/1088357619842858

Lareau, A. (2003). *Unequal childhoods: Class, race, and family life.* University of California Press.

Mann, D. R., & Honeycutt, T. (2016). Understanding the disability dynamics of youth: Health condition and limitation changes for youth and their influence on longitudinal survey attrition. *Demography, 53*(3), 749–776. https://doi.org/10.1007/s13524-016-0469-7

Martins, C., & Gaffan, E. A. (2000). Effects of early maternal depression on patterns of infant-mother attachment: A meta-analytic investigation. *Journal of Child Psychology and Psychiatry, 41*(6), 737–746. https://doi.org/10.1111/1469-7610.00661

Meyer, K. A., Ingersoll, B., & Hambrick, D. Z. (2011). Factors influencing adjustment in siblings of children with autism spectrum disorders. *Research in Autism Spectrum Disorders, 5*(4), 1413–1420. https://doi.org/10.1016/j.rasd.2011.01.027

Mitra, S., Findley, P. A., & Sambamoorthi, U. (2009). Health care expenditures of living with a disability: Total expenditures, out-of-pocket expenses, and burden, 1996–2004. *Archives of Physical Medicine and Rehabilitation, 90*(9), 1532–1540. https://doi.org/10.1016/j.apmr.2009.02.020

National Center for Education Statistics. (2017). *Children and youth with disabilities.* U.S. Department of Education, Institute of Education Sciences. https://nces.ed.gov/programs/coe/indicator/cgg

National Longitudinal Surveys. (n.d.). *Sample design & screening process.* Bureau of Labor Statistics. https://www.nlsinfo.org/content/cohorts/nlsy79/intro-to-the-sample/sample-design-screening-process

Noonan, K., Reichman, N. E., & Corman, H. (2005). New fathers' labor supply: Does child health matter? *Social Science Quarterly, 86,* 1399–1417. https://doi.org/10.1111/j.0038-4941.2005.00352.x

Oliver, M. (1983). *Social work with disabled people.* Macmillan.

Priestley, M. (2001). *Disability and the life course: Global perspectives.* Cambridge University Press.

Rum, Y., Genzer, S., Markovitch, N., Jenkins, J., Perry, A., & Knafo-Noam, A. (2022). Are there positive effects of having a sibling with special needs? Empathy and prosociality of twins of children with non-typical development. *Child Development, 93*(4), 1121–1128. https://doi.org/10.1111/cdev.13740

Ryan, C. L., & Bauman, K. (2016). *Educational attainment in the United States: 2015.* US Department of Commerce, Economics and Statistics Administration, US Census Bureau.

Seltzer, M. M., Greenberg, J. S., Orsmond, G. I., & Lounds, J. (2005). Life course studies of siblings of individuals with developmental disabilities. *Mental Retardation, 43*(5), 354–359. https://doi.org/10.1007/s10995-005-4870-x

Settersten, R. A. (2017). Propositions and controversies in life-course scholarship. In R. A. Settersten Jr. (Ed.), *Invitation to the life course: Toward new understandings of later life* (pp. 15–48). Routledge.

Shandra, C. (2018). Disability as inequality: Social disparities, health disparities, and participation in daily activities. *Social Forces, 97*(1), 1–35. https://doi.org/10.1093/sf/soy031

Siegal, B., & Silverstein, S. (2007). *What about me? Growing up with a developmentally disabled sibling.* Plenum.

Sofaer, S. (2009). Navigating poorly charted territory: Patient dilemmas in health care 'nonsystems'. *Medical Care Research and Review, 66*(1), 75S–93S. https://doi.org/10.1177/1077558708327945

Williams, J. C. (2010). *Reshaping the work-family debate: Why men and class matter.* Harvard University Press.

Wolfe, B., Song, J., Greenberg, J. S., & Mailick, M. (2014). Ripple effects of developmental disabilities and mental illness on nondisabled adult siblings. *Social Science & Medicine, 108*, 1–9. https://doi.org/10.1016/j.socscimed.2014.01.021

Ybema, J. F., Kuijer, R. G., Hagedoorn, M., & Buunk, B. P. (2002). Caregiver burnout among intimate partners of patients with a severe illness: An equity perspective. *Personal Relationships, 9*(1), 73–88. https://doi.org/10.1111/1475-6811.00005

Zaidman-Zait, A., Yechezkiely, D., & Regev, D. (2020). The quality of the relationship between typically developing children and their siblings with and without intellectual disability: Insight from children's drawings. *Research in Developmental Disabilities, 96*, 1–12. https://doi.org/10.1016/j.ridd.2019.103537

NEGOTIATING THE SPOUSAL CAREGIVING RELATIONSHIP FOLLOWING SPINAL CORD INJURY

Alexis A. Bender

AUTHOR BIOGRAPHY

Alexis A. Bender, PhD, is an Assistant Professor in the Department of Medicine at Emory University with a secondary appointment in the Department of Rehabilitation Medicine. Dr. Bender completed her PhD in Sociology with a concentration in family, health, and the life course and received an interdisciplinary certificate in gerontology. Her research broadly focuses on aging with disability and chronic disease with an emphasis on relationships over the life course. Dr. Bender is a fellow in the NIMH-funded UCSD Sustained Training in Aging & HIV Research (STAHR) program and receives funding from the National Institute on Aging and the National Institute on Drug Abuse. Select work has appeared in *The Gerontologist, Journals of Gerontology, Social Sciences, Journal of the American Geriatric Society*, and *Journal of Applied Gerontology*, where she also serves on the editorial board.

ABSTRACT

Sustaining a spinal cord injury (SCI) at any point in time is life-altering – physically, emotionally, and financially – for all persons affected by the injury, but it can place unique challenges on younger married couples. This study examines the transition to injury for 18 couples (ages 21–55). Data were collected using individual interviews with each partner at three time points following injury and observation in the rehabilitation setting (Creekview). This resulted in 96 individual interviews and 300 hours of observation. Using the life course perspective as a guiding theoretical framework and thematic analysis, I examined how the healthcare institution influenced the couples' relationship during their rehabilitation stay and the subsequent transition home. Creekview staff and couples accepted and reinforced the dominant

Disabilities and the Life Course
Research in Social Science and Disability, Volume 14, 145–165
Copyright © 2023 Alexis A. Bender
Published under exclusive licence by Emerald Publishing Limited
ISSN: 1479-3547/doi:10.1108/S1479-354720230000014009

cultural narrative that women are natural caregivers, but larger social struc-
tures of class, gender, and the division of paid and unpaid labor worked
together to push some women into caregiving faster or prevented other women
from engaging in caregiving. This study examines how younger couples move
through the caregiving career during an off-time transition when the expected
outcome is not long-term care placement or death. This study identified three
main types of caregivers, each with their own path of caregiving – naturalized,
constrained, and resistant caregivers. Overall, the transition to injury is
complex and this study highlights some of the ways the marital relationship is
affected by a nonnormative, unexpected transition.

Keywords: Caregiving; spinal cord injury; qualitative research; spousal
relationships; rehabilitation; longitudinal research

Sustaining a spinal cord injury (SCI) at any point in time is life-altering –
physically, emotionally, and financially – for all persons affected by SCI, but it
can place unique challenges on younger married couples. Both partners involved
in the injury face uncertainty about the future and the concern about whether the
relationship will "survive" might be equally strong for the noninjured spouse as it
is for the injured spouse (Kreuter, 2000). The presence of SCI might magnify or
modify existing problems in a relationship, create a burden for one partner, or
impede life satisfaction for both partners (Chan, 2000). It has been argued that
the marital dyad and other intimate relationships are perhaps the most important
"social context within which the psychological aspects of chronic illness are
managed" (Rodgers & Calder, 1990, p. 25). I assert that the sociological aspects
of chronic illness and injury are also negotiated within the context of the rehabilitation setting.

Being married can be beneficial for people experiencing SCI, as married
individuals report higher levels of life satisfaction, lower levels of disability
(Putzke et al., 2001), and higher levels of acceptance of disability (Harrison et al.,
2004) compared to unmarried individuals. While marriage serves as a buffer to
some of the effects of disability, spouses also can be a source of criticism or may
reinforce disability by helping too much (Holicky & Charlifue, 1999; Mills &
Turnbull, 2004; Putzke et al., 2001).

Spousal caregiving is unique from other kinds of caregiving because spouses
provide care for longer periods and tolerate higher levels of disability than other
types of care partners (Biegel et al., 1991). Additionally, spouses provide 25% of
care to older adults (Calasanti & Slevin, 2006) and a married person will turn to
their spouse first for care, regardless of gender (Kaye & Applegate, 1990).
Caregiving relationships can be difficult for both partners in the relationship.
Often the care partner must play the roles of lover and care partner, which can
negatively impact the relationship (Eriksson & Svedlund, 2006; Jeyathevan et al.,
2019; Kreuter, 2000). Caregiving spouses also have higher rates of depression and
decreased marital satisfaction compared to non-caregiving couples (Choi &
Marks, 2006; Jeyathevan et al., 2019).

Inequalities in the caregiving relationship also exist. Ingersoll-Dayton and Raschick (2004) found a gendered relationship between care partner stress and problem behaviors of the care recipient. They found a moderating effect on the relationship between problem behaviors and care partner stress when care-receiving wives engage in helping behaviors. However, they did not find a similar effect when husbands were the recipients of care. Married women with SCI are more likely to have a paid care partner while married men with SCI are more likely to receive their care from their spouse (Shackelford et al., 1998) and wives with disabling conditions receive fewer hours of care than husbands (Noël-Miller, 2010) and benefit less from spousal care (Spitze & Ward, 2000).

Care is complicated. Few scholars recognize the paths that people take when entering and exiting informal caregiving relationships and how care recipients and care partners negotiate everyday caregiving relationships. People who engage in care daily often do not recognize how social institutions, such as hospitals, communities, and places of employment, shape these paths. This oversight is especially true for women who provide care because of the socially constructed division of household labor and the pervasiveness of the cultural expectation of women to be better care partners (Hooyman & Gonyea, 1995). In this chapter, I explore how injured and noninjured spouses negotiate the spousal caregiving relationship within the context of these broader communities. There is a significant gap in the literature examining these dynamics among spouses immediately following injury.

THE LIFE COURSE PERSPECTIVE

The life course perspective is a valuable tool for examining life events and life changes. The life course perspective has theoretical roots in the study of social history and theories of individual and family development (Bengtson & Allen, 1993). Much of the life course scholarship has conceived of the life course as a natural, systematic progression of individuals' experiences as they move through time (Clausen, 1986). This tradition of scholarship is guided by how the events in an individual's life, in the form of event histories or trajectories, compare to other persons or groups in terms of timing, duration, and rates of change (Giele & Elder, 1998). For the couples in this study, the event of SCI might vary depending on multiple aspects of their lives. The life course perspective, like developmental psychology, says that what a person experiences before injury will affect how they experience life after injury. The life course examines all the experiences in one's life, which allows for various roles and events that might or might not proceed in any sequence. While we anticipate events will occur in a structured order (e.g., aging then disability), we know that events frequently do not follow our anticipated sequence (e.g., disability at 30). Additionally, the life course perspective allows us to examine the impact of change at different points in a person's life and there are many benefits of using this perspective, all of which stem from the guiding principles of the framework.

The life course perspective in its original conceptualization relies on four basic principles: location in time and place, timing in lives, linked lives, and human agency (Giele & Elder, 1998). The first three are most applicable to this study. First, *location in time and place* refers to the cultural background that individuals experience both in terms of social and physical context. Time and place shape the trajectories of family, education, and work, and they in turn influence behavior. For example, a person who experienced SCI in 2018 will have a vastly different experience than a person who experienced one in 1985 before the passage of the Americans with Disabilities Act that shaped the cultural context of disability in America. Because of the importance of time and place in life course scholarship, this project aims to capture how these couples transition through time by using three interview points. The three interviews will use a combination of retrospective and prospective questions to examine how these couples experience this transition over time. The second principle, *timing in lives*, refers to when events occur and it is most crucial to understanding events in the life course (Giele & Elder, 1998). The way individuals measure their successes in life is frequently through the element of timing; thus, the ways people view their life events as being "off-time" can have social ramifications and result in different trajectories in their life course. Focusing on younger couples (before the age of 50) allows me to examine the transition to injury as an off-time event for both partners. This event, because of its timing, could have ripple effects in terms of social interaction with friends and family as well as feelings of isolation within the couple. The third aspect of the life course perspective is the concept of *linked lives* (Giele & Elder, 1998). All aspects of an individual's life are interdependent, rather than separated from one another. People who experience SCI might find that it will affect other aspects of their life such as social relationships and workforce transitions, not just physical changes. Additionally, lives are linked when people share the same social worlds. This concept is especially true in families and dyadic relationships. These couples' lives also are linked to the rehabilitation professionals they interact with following injury. Both partners' understanding of injury is shaped by the information they do, or do not, receive from counselors, physicians, and family educators.

METHODS

Design

This prospective, life course-informed, qualitative study included 18 married couples ages 21–55 where one partner experienced a traumatic SCI within 1 month of our first interview. Recruitment for this study took place at a specialty spinal rehabilitation center that is part of the SCI Model System, which provides the highest and most comprehensive level of care. The decision to use three time points for interviews was based on the average progression of care in this center: about 1 month following SCI while in inpatient care, but after acute care (Int. 1); about 3 months after Int. 1 (Int. 2), which often aligned with intensive outpatient care; and approximately 6 months following Int. 1 after the transition home (Int.

3). The Institutional Review Boards at both [blinded] the University and the center approved this research. Participant and the rehabilitation center names reported here are pseudonyms.

Sample and Setting

To be included in the study, respondents had to meet the following criteria: one partner had to have sustained a new SCI without cognitive impairment and have started inpatient acute therapy 1 month before the first interview and they had to be married and under the age of 55 at the time of injury. Social workers in the setting served as gatekeepers by identifying eligible participants, sharing information about the study, and asking injured partners for consent for researchers to contact the couple. Participants (injured partners and care partners) were recruited for the study for 14 months and efforts were made to diverse sociodemographic and injury characteristics where feasible. Participants were recruited until we reached saturation at the first interview point. Twenty-four eligible couples provided consent to contact, of which 18 participated.

Data Collection and Analysis

Semistructured interview guides were informed by the life course perspective, literature, previous interviews, and observations in the rehabilitation center. As data collection progressed, the guide was modified to achieve data saturation. Interviews were conducted with each partner separately. The interviews began with a broad question about the respondent's current and recent life events, including details surrounding the SCI at Int. 1. Participants were then asked questions about their routine, relationship history, formal and informal social supports, sexuality and intimacy, and interactions with rehabilitation providers. The three interviews used a combination of retrospective and prospective questions to examine how participants experience this transition over time.

Interviews were digitally recorded, transcribed verbatim, and analyzed using a combination of inductive and deductive thematic analysis (Braun & Clarke, 2006) guided by the life course perspective and a model of the caregiving career adapted from (Aneshensel et al., 1995). When examining the caregiving relationships among the dyads in this study, I asked questions of the data like: "How willing are partners to engage in caregiving tasks?" "What are patients paying attention to in regard to their caregiving relationship?" "What are partners paying attention to during this process?" "Do they draw boundaries about what is acceptable and unacceptable in the caregiving relationship?", and "Are there self-imposed boundaries in care?" I initially analyzed data line by line inductively by constantly comparing instances within the data and applying codes to the text as concepts emerged. Related concepts were combined into categories and grouped into themes to summarize the key ideas and experiences discussed by the participants (Creswell, 1998). As coding progressed, I examined participant narratives across and within themes deductively to identify common experiences before and after injury and as they moved along the caregiving trajectory, resulting in

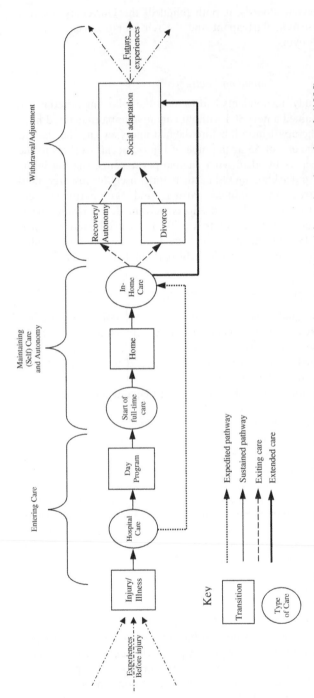

Fig. 1.   Caregiving Careers Following Spinal Cord Injury. *Source:* Adapted from Aneshensel et al. (1995).

the typology of care partner relationships described below and on Table 2. NVivo qualitative software versions 9 and 11 (QSR NVivo) were used to facilitate data organization.

FINDINGS

Sample Characteristics

Injured partners were predominately White, middle-aged, educated, and male. Care partners were primarily female and most earned less than their spouses (See Table 1). There was a range in household income at the time of injury, but most couples were above the US median household income for married couples

Table 1. Demographic and Injury Characteristics.

	Injured Partner ($N = 18$)	Care Partner ($N = 18$)
Characteristic	Number (%)	Number (%)
Female gender	2 (11%)	16 (89%)
White	16 (89%)	15 (83%)
Age		
Under 30	3 (17%)	4 (22%)
30–39	4 (22%)	4 (22%)
40–49	9 (50%)	6 (33%)
50+	2 (11%)	4 (22%)
Education		
HS or less	6 (33%)	5 (18%)
Some college	5 (18%)	6 (33%)
College graduate	7 (39%)	7 (39%)
Income		
≤$25,000	2 (11%)	8 (44%)
$25,001–50,000	6 (33%)	8 (44%)
$50,001–75,000	6 (33%)	1 (6%)
>$75,001–100,000	4 (22%)	1 (6%)
Cause of injury		
Internal (stroke, viral, abscess)	6 (33%)	
Auto	4 (22%)	
Fall	2 (11%)	
Sport	2 (11%)	
Violence	1 (6%)	
Work-related	3 (17%)	
Severity/Type of injury		
Complete quadriplegia	3 (17%)	
Complete paraplegia	6 (33%)	
Incomplete quadriplegia	4 (22%)	
Incomplete paraplegia	5 (18%)	

($61,335). Participants' length of marriage varied from 2 weeks to 37 years with a mean marriage length of 11.5 years at the time of injury. It was the second marriage for two participants and the only long-term intimate relationship for five participants. Causes of injury included external events (e.g., auto accidents, falls) and health-related events (e.g., spinal stroke, abscess) (Table 1).

This study included 18 couples (36 individuals) at the first interview point, 16 couples (32 individuals) at the second interview point, and 15 couples (30 individuals) at the third interview point for a total of 98 individual interviews. Although these respondents fell into dichotomous medical categories of paraplegia/quadriplegia and complete/incomplete, there was significant variation in the function and ability across these groups. Because of the longitudinal nature of this study, changes in ability and function over time were noted.

Caregiving Types and the Caregiving Career

Inductive analysis of the data resulted in three main types of caregiving relationships – *naturalized, constrained, and resistant*. Next, I overlaid these types on the caregiving career trajectory to examine similarities and differences among these three groups at key points of the career. Here I present how each type of care relationship moved along the career (Fig. 1) including the ways they (1) enter into caregiving relationships and the ways this entry is shaped by individual and structural forces (*Entering care*); (2) how couples negotiated the caregiving relationship daily and how they acted to create or limit their participation in caregiving spaces (*Maintaining (self) care and autonomy*); and (3) how the negotiation of the caregiving relationship can alter the trajectories for some couples and not for others (*Withdrawal/Adjustment of caregiving*). All three types moved along this trajectory, yet there were differences in previous life experiences and in the level and intensity of care that was provided at various points along the trajectory (Table 2). As couples moved through this career, the paths they took and their interactions along the way resulted in differing levels of social readjustment following injury and different relationship outcomes. It should be noted that the types presented in this chapter are ideal types and that the caregiving relationship is constantly negotiated. Additionally, some couples moved between these types at different time points depending on other life factors occurring simultaneously. The numbers I present are based on the dominant type of caregiving style presented in a dyad.

Naturalized Care Partners

Couples who offered naturalized narratives conceptualized caregiving as a job that had to be done out of love and necessity and as something they were good at providing. All caregivers in this category were women and, as will become more apparent, had internalized the cultural ideals that women are natural caregivers (Hooyman & Gonyea, 1995). Caregivers in this category neglected their own emotional and physical health to accomplish caregiving tasks. Naturalized caregivers could be characterized as willing to do what needed to be done for

Table 2. Conceptual and Demographic Attributes of Caregiving Types.

Primary Type	Naturalized	Constrained	Resistant
Number of couples	6	10	2
Mean length of marriage	15 years (Range 10–37 years)	10 years (Range 2 weeks–24 years)	8 years (Range 2–15)
# Working	2/6 care partners 6/6 patients	8/10 care partners 10/10 patients	1 care partner 2 patients
Gender of care partner	All women	9 women	1 woman
Children living at home	4/6 couples	7/10 couples	Both couples
Education	Less than high school to some college (1/6 patients had a college degree)	Most with some college or greater (1/10 patients had HS degree); 5 patients and 5 care partners were college graduates; one care partner had postgraduate education.	Partners were equal: One couple were HS graduates; one couple were college graduates
Income	Unequal: Care partner model category <$12,500, none earned more than $37,000 Partners with injury all earned at least $12,00 with two earning greater than $75,000	Higher than naturalized and more equal. Care partner model category was 37,500–$50,000; Patient modal category was $50,000–$62,500	Correlated with the level of education
Type of injury	4 quad/2 para	3 quad/7 para	1 quad/1 para
How they identify themselves and their roles	Care partners could be characterized as willing to do what needs to be done for their partner to be safe, comfortable, and happy. Partners with injuries expected their spouses to provide care.	Described being torn between the amount of care they could provide and the amount they wanted to provide. Care was given as part of a reciprocal agreement with the goal of building independence.	Not willing to engage in caregiving until pushed by care workers at Creekview. More likely to see care as a burden before starting care. Only pushed into taking on caregiving tasks when necessary.
Previous care experiences	Many, but not all, had previous experiences caring for family, especially among women with fewer resources	Minimal care work beyond raising children	Minimal care work beyond raising children
Social support	Minimal, and often did not ask for help	Moderate. Had resources to pay for care and willing to ask children for help	Low. Expressed high levels of loneliness and isolation
Sources of stress	High levels of emotion work; limited self-care	Work; tension between desired care and ability to provide care	Previous marital discord; substance use

Table 2. (*Continued*)

Primary Type	Naturalized	Constrained	Resistant
Balance of care and autonomy	Great concern about further injury; little separation or outside assistance	More autonomy than naturalized couples, likely due to level of injury and recovery	Autonomy and refusal to provide care
Path for exiting care	Burnout; exhaustion	Returned to work; boundary around care; push spouse to take care back	Unknown/began divorce proceedings

their partner to be safe, comfortable, and happy. Many caregivers in this category, especially those with few social resources, had previous experiences with caring for other family members.

Entering Care

Naturalized care partners moved quickly into caregiving and were the initiators of care responsibilities. For example, Shirley spoke about her entry into caregiving at Int. 2. She said: "I was always there to learn, you know, they didn't have to ask me, I did it on my own. . .I asked 'em this and that, and so they would show me and stuff." Like most of the women in this category, Shirley did not work when her husband was injured and perceived the caregiving relationship as an extension of the unpaid labor she already provided in their household. All partners in this category willingly moved into a caregiving role, and the training and classes at Creekview provided an orientation into caregiving. As Shirley said:

> I went to the class yesterday, what I have to do for Jim, what he's gonna go through and stuff. But it was an eye-opener. . . .my work is cut out for me. But I know most of it Jim has to do. He's gonna be able to handle it, but I know I have to be there for him. And it doesn't bother me. I tell Jim to just focus on getting well. Let me handle it, you know, take of everything.

Perceiving the caregiving relationship as a job was not only done by care partners but also by injured partners as well. Jim, Shirley's husband, described how Creekview informed his view:

> When I was in the hospital, Shirley was encouraged to learn everything she could and they do that for everybody. . .they encourage. . .I've seen it, you know. Shirley loved it. . .it just has given her something to do, or given her a job, you know. Before this, she didn't have a job. . .I think it's good for her.

Most of the injured partners in this category did not question the encouragement their partners received to become care partners. They did not question the structures of their lives before the injury which would cause some care partners to feel as though they did not have a purpose in the relationship. Like the women in this category, these men had internalized the cultural ideal that women are care partners and would naturally assume this role. These ideas about natural gender roles further reinforced gender inequality in the home. Some injured partners in this category recognized the power the rehabilitation institution had in constructing the caregiving relationship yet were still unaware of the unequal balance of power in their own homes. As John, who has been married to Geraldine for 37 years, said:

> They kinda, to me, a little bit, kinda took advantage of that she was doin' for us…like the lady in the room with us, her husband was almost completely paralyzed, but she wouldn't step in and do their job for 'em, but Geraldine would…but it wasn't because they wanted her to do it, she wanted to do it, you know…but she's just that way…Geraldine's like, I mean she's not gonna set back and just watch somebody do somethin'…so she helped take a lot off [the nurses]…but I loved for her to do it, too (chuckle).

Maintaining Care and Autonomy
Emotion Work Among Naturalized Care Partners. As people moved along the caregiving career, every person in this study engaged in some level of emotion work. Naturalized care partners tended to engage in emotion work more often than couples in the other two groups. In the first few months following injury, emotion work frequently began as a form of reassurance. This included reassurance about having a strong relationship, sticking through the injury, and general "love." Anita shared:

> I think he might of felt because he was [injured] that I probably leave him or somethin'…and I said 'you know we love you, we gone be right here for you, anything you need, we gone be right here for you, we ain't goin' nowhere,' so I just try to let him know, cuz I don't want him to fall into a depression

In general, most care partners were concerned about injured partners' mental health and aimed to keep their spirits up. Care partners encouraged injured partners and rarely the other way. For example, John spoke about how his wife's encouragement helped him every day. He said:

> Uh…my wife…she encourages me (chuckle)…she says, 'you can do it, you can do it…it just takes you a little longer, but you can do it.' When I get through, she says, 'look at that…that's professional lookin'…you know, it makes you feel good…and she really encourages me.

Balancing Care and Autonomy Among Naturalized Couples. Balancing giving and receiving care with autonomy was especially difficult for couples in the naturalized category. Because injured partners in this category were more likely to have quadriplegia, care partners expressed greater concern about safety and possible health problems. Geraldine, whose husband John was walking and managing his daily life at the time of our third interview, explained:

> I had to watch him and uh, help him with you know, watchin' him when he gets steppin' in out the bathtub and goin' up down the steps, uh, he's not drivin' a car yet, stuff like that, no, no…he wants to, but, it's not safe that wouldn't be safe. He's just, he's just that naturalized.…and uh, I have to really watch him 24 hours a day because he try anything. (laugh)

Simultaneously, John expressed frustration with the constant oversight. He said: "I get kinda aggravated cuz I can't do the things I wanta do and sometimes that I know I can do, but she thinks I can't do, you know, and I'll try to do 'em and she'll get kinda aggravated, cuz she just, she don't want me to hurt myself."

Exiting Care
Self-Care and Care Partner Overload. Over time, naturalized care partners recognized the need to care for their health to prevent illness and burnout. Concerns about illness increased over time and were more common among the older women in this category than among the younger women. However, all women mentioned it at some point. In the following excerpt, Shirley described how she wanted her husband to be as independent and healthy as possible because of concerns about her health:

> I know it's so important for Jim to be independent, be able to really take care of himself. But sometimes I think about when I get sick...I think about that. And I know anything could happen with Jim because I told him, I said, "We are gonna be on top of things." I said, "We're gonna go by the book."

Care partners in this category all got to a point where they were "just tired" and had to say no to engaging in physical and emotional work. During our third interview, care partners in this category provided narrative after narrative about "needing to rest," "being tired," "losing sleep," and "wanting to relax." Because none had exited caregiving during this study, the construction of caregiving boundaries was a key to mental health survival for the care partners in this category. One injured partner, Jim, started playing a wheelchair sport during the study period and, although Shirley had to increase some of her responsibilities to get him back and forth to practice, she found the time he was in practice to be vital for her mental and emotional well-being. She said:

> It gives me some time to be by myself, too, you know, I need that break...cuz when he comes here on Saturday, he [has practice] and has to be here 10:00 and he's done at 1, so that gives me time...I mean, during that time I can wash clothes and stuff.

Constrained Care Partners

Partners who offered constrained narratives ($n = 10$) felt torn between the amount of care they could provide and the amount of care they wanted to provide. Compared to those in the naturalized category, constrained couples had more equitable relationships before injury and both partners were likely to be employed outside of the home. Care was frequently given because of an expectation of reciprocity and equality, rather than as work. Additionally, couples in this category were slightly more likely to have children in the home. Caregivers in this category often neglected their own emotional and physical health to an extent to accomplish caregiving tasks and other life commitments. However, constrained couples were more likely to draw clear boundaries of acceptable amounts of care and self-care early in the caregiving career. Constrained caregivers expressed concerns about their ability to provide appropriate care.

Entering Care

Constrained care partners described their entry into care as being on their terms and did so with a level of comfort. As Sarah noted:

> I guess they [nurses] made me feel comfortable as far as knowledge and instruction...He is not your typical situation for there wasn't near as much for me to do, but they made me feel like I needed to make him as independent as possible, so they told me to stand back, but they helped me know what to do when I needed to help.

Both spouses perceived the staff to be understanding and willing to work within the structural limitations (e.g., work, children at home, distance) that kept care partners away from Creekview. Many constrained care partners wanted to be more involved in everyday care but could not. Marie explained:

> I can't be there and that is hard – well, I wish I could be up there, you know, all the time, with Chuck, because like in the beginning when he needed to be bathed and things like that, you know, I felt kinda bad because I wasn't there to help out except for on the weekends, but um, I, the one thing that I wish that I could be there more than I'm able to...that would be one of the main things that I would change for myself.

Because they had fewer opportunities to provide care in the hospital setting, constrained care partners worried about the quality of care they provided once they transitioned home. Constrained partners often talked about being nervous about their abilities more than they did about their worries about injured care partners' safety or being alone. For example, Marie said: "the only thing that bothers me...is just cuz I don't know for sure and you know, if I'm doin' a good enough job meeting his needs in regards to [care]." Marie was concerned that because of her work or having to care for her teenage child she was not meeting her husband's daily needs. Diane was also worried about the care she provided, but she was more afraid about hurting Jack. She said: "I'm just nervous, that I'm gonna hurt him, I probably won't, but that's my biggest fear, that I'm gonna do something wrong (laugh), you know..." For both women, their biggest fear was centered on their ability to provide good care.

Constrained couples engaged in more boundary work surrounding issues of care earlier than couples in the naturalized category. Constrained care partners spoke up often if they felt the injured partner was crossing a boundary related to caregiving. As Brandy said:

> I have to set boundaries for his, our new relationship as far as the way [Steve] talks to me, like I was tryin' to do his catheterization the other day and he spouted out, I mean just, you did it wrong, start over, screamed, you know, and I'm like, ok, God, and he's "jeez" everywhere, blah, blah, blah, anyway and the nurse is standin' there, I'm like, you know, tryin' to get checked off, and I'm like (laugh)...I'm gonna put it in your nose, but that kinda part, the one thing that we have to, they said bickering's good, just that you have to set boundaries, you know, as far as he's not gonna treat you any differently than you did before...it's just that we both have a new, a different way of communicating that way, I guess...

Constrained care partners frequently discussed the active negotiation of boundaries during the transition to care, especially early in the care process. When Steve felt his care was not being done correctly, he spoke up about his needs. When Brandy felt she was being attacked for providing care, she spoke up. These negotiations were more common among couples in this category than in the other categories.

Injured partners in this category also worked at creating boundaries around caregiving. Injured partners in the constrained category protected their care partner's time and advocated for their health earlier in the process. As Chuck explained:

> [Marie's] comin' up on weekends. I think it's important for her to still stay in her daily routine, you know, not to get too caught up in mine although she wants to know everything about what's goin' on with me…We had a conference today with the Dr. and my wife, and myself…well, she didn't come up, but I called her on the phone, put it on speaker and I said, "here you go." There wasn't, I mean, 15 or 20 minutes, for her to travel 2 hours, on a Thursday and take that day off work, to me, I just didn't see that as necessary…it's important that she still do her like, tonight, I would expect that she goes to yoga. I'll call her, and if she doesn't, I'll be highly upset, because I think she needs it…I don't want her going crazy.

Before the injury, both partners were balancing work and home life and as such, they held multiple roles in the community and their relationship. Following injury, most people in the constrained category continued to wear multiple hats and care partners were not relegated to assuming a singular identity as care partners. Because of the complicated intersections of class, gender, age, employment, and recovery, it is difficult to say if the care partners in the constrained category benefited or suffered from the multiple roles they maintained.

Maintaining Care
Emotion Work and the Constrained Care Partner. Although everyone in this study engaged in some form of emotion work, the intensity of emotion work varied based on several factors. Timing in lives and other family obligations contributed to this variability. For example, Sarah hid her concerns about fertility and health not only because she wanted Phil to focus on his health but also because of their newlywed status. She said:

> When we had the medical conference, the big thing that came up that I really just had to swallow and bite down on was the potential fertility problems that come along with [injury]…it's not so much the sex, it's the idea of having kids and knowin' we want family at some point…was kinda scary, cuz this is a big deal, especially newly married, the, that's not what we're thinkin' about today, but in a year or two, we're definitely gonna be thinkin' about it…now, since the accident, if I had a concern that related directly to his situation, I might not approach it with him right now…I might share it with him, but for now, if I needed to talk it through with somebody, it probably wouldn't be him, cuz I don't want to bring him down with my questions, my concerns about his health, because that's the last thing he needs right now.

Constrained care partners described their relationships as equitable before SCI. However, because of the injury, partners noted a change in balance. Brandy, for example, exclaimed her husband's shifting attitude was starting to wear on her by our second interview. She said: "You know, his attitude and state of mind kind of thing, it goes up and down and I'm constantly feeling like I have to be the cheerleader, so, you know, I'm just tired…I'm just tired."

Household Labor, Autonomy, and the Constrained Care Partner. Injured partners in this category had more freedom than injured partners in the naturalized category. Constrained care partners expressed a desire for their spouses to do more independently because they could not be always present. Care partners had similar concerns their spouse might do something risky or hurt themselves but recognized they could not always be in control of their partner's actions. Diane explained:

> Right now, I'm more on just kinda wantin' to do it for him, Creekview would probably slap me on the back of the hand for that, cuz, yeah, they do try to teach you to let go, but it is hard, it really is hard. And I hate to think, like ok, I told him he can do it and something happens...how would I feel, you know? If he falls, so what if this happens, you know...but I know, I bet if I weren't here, he'd probably do more things, you know.

Care partners in this category also expected their spouses to contribute around the house. They did not take over care and they initially did not push for self-sufficiency. Rather, they let the injured partner take up tasks as needed. Again, Diane offered a good example:

> I mean he does what he can, but I do notice that sometimes I'm afraid to ask him, are you capable of doin' this. I don't know if it's something he's capable of doing and but I don't want to push it cuz I don't want think, well why don't you do this if he's not capable of it (whisper)... I don't know where we are as far as should I push it or should I like kinda hold back a little bit about it. Like, making his own breakfast or making his own coffee, should I just say, you know what, why don't you do it, you know (laugh)...

While Diane was willing to let the caregiving relationship just work itself out, Cindy was more insistent on asking for help with household tasks. Cindy had to go from part-time work to full-time work to help make ends meet while her husband was not working, and she felt he needed to do more around the house. She said:

> He feels like, that if he does the little things, such as...maybe puttin' the kids to bed tonight or runnin' me a bath or that kind of stuff, he feels like if he does that kind of stuff, that he's done something grand...but in my eyes, and I've told him this, if he's not pullin' his end of the marriage as a whole, then the little things don't really matter... he doesn't do anything in the household to keep things clean or organized or laundry...so I feel like I'm pullin' way more than my share of the load...the little things really don't matter to me.

Achieving autonomy and independence was more complex than just sharing household labor. Injured partners in this category were frequently left alone or asked to do things quicker than injured partners in naturalized couples. Brandy's husband, Steve, had to return to Creekview for intense outpatient care without her. She wanted to be with him, but because she was the sole earner in the family, she had to push him to be more independent than he might have otherwise been. She said: "He's done really great; I mean he can turn himself. He's very independent. He's stayed in the apartment by himself in Atlanta...he just told me last night, he said, 'I'm scared, I'm worried...about living by myself up there' and I said, 'Well, I have to work, you know'."

Injured partners in this category took a more direct approach to regaining autonomy than injured partners in the naturalized category. For example, Chuck took his body care back from his wife. He recognized the work she was doing outside of the home in addition to the care she was providing in the home. Chuck explained:

> She was [cleaning up after bowel and bladder care] and uh, I finally, she maybe did about 3 or 4 days of that, and I said, you know what, this is crazy…I gotta find a way…so, I would get myself as far as I could into the doorway of the toilet, where the toilet was at and I could actually reach and, you know, dump my bladder bag and dump the pail, my bowel, the bowel pail from the thing, and I said, listen, you don't have to do this for me anymore, and you shouldn't have had to in the first place… this is something I have to do and I should be doin,' so I just took that right off the table.

Adjusting to Care
Self-Care and Care Partner Concern Among Constrained Care Partners. Both partners in this category were aware of the need to engage in self-care. Injured partners were quicker to respond to concerns about their care partners' mental and physical health than injured partners in the naturalized category. For example, in our first interview, Gary said his biggest concern about going home was "worrying about [his wife] getting just totally worn out, exhausted." Injured partners in this category were much more worried about care partner burnout and overload than the other two groups of injured partners.

Because constrained care partners were pulled in so many directions, self-care for these care partners required actively setting boundaries around what they could realistically accomplish and acknowledging their limitations. As Marie said:

> I kinda have to take a step back and tell myself that I'm not gonna be able to get everything done, and so I do what I can do and just leave the rest for when I can get to it.

Care partners in this category also were more vocal and assertive about doing things to take care of themselves. During my first interview with Diane, she expressed a desire to go to a concert and her husband wanted her to stay with him at the hospital. She explained:

> I first told him, I still wanted to go to the Kenny Chesney concert 'cuz I love him, he puts on a great concert. I still wanted to go…at first, he didn't want me to go… "I want you to stay with me" and I said, "You know, that's kind of selfish. I am spending all my time with you." We've got 13- and 15- and 16-year-old kids that are here by themselves because their parents have to go back to work…you're a 40-year-old man and you want me to stay with you, you know?

Resistant Care Partners
Only two couples were classified as primarily resistant and were outliers in this study. These two couples were quite different from each other demographically, yet they had similar tensions in their relationships before the injury. Before injury, both couples had been experiencing other marital strains. One couple was dealing with the resolution of an extramarital affair while the other couple was handling the transition to parenthood and marriage. Resistant caregivers were not very

willing to engage in caregiving until pushed by care workers at Creekview. They were marginalized in the caregiving relationship by staff at Creekview and were more likely to see care as a burden before starting care.

Entering Care

Before Brenda's injury, Eddie worked two jobs and Brenda worked full time and was responsible for all the housework and parenting. She was injured in a car accident after she left the house after learning about Eddie's extramarital affair. While in the hospital, Eddie was resistant to helping with her care and he shared he had "gone on a bender" after the injury. He was sober for three days at the time of our interview and it was the longest he had stayed sober and with his wife since the accident a month earlier. Eddie described his transition into providing care for his wife:

> It's just like, there was a nurse upstairs, she said, "You're gonna have to catheterize your wife before you can leave." I said, "I ain't doing that." She said, "Well, you got to." I said, "Lady, the only thing I got to do is die. That's the only thing I got to do in life." I apologized; I didn't mean to be disrespectful to her, but it's just hard to think of doing that, and the other thing, it's just a lot....I've just got real issues with bladder care. And bowel care. Will I end up doing it? Yeah. I won't like it, let's put it that way. I'll hire someone at home if I have to.

Nan, the other resistant care partner, was not as combative or resistant to care. Yet, the idea of care was overwhelming. Nan and Sidney were high-school sweethearts who married when she got pregnant following high-school graduation. Sidney came from a religious family. His parents pushed the couple into getting married and having the baby. They were struggling financially and emotionally with an infant before the injury. Sidney was apprenticing to learn skills for future work. Nan did not work and Sidney was opposed to her working outside the home. In the months following Sidney's injuries, Nan struggled with depression and substance abuse and was generally overwhelmed at the thought of caring for her child and her husband simultaneously. She explained her transition into caregiving in the following way:

> I know that I feel like out of my mind, sometimes. I just feel really overwhelmed and like I'm just crazy, but I don't really know what Creekview could do to help that. I guess that's just something I kinda need to work on...I don't really know what they could do.

For Nan, care was too much to think about. Compared to the first two types, there were unique features about resistant couples. Both partners in these relationships had dealt or were dealing with substance abuse and mental health problems, which were obstacles during this time of transition. Additionally, they were not receiving support within Creekview for their needs related to existing relationship problems. When I asked a counselor about couples with existing problems, he explained their focus is solely on the injured partner's current mental state. He said: "couples will eventually work out whatever it is they need to work out. This injury provides kind of a band-aid for their problems. I don't want to be responsible for pulling off the band-aid." This approach to relationships in the rehabilitation setting could be setting couples up for failure when they return home to find out the band-aid fell off on the way.

Managing Care
Emotion Work and Stress. The couples in the resistant category engaged in emotion work less, or differently than other couples. Injured partners tended to do more reassurance and work to keep their care partner happy and comfortable with the injury. Brenda offered the following story about how her husband tried to comfort her:

> [Before] he would like me to do my nails and do my hair and do my makeup two or three times a day. I'm just not like that. I'm just kind of like, I don't care what people think…Since I've been here, he has made sure that I do my nails and put on my makeup. He's actually wanted me to take my picture and send it to him on his phone to make sure I'm putting my makeup on every day. He asked me last night, "Where's my picture?" I'm like, "I already washed it off now." I'm sure today he'll ask me where his picture is because he knows that my spirits are better and my mindset's better when I do something for myself.

Nan and Sidney seemed more protective of one another's emotions and needs than Eddie and Brenda, and Nan had a tough time watching her husband get dressed in the morning. Nan said:

> The hardest thing for me to see is him try and dress himself because it's just …something you learn when you're two.…I get really upset even talking about it because it's really hard for him to do, and it's so hard seeing him struggle just to put pants on. And he's having to like pull himself 20 times just to get something over his ankle, and it's just really difficult to watch. And I try not to let him see that I feel sorry for him or anything because that can kind of hurt his ego for me to feel bad.

The timing of Sidney's injury also was difficult. During our second interview, their daughter was just starting to walk, which caused a lot of stress for Nan. As she said:

> For me, it's just taking care of him and a baby at the same time. Trying to learn how to do things for him and – it's just her age…she's getting into toddler stages right at the same time I'm trying to learn about what I need to be doing with him. Like she just started walking and she's into everything and is getting very opinionated and pitching fits so much more. It's just been really hard on those days when he's just acting like kind of a jerk and then she's just crying nonstop and just clinginess and I just want to pull my hair out. That's been the biggest thing for me. I'm trying not to get too stressed out about things, which I do…I just get really tired of everything.

Exiting Care
For these couples, exiting the caregiving relationship looked different than other couples. Eddie and Brenda did not complete the third interview, but upon returning home Eddie hired home health and he did not continue any bladder or bowel care. Nan left Sidney and her child 2 months after returning home. In our last interviews, Sidney expressed he had a lot of guilt about her leaving and wondered if he "had done enough." Nan did not express guilt over her decision.

She had moved in with a friend and "was living the life" she wanted and was able to "just be in [her] 20s."

DISCUSSION

Much of what we know about trauma, disability, and the marital dyad focuses on emotional, financial, and marital strain (Chan, 2000; Gosling & Oddy, 1999; Kowal et al., 2003; Kreuter, 2000), changes in relationships as a result of caregiving (Degeneffe, 2001), and changes in sexuality and intimacy following injury (Mills & Turnbull, 2004). Additionally, much research about trauma and illness in the family focuses on stress (Boss, 1987) and poor health outcomes (Aneshensel et al., 1995) for family care partners. I found the dominant cultural narrative of women being natural care partners was accepted and reinforced by the practitioners at Creekview as well as the couples in this study. This study advances the concept of a caregiving career to examine how younger couples move through the caregiving career when the expected outcome is not long-term care placement or death. Additionally, this study highlights the ways principles of the life course – timing in lives, location in time and place, and linked lives in particular – impact the caregiving career.

Transitioning in and out of the caregiving relationship along the caregiving career impacts the relationship trajectory. Every couple in this study moved along the caregiving career (Aneshensel et al., 1995), but differences existed in the ways couples entered into care, how they negotiated the caregiving relationship including autonomy and self-care, and how they transitioned out of or adapted to the caregiving relationship. There is a pervasive ideology that caregiving is natural for women (Calasanti & Slevin, 2006), and this ideology impacted the caregiving career of couples in this study. Additionally, larger social structures of class, gender, and the division of paid and unpaid labor work together to push some women into caregiving faster or prevent other women from engaging in caregiving (Calasanti & Slevin, 2001). When ideologies about housework and care are at odds with one another, tensions arise, which can impact the stability of the marriage (Hochschild, 1989). For care partners in this study who also worked outside the home, caregiving for their spouse was often a third or fourth shift on top of everything they were already doing. In Hochschild's (1989) analysis of the division of labor, she found that couples who espoused the ideology of equality in the home and family care engaged in several strategies to meet these ideological expectations. Within this study, both partners engaged in emotion management as a strategy for negotiating the caregiving relationship, with some having more success than others.

The results from this study expand our understanding of transitions and caregiving to include younger marital couples and show how people experience transitions and trajectories differently based on their life course experiences and social locations. By examining what people pay attention to during the transition to injury, we can examine how they construct meaning associated with the life course (Holstein & Gubrium, 2000). My research indicates that while the individual experiences matter, the rehabilitation setting plays a key role in shaping experiences following injury. This adds a new dimension to our understanding of the caregiving career not only for couples who are experiencing SCI but for all people with injury and illness who transition in and out of institutions during their life course. In particular, this study builds on existing research about transitions into and out of caregiving over the life course (Pavalko & Woodbury, 2000; Seltzer & Li, 2000).

As with much feminist scholarship, Hooyman and Gonyea (1995) remind us the "personal is political" and the interactions women have with health systems and public policies shape how they experience this relationship. When considering caregiving relationships, it is important for counselors and other healthcare professionals to be aware of the various kinds of caregiving relationships and how these relationships can alter individual and relationship trajectories when people transition home.

ACKNOWLEDGMENTS

Most importantly, I want to thank the individuals who took the time to talk with me during an overwhelming life transition. I also thank Elisabeth O. Burgess, Candace L. Kemp, and Ralph LaRossa for their outstanding mentorship on this project.

REFERENCES

Aneshensel, C. S., Pearlin, L. I., Mullan, J. T., Zarit, S. H., & Whitlatch, C. J. (1995). *Profiles in caregiving: The unexpected career*. Academic Press.

Bengtson, V. L., & Allen, K. R. (1993). The life course perspective applied to families over time. In P. G. Boss, W. J. Doherty, R. LaRossa, W. R. Schumm, & S. K. Steinmetz (Eds.), *Sourcebook of family theories and methods: A contextual approach* (pp. 469–504). Plenum Press.

Biegel, D. E., Sales, E., & Schulz, R. (1991). *Family caregiving in chronic illness*. Sage.

Boss, P. (1987). Family stress. In M. B. Sussman & S. K. Steinmetz (Eds.), *Handbook of marriage and the family*. (pp. 695–723). Plenum Press.

Braun, V., & Clarke, V. (2006). Using thematic analysis in psychology. *Qualitative Research in Psychology*, *3*(2), 77–101.

Calasanti, T. M., & Slevin, K. F. (2001). *Gender, social inequalities, and aging*. AltaMira Press.

Calasanti, T. M., & Slevin, K. F. (2006). Gender and old age: Lessons from spousal care work. In T. M. Calasanti & K. F. Slevin (Eds.), *Age matters: Realigning feminist thinking* (pp. 1–18). Routledge.

Chan, R. C. K. (2000). How does spinal cord injury affect marital relationship? A story from both sides of the couple. *Disability and Rehabilitation*, *22*(17), 764–775.

Choi, H., & Marks, N. F. (2006). Transition to caregiving, marital disagreement, and psychological well-being: A prospective U.S. national study. *Journal of Family Issues*, *27*, 1701–1722.

Clausen, J. A. (1986). *The life course: A sociological perspective*. Prentice-Hall.

Creswell, J. W. (1998). *Qualitative inquiry and research design: Choosing among five traditions*. Sage Publications, Inc.

Degeneffe, C. E. (2001). Family caregiving and traumatic brain injury. *Health and Social Work*, *26*(4), 257–268.

Eriksson, M., & Svedlund, M. (2006). 'The intruder': Spouses narratives about life with a chronically ill partner. *Journal of Clinical Nursing*, *15*(3), 324–333.

Giele, J. Z., & Elder, G. H. (1998). Life course research: Development of a field. In J. Z. Giele & G. H. Elder (Eds.), *Methods of life course research: Qualitative and quantitative approaches* (pp. 5–24). Sage.

Gosling, J., & Oddy, M. (1999). Rearranged marriages: Marital relationships after head injury. *Brain Injury, 13*(10), 785–796.

Harrison, T., Stuifbergen, A., Adachi, E., & Becker, H. (2004). Marriage, impairment, and acceptance in persons with multiple sclerosis. *Western Journal of Nursing Research, 26*(3), 266–285.

Hochschild, A. (1989). *The second shift: Working parents and the revolution at home*. Avon Press.

Holicky, R., & Charlifue, S. (1999). Ageing with spinal cord injury: The impact of social support. *Disability and Rehabilitation, 21*(5/6), 250–257.

Holstein, J. A., & Gubrium, J. F. (2000). *Constructing the life course* (2nd ed.). AltaMira Press.

Hooyman, N. R., & Gonyea, J. (1995). *Feminist perspectives on family care: Policies for gender justice*. Sage.

Ingersoll-Dayton, B., & Raschick, M. (2004). The relationship between care-recipient behaviors and spousal caregiving stress. *The Gerontologist, 44*(3), 318–327.

Jeyathevan, G., Cameron, J. I., Craven, B. C., Munce, S. E. P., & Jaglal, S. B. (2019). Re-building relationships after a spinal cord injury: Experiences of family caregivers and care recipients. *BMC Neurology, 19*(1), 117. https://doi.org/10.1186/s12883-019-1347-x

Kaye, L. W., & Applegate, J. S. (1990). *Men as caregivers to the elderly: Understanding and aiding unrecognized family support*. Lexington Books.

Kowal, J., Johnson, S. M., & Lee, A. (2003). Chronic illness in couples: A case for emotionally focused therapy. *Journal of Marital and Family Therapy, 29*(3), 299–310.

Kreuter, M. (2000). Spinal cord injury and partner relationships. *Spinal Cord, 38*, 2–6.

Mills, B., & Turnbull, G. (2004). Broken hearts and mending bodies: The impact of trauma on intimacy. *Sexual and Relationship Therapy, 19*(3), 265–288.

Noël-Miller, C. (2010). Longitudinal changes in disabled husbands' and wives' receipt of care. *The Gerontologist, 50*(5), 681–693.

Pavalko, E. K., & Woodbury, S. (2000). Social roles as process: Caregiving careers and women's health. *Journal of Health and Social Behavior, 41*(1), 91–105. http://www.jstor.org/stable/2676362

Putzke, J. D., Elliot, T. R., & Richards, J. S. (2001). Marital status and adjustment 1 year post-spinal-cord-injury. *Journal of Clinical Psychology in Medical Settings, 8*(2), 101–107.

Rodgers, J., & Calder, P. (1990). Marital adjustment: A valuable resource for the emotional health of individuals with multiple sclerosis. *Rehabilitation Counseling Bulletin, 34*, 25–32.

Seltzer, M. M., & Li, L. W. (2000). The dynamics of caregiving: Transitions during a three-year prospective study. *The Gerontologist, 40*(2), 165–177.

Shackelford, M., Farley, T., & Vines, C. L. (1998). A comparison of women and men with spinal cord injury. *Spinal Cord, 36*, 337–339.

Spitze, G., & Ward, R. (2000). Gender, marriage, and expectations for personal care. *Research on Aging, 22*(5), 451–469. https://doi.org/10.1177/0164027500225001

DISABILITY AND PRECARIOUS WORK OVER THE LIFE COURSE: AN APPLICATION OF KEY CONCEPTS

Robyn Lewis Brown

AUTHOR BIOGRAPHY

Robyn Lewis Brown, PhD, is a Quantitative Sociologist who specializes in the study of stress and health among women and people with disabilities. She is an Associate Professor of Sociology at the University of Kentucky (the United States), where she also serves as Director of the Health, Society, and Populations Program.

ABSTRACT

This study examined changes in work precarity (i.e., job insecurity and income insecurity) and involuntary job loss following the start of the Great Recession in 2007 among people with and without disabilities. Using five waves of nationally representative data from the Americans' Changing Lives (ACL) panel study, the findings demonstrated that people with disabilities who had early experiences of income insecurity were more likely to experience later income insecurity than people without disabilities. Those who had a functional disability and experienced job insecurity and income insecurity at W1, in 1986, were also significantly more likely to experience involuntary job loss following the start of the Great Recession. These findings highlight the disproportionate impact of early work precarity for people with disabilities and are discussed as an application of the life-course concept of cumulative disadvantage.

Keywords: Disability; precarious work; involuntary job loss; Great Recession; life course; cumulative disadvantage

Does work precarity – defined as both the experience of job insecurity and income insecurity (Kalleberg, 2009; Mai et al., 2019; Vosko, 2006) – predict greater

Disabilities and the Life Course
Research in Social Science and Disability, Volume 14, 167–181
Copyright © 2023 Robyn Lewis Brown
Published under exclusive licence by Emerald Publishing Limited
ISSN: 1479-3547/doi:10.1108/S1479-354720230000014010

disadvantage for people with disabilities compared to people without disabilities over time? And, if so, is this association impacted by age and/or historic context? The focus of these questions on variation by age and historic time and place are consistent with the life course paradigm, which is defined as a set of conceptual and methodological approaches to understanding the synergistic influences of individual biography, history, and social change for health outcomes (Ben-Shlomo & Kuh, 2002; Elder, 1995; O'Rand, 1996). The consideration of disability as a predictor of inequality rather than an outcome of inequality, however, is not.

Indeed, a challenge this study addresses related to incorporating life course concepts into disability research concerns the tendency of life course scholars to treat disabling health conditions as outcomes to be avoided by the able-bodied in later life. This approach is fundamentally different from the approach taken by most disability researchers, who typically consider disability as a starting point for inquiry rather than an outcome. The outcomes approach is also limited because it cuts out all of the life course of people born with disabilities and a significant portion of the life course for many others.

At the same time, life course concepts and methods have been used sporadically for understanding differences in life experiences over time for people with disabilities compared to people without disabilities. Conceptualizing disability within this framework – other than as an outcome – is worth further consideration because quantitative disability researchers do not have well-established methodological and theoretical frameworks to draw on for assessing continuity and change over time. In employment research (and other areas), a consequence is that most research is cross-sectional. This research has provided important information on the comparatively lower earnings, greater unemployment, and experience of unstable employment among people with disabilities (Brown & Moloney, 2019; Iezzoni, 2011). But data capturing a single snapshot in time can only speculate about employment trajectories and causal patterns associated with work.

In the adaptive spirit that characterizes much quantitative disability research, it is noteworthy that life course concepts are already well utilized in research addressing employment trajectories and consequences of other social statuses, such as gender (Bracke et al., 2020), race or ethnicity (Shuey & Willson, 2008), and sexuality (Carpenter, 2010). They have also been widely used in mental health research in examining the life course trajectories of people with mental illness compared to those without mental illness (Dohrenwend et al., 1992; Hudson, 2005; Johnson et al., 1999; Turner & Turner, 2004), though notably life-course scholars also tend to consider psychological symptoms as outcomes rather than predictors (Mirowsky & Ross, 1989). Their application in this area has yielded significant developments related to the social selection hypothesis or "drift" hypothesis, which posits that individuals with mental illness face difficulty in gaining or maintaining steady employment, and thus tend to "drift" into positions of disadvantage or fail to rise out of such positions over time (Dohrenwend et al., 1992; Hudson, 2005; Johnson et al., 1999).

Drawing on this work, this investigation incorporates three often-utilized life course concepts (i.e., cumulative disadvantage, age effects, and period effects) into a study of employment consequences associated with disability. This analysis used five waves of data from the nationally representative Americans' Changing Lives (ACL) panel survey to assess three aspects of work precarity for people with disabilities compared to people without disabilities across a 26-year period: perceived job insecurity, perceived income insecurity, and involuntary job loss during or after the Great Recession. Longitudinal regression analysis and continuous-time, discrete-state event history modeling were used to specify changes in these aspects of work precarity across the study period and after the beginning of the Great Recession.

BACKGROUND

The Life Course, the Great Recession, and Precarious Work

The life course paradigm is not a single cohesive perspective, but a combination of perspectives guided by four principles and methodological considerations, which can be briefly summarized as thus (Elder, 1995; Ferraro & Shippee, 2009; George, 1996; O'Rand, 1996): The first principle is that individual experience is shaped by age, period, and cohort effects (Elder, 1995; George, 1996). Second, life course research recognizes the important interplay between individual experience and history (Ben-Shlomo & Kuh, 2002; O'Rand, 1996). Third, although individual experience is shaped by historical influences, individuals also have agency in shaping their lives (George, 1996). Fourth, the culmination of one's life experiences is shaped by their personal experiences and by those individuals, institutions, and structures to whom their life is linked (Moody et al., 2019; O'Rand, 1996). Finally, life course research requires statistical techniques that allow for such factors as the mapping of individual change over time; increased heterogeneity among respondents over time; the potential of multiple health trajectories over time; and the emergence of different risk and protective factors over time (Berkman et al., 2014; Ferraro & Farmer, 1996; Ferraro & Schafer, 2017; Ferraro & Shippee, 2009).

Three aspects of the life course paradigm have been influential in studying variation by social status or in making group comparisons (i.e., differences by gender, etc.). Perhaps most influential is the consideration of *cumulative disadvantage*. As O'Rand (1996) noted, Merton first articulated this concept based on observations that early success made scientists more likely to experience subsequent success throughout life, whereas early-career scientists whose work was devalued or unnoticed tended to experience more mediocre career trajectories. These observations have been generalized for understanding increased heterogeneity among people who are socially disadvantaged compared to those who are not over time (Berkman et al., 2014; Ferraro & Schafer, 2017). A key point is that disadvantages in later life are shaped by much earlier experiences of disadvantage and the constraints they place on the possible paths an individual's life can take (Berkman et al., 2014; Ferraro & Shippee, 2009; O'Rand, 1996).

This extended view of individual biography is further informed by two other influential aspects of life course theory. The first is the distinction drawn between *age effects*, which refer to both variation associated with chronological changes over time among individuals and age variation across the population at a single time point, from cohort effects, which are generational differences at a comparable point in the life course (Berkman et al., 2014; Ferraro & Farmer, 1996; George, 1996). The second is its consideration of *period effects*, or the ways in which the time and place in history we occupy influences our life experiences (O'Rand, 1996). For example, a significant portion of early life course research was devoted to understanding the consequences of the Great Depression for generations of American families (Elder, 1995; O'Rand, 1996).

Period effects are crucial to an understanding of cumulative disadvantage as well because they remind us that cumulative disadvantage processes arise out of the historic time and place we occupy. Because of methodological advances, this has been most clearly demonstrated in considering the impact of the Great Recession, which occurred between December 2007 and June 2009 and had lingering effects in the subsequent decade (Cochrane, 2011; Kalousová & Burgard, 2022; Richman et al., 2012). Considered the most serious economic crisis in the United States since the Great Depression, the recession was an economic shock that unmoored many people who were already socially disadvantaged (Brown et al., 2019; Kalousová & Burgard, 2022; Richman et al., 2012). My colleagues and I have described this shock as a form of differential stress proliferation through which the greater stress burden already experienced by socially disadvantaged groups made it more difficult for them to weather the recession years and avoid financial hardship (Brown et al., 2017, 2019). But it could also be said that the recession exacerbated cumulative disadvantage processes. This is because socially disadvantaged groups were less protected from financial hardship, and came out of the recession comparably more economically disadvantaged (Brown et al., 2019; Burgard & Seelye, 2017; Rugh et al., 2015). As Rugh et al. (2015) have noted, the recession further demonstrated that cumulative disadvantage processes are supported by institutional policies and practices that promote members of some groups at the expense of members of other groups.

In the employment sphere, this consideration is supported by research on work precarity during and after the Great Recession. This research has considered both the degree to which one's job is unstable or erratic and offers few prospects for advancement (i.e., job insecurity) and income uncertainty, which refers to being underpaid, experiencing salary/pay cuts, or lacking stability in meeting financial commitments despite working regularly (Kalleberg, 2009; Mai et al., 2019; Vosko, 2006). This work consistently indicates that employment and income changes during the recession years were not experienced equally among the paid labor force. The greatest employment and income effects of the recession have been observed among younger people, African Americans, and individuals who have completed less education (Brown et al., 2019; Kalousova & Burgard, 2014, 2022; Surn & Khatiwada, 2010).

Disability and Work Precarity

There is further evidence that people with disabilities were more likely to experience unemployment and earned less during the recession compared to people without disabilities (Braddock et al., 2017; Fogg et al., 2010; Fraser et al., 2011). Provided the evidence, Fogg et al. (2010) concluded: "It is clear that the Great Recession imposed a far greater level of hardship on people with disabilities in America when measured by various aspects of unemployment," further noting that "personal characteristics which tend to 'soften the blow' in hard economic times, such as age, experience, and education, were less effective" (pp. 200–201).

However, this is not a foregone conclusion. The few studies that have considered differences by disability status in employment markers during the recession have been cross-sectional or used pooled data from during the recession (i.e., December 2007 to September 2009) and have been limited to comparing people across age groups or different levels of experience. The limits of this analytic approach are elaborated upon in life course research in several key ways: First, the consideration of how period effects impact cumulative disadvantage processes centers the need to consider whether the differential risk observed during the recession among people with disabilities varies from the disadvantages experienced by people with disabilities as a group before the recession. This would provide a clearer answer to the question of whether the impact of the recession was *disproportionate* for people with disabilities. This analytic approach could also consider the impact of earlier adversity. It seems highly intuitive, for instance, that people with disabilities might have been comparatively disadvantaged by the recession because of the accumulation of disadvantages associated with earlier work precarity. Additionally, the life course consideration of age effects supports thinking beyond age variation within the population at a single time point. Further information on age variation in length of employment, or a sense of how long people have experienced employment benefits or disadvantages, could more clearly identify the kinds of resources that are effective in "softening the blow" of a recession.

To these points, this analysis addressed three hypotheses: First, and consistent with the cumulative disadvantage perspective, *H1* predicted that people with disabilities who had early experiences of work precarity would be more likely to also experience later work precarity compared to people without disabilities. Second, recognizing "age effects" or the potential benefits of age as a proxy for the length of time one has been employed, *H2* predicted that chronological age would buffer the impact of disability on later work precarity. Finally, addressing whether the recession had a disproportionate impact on people with disabilities, *H3* predicted that early work precarity and disability would increase the likelihood of experiencing involuntary job loss following the start of the Great Recession, whereas age would decrease this hazard.

METHOD

Data

Data to address these hypotheses were derived from the five available waves of the nationally representative ACL panel study (House, 2018). The baseline study, conducted in 1986, drew from a multistage stratified area probability sample of community-dwelling adults aged 25 or older, with African Americans and individuals over 60 sampled at twice the rate of their counterparts. The first wave of the study achieved a response rate of 70% (N = 3,617). This analysis was limited to the respondents who reported some form of employment at W1 (n = 1,867) and provided information on working conditions or employment transitions in a subsequent study wave (n = 1,686). Nearly three-quarters (72%) of this subsample was between the ages of 25 and 45 at baseline and, thus, the five study waves capture the majority of most respondents' working lives.

Sample weights were utilized to account for variation in selection probability at each wave and adjusted the data to match US Census estimates of the community-dwelling population in 1986. It should be noted, however, that those lost to attrition were significantly more likely to identify as having a disability and to report greater income uncertainty at W1.

Principal Measures

I examined two aspects of precarious employment – perceived job insecurity and perceived income insecurity – as outcomes and as predictors of the likelihood of experiencing involuntary job loss following the start of the Great Recession. *Perceived job insecurity* was assessed with a single item asked of employed respondents at each study wave: "How likely is it that during the next couple of years you will involuntarily lose your main job – not at all likely, not too likely, somewhat likely, or very likely?" *Perceived income insecurity* was assessed using three items (W1 α = 0.79) gauging how difficult respondents found their financial situation, meeting monthly payments on bills, and their finances working out at the end of the month. Responses ranged from not difficult (0) to extremely difficult (4). In models predicting involuntary exits from employment, *involuntary job loss since the recession* was calculated as the hazard any one respondent had each year from 2007 to 2011 of losing their job. This measure utilized self-reports of involuntary job loss and the year in which it occurred. Similarly, *involuntary job loss before the recession* was measured with self-reports of years in which involuntary job loss occurred over the study period. It was calculated as the hazard of respondents losing their job after the first wave of data collection but before the recession – from 1987 to 2006.

Because I was interested in whether or how disability predicts these employment consequences over time, I treated disability as a time-invariant variable based on W1 responses to an index of *functional disability*. This count index was scored so that the lowest value (0) indicates no disability, whereas the highest score (4) indicates significant functional disability, such as being confined to a bed or chair (House et al., 2005). Consistent with a prior study (House et al., 2005), this item was dichotomized to differentiate respondents with no functional disability (0) from respondents with functional disability (1).

Control Variables
Other time-invariant variables included in the analysis were *gender* (1 = female, 0 = male), *race/ethnicity* (1 = African Americans, 0 = Whites), and *education*, assessed by the number of years of school completed at W1, ranging from 0 to 17.

Respondent *age* was included as a time-varying control variable measured in years. Additional analyses considered the nonlinear function of age and variation by age cohorts. These analyses are not presented because the coefficients for these variables were not significant in any of the regression models, nor did their inclusion significantly improve model fit.

Analytic Strategy
A series of longitudinal OLS regression models were used to examine changes in perceived job insecurity and perceived income insecurity from W1 to W5. Although fixed effects methods are often preferred to OLS methods in longitudinal modeling, a key limitation of fixed effects regression, in this case, is that it would exclude those respondents whose perceived job and income insecurity remained constant over time. Following the recommendations of prior investigations using these data (e.g., Burgard et al., 2009), OLS regression analyses of continuous measures of perceived job insecurity and perceived income insecurity, respectively, at W5 included the W1 measures of these variables as predictors to assess change over time. Three models were considered for each outcome. The first model considered whether baseline (W1) functional disability, baseline age, and the control variables were associated with increases or decreases in perceived insecurity from W1 to W5. The linear measure of age is retained in this model because, as noted, nonlinear and categorical measures were not significant and did not significantly improve model fit. This approach also allows for a more straightforward examination of whether experiencing disability and work precarity at an early age would be linked with later work precarity (*H1*). The second model considered whether age moderated the effects of functional disability (*H2*). The third model further assessed *H1* by testing whether functional disability moderated the impact of early job or income insecurity on later insecurity.

Continuous-time, discrete-state event history modeling was then used to analyze involuntary job loss following the start of the Great Recession in 2007. This approach enabled the inclusion of censored cases (i.e., people who remained employed at the fifth wave of the study) in calculating the hazard of involuntary job loss (Jones & Box-Steffensmeier, 2004). Because these models address the hypothesis that early work precarity and disability increased the likelihood of experiencing involuntary job loss following the start of the Great Recession (*H3*), the baseline (W1) measures of work precarity and disability were included as predictors. I tested four models for the hazard of involuntary job loss: Model 1 considered the impact of early work precarity and disability (i.e., W1 perceived job insecurity, perceived income insecurity, and functional disability), net of the control variables. Models 2–4 added interaction terms of W1 functional disability with age (Model 2), W1 perceived job insecurity (Model 3), and W1 perceived income insecurity (Model 4) for the hazard of involuntary job loss after the start of the recession.

RESULTS

Descriptive statistics of the study variables for the full sample and by disability status are presented in Table 1. Notably, functional disability was significantly associated with variation in each of the three dependent variables: People with functional disability at baseline were significantly more likely than those who did not begin the study with a disability to experience perceived job insecurity – both at baseline, and 26 years later at W5 – and involuntary job loss following the start of the recession. They were also more likely to experience perceived income insecurity at both the beginning and end of the study period. Significant differences by disability status were additionally observed such that people with a functional disability at baseline completed fewer years of education and were more likely to be female, African American, and older than people without a functional disability.

Table 1. Means and Standard Deviations or Percentages of Study Variables by Disability Status.

Dependent Variables	Full Sample (N = 1,686)	Has Functional Disability (n = 801)	No Functional Disability (n = 885)
Perceived job insecurity	1.690	1.955**	1.497
	(0.862)	(0.888)	(0.852)
Perceived income insecurity	0.095	0.129**	0.046
	(0.960)	(0.935)	(0.994)
Hazard of involuntary job loss	0.479	0.535**	0.418
	(0.500)	(0.499)	(0.494)
Independent variables			
Baseline perceived job insecurity	1.779	1.854**	1.709
	(0.884)	(0.933)	(0.851)
Baseline perceived income insecurity	0.059	0.091**	0.029
	(0.972)	(1.022)	(0.922)
Gender (% female)	49%	57%***	42%
Race/ethnicity (% African American)	33%	37%**	30%
Education	12.9422	12.118***	13.921
	(2.834)	(2.925)	(2.633)
Age	43.274	48.359***	38.482
	(13.040)	(13.252)	(10.843)

Notes: All coefficients are weighted estimates. $*p < 0.05$; $**p < 0.01$; $***p < 0.001$ (significantly different than people without functional disability based on two-tailed tests). $N = 1,686$.

Table 2. Unstandardized Coefficients From Longitudinal OLS Models of Perceived Job Insecurity or Perceived Income Insecurity at W5 on Functional Disability (*n* = 488[a]).

	Perceived Job Insecurity			Perceived Income Insecurity		
	Model 1	Model 2	Model 3	Model 1	Model 2	Model 3
Baseline perceived job insecurity	0.186***	0.188***	0.061	–	–	–
	(0.046)	(0.045)	(0.175)			
Baseline perceived income insecurity	–	–	–	0.199***	0.199***	0.205***
				(0.031)	(0.031)	(0.031)
Functional disability	0.345**	0.333***	0.571	0.326***	0.319***	0.348***
	(0.139)	(0.141)	(0.344)	(0.073)	(0.074)	(0.074)
Gender (1 = Female)	0.072	0.076	0.023	0.038	0.034	0.042
	(0.078)	(0.078)	(0.078)	(0.060)	(0.060)	(0.060)
Race/ethnicity (1 = African American)	0.269**	0.272**	0.271**	0.286***	0.283***	0.299***
	(0.090)	(0.090)	(0.090)	(0.065)	(0.065)	(0.065)
Education	−0.031*	−0.033*	−0.033*	−0.027*	−0.025*	−0.029*
	(0.018)	(0.017)	(0.017)	(0.012)	(0.013)	(0.012)
Age (in years)	0.001	0.002	0.001	0.021***	0.029***	0.021***
	(0.005)	(0.005)	(0.005)	(0.003)	(0.003)	(0.003)
Functional disability * age	–	0.001	–	–	0.001	–
		(0.002			(0.002)	
Functional disability * baseline perceived job insecurity	–	–	0.129+	–	–	–
			(0.162)			
Functional disability * baseline perceived income insecurity	–	–	–	–	–	0.058*
						(0.025)
Constant	2.281***	2.249***	2.536***	0.576***	0.589***	0.602***
	(0.361)	(0.366)	(0.501)	(0.243)	(0.243)	(0.243)
R^2	0.073	0.074	0.074	0.156	0.157	0.161

[a]Analyses are limited to respondents who remained employed at W5.
Notes: All coefficients are weighted estimates. Standard errors are in parentheses. +$p < 0.10$; *$p < 0.05$; **$p < 0.01$; ***$p < 0.001$.

Table 2 presents the results of longitudinal OLS regression analyses that examined changes in perceived job insecurity and perceived income insecurity from W1 to W5 among survey respondents who remained employed at W5 (*n* = 488). A similar pattern of findings was observed for both outcomes. Net of the control variables, higher levels of perceived job insecurity at baseline predicted greater perceived job insecurity 26 years later. Similarly, greater perceived income insecurity at baseline was associated with greater perceived income insecurity at W5. Experiencing a functional disability at baseline was also associated with greater job insecurity and greater income insecurity at W5.

The second model, which included interaction terms for functional disability by age, provided no indication that the associations of baseline functional disability with greater perceived job insecurity and perceived income insecurity are conditioned by age. Model 3 tested whether there are differences by functional disability status in the extent to which employment disadvantages experienced earlier in life are associated with greater employment disadvantages later in life. The coefficient for the functional disability by baseline perceived job insecurity interaction was marginally significant in the prediction of later perceived job insecurity ($p < 0.07$). However, it demonstrated a pattern consistent with the significant effect observed for the interaction of functional disability by baseline income insecurity in the prediction of perceived income insecurity. As illustrated in Model 6, the association of early income insecurity with later income insecurity was significantly greater for people with a functional disability at baseline compared to those who were not disabled at that time.

Both baseline job insecurity and income insecurity predicted the hazard of involuntary job loss following the start of the Great Recession, as shown in Model 1 of Table 3. Each one-unit increase in baseline job insecurity was associated with about a 2% increase in the likelihood of losing one's job two decades later. Incremental increases in perceived income insecurity were associated with larger increases. Each one-unit increase in baseline income insecurity predicted about a 24% increase in the likelihood of experiencing involuntary job loss in the wake of the Great Recession. Furthermore, having a functional disability at baseline increased the likelihood of losing one's job involuntarily in the recession years by about 42%. These effects remained robust despite the inclusion of other social factors known to influence work precarity, including gender, race/ethnicity, education, and age.

Having a functional disability was also found to increase the hazard of involuntary job loss associated with other characteristics. While no differences by functional disability status were found in the association of older age with less involuntary job loss (Model 2), functional disability had a stronger effect on involuntary job loss among those who experienced early job insecurity (Model 3). The adverse effects of early income insecurity for later job loss were also significantly greater among people with a functional disability at baseline compared to those without disability (Model 4).

DISCUSSION

The starting point for this study was the question of whether people with and without disability vary in the extent to which early experiences of work precarity predict later work-related disadvantages. In addressing this question, I utilized three life course concepts: cumulative disadvantage, age effects, and period effects (Berkman et al., 2014; Ferraro & Schafer, 2017; O'Rand, 1996). Study findings provided a clear indication that people with disabilities who had early experiences of income insecurity were more likely to experience later income insecurity compared to people without disabilities, partly supporting *H1*. The trends observed in assessing the impact of early job insecurity and disability on later job insecurity were also consistent with this hypothesis but failed to reach significance. Aging did not significantly impact the effects of disability in the prediction of work precarity (*H2*) or involuntary job loss following the start of the Great Recession (*H3*). However, some support for a cumulative adversity hypothesis

Table 3. Hazard of Involuntary Job Loss Following the Great Recession ($N = 1,686$).

	Model 1		Model 2		Model 3		Model 4	
	Parameter Estimate	Hazard Ratio	Parameter Estimate	Hazard Ratio	Parameter Estimate	Hazard Ratio	Parameter Estimate	Hazard Ratio
Baseline perceived job insecurity	0.015** (0.002)	1.019	0.011* (0.002)		0.015* (0.003)		0.050* (0.002)	
Baseline perceived income insecurity	0.428*** (0.079)	1.246	0.174** (0.086)		0.423*** (0.081)		0.423*** (0.081)	
Functional disability	0.355** (0.194)	1.427	1.593* (1.200)		0.394* (0.203)		0.301* (0.208)	
Gender (1 = Female)	0.133 (0.193)		0.126 (0.194)		0.060 (0.184)		0.074 (0.184)	
Race/ethnicity (1 = African American)	0.034 (0.205)		0.034 (0.206)		0.212 (0.202)		0.227 (0.202)	
Education	−0.112** (0.041)	0.891	−0.108** (0.042)		−0.181** (0.035)		−0.178** (0.036)	
Age (in years)	−0.129*** (0.011)	0.885	−0.099*** (0.017)		−118*** (0.011)		0.118*** (0.011)	
Functional disability * age			−0.037 (0.023)		—		—	
Functional disability * baseline perceived job insecurity	—		—		0.081* (0.004)	1.075	—	
Functional disability * baseline perceived income insecurity	—		—		—		0.087** (0.003)	1.088
Pseudo R^2	0.241		0.246		0.242		0.244	

Notes: All coefficients are weighted estimates. Standard errors are in parentheses. $^+p < 0.10$; $^*p < 0.05$; $^{**}p < 0.01$; $^{***}p < 0.001$. Hazard ratios are reported only for significant coefficients in Model 1, and only for significant interaction coefficients in Models 2–4.

(*H3*) was observed. Those individuals in the study who had a functional disability and experienced job insecurity and income insecurity in 1986 were significantly more likely to experience involuntary job loss following the start of the Great Recession – more than 20 years later – than their counterparts without disabilities or precarious employment. These effects were both direct and synergistic. That is, in addition to baseline disability and work precarity independently predicting later involuntary job loss, interaction effects indicated that the disproportionate rate of unemployment among people with disabilities following the start of the Great Recession was exacerbated by their greater tendency to experience job insecurity and income insecurity earlier in life.

These effects are generally consistent with other research indicating that early adversity places individuals on distinct trajectories that influence later life experiences (Ferraro & Shippee, 2009; O'Rand, 1996). They also support the view that acute events can exacerbate processes of cumulative disadvantage (Brown et al., 2019; Burgard & Seelye, 2017; Rugh et al., 2015). In these respects, life course theory and methods have proven useful in modeling the long-term association of disability with precarious employment.

Along with highlighting the relevance of cumulative disadvantage for people with disabilities, an important implication of these findings is that people who experience disability in early adulthood may languish professionally without adequate workplace supports or protections. To this point, this study documents a consistent pattern of work precarity from 1986 to 2011, a span of time that included the passing of the ADA and other legislation to offer workplace protections to people with disabilities that ostensibly should have reduced work precarity. It is possible that people who were already established in careers when the ADA passed in 1990 benefitted less from its mandates, and that people who entered the workforce after its passing have experienced different career trajectories. Because this study followed the same respondents over the study period, though this is a strength in many respects, it cannot address the work experiences and trajectories of younger cohorts of people with disabilities. But these findings raise important questions about the extent to which legislative efforts have impacted work precarity, which is recommended for future research.

Another promising direction for research concerns the causal pathways linking disability and the accumulation of disadvantage in employment and other spheres of life. This study demonstrates the utility of a model considering disability as a predictor rather than an outcome of disadvantage. This is generally consistent with the cumulative disadvantage framework, or perhaps more accurately an application of this framework to a related topic. As noted, mental health scholars previously examined similar processes, which they termed social selection processes, whereby mental illness was found to predict greater social and economic disadvantage over time (Dohrenwend et al., 1992; Hudson, 2005; Johnson et al., 1999).

Several ways the social selection subfield was developed could be useful in thinking about next steps for disability research on similar processes. First, the concept of social selection was framed as the reverse of the social causation process more typically considered in life course research, which posits that poor mental health (or disability) is the product of economic disadvantage (Dohrenwend et al., 1992). This is because many correlates of economic disadvantage, such as crowded living conditions, ambient strain, physical hardship, less rewarding and autonomous employment, and disrupted family life, are mental health risk factors (Hudson, 2005; Mirowsky & Ross, 1989). Rather than considering this an either/or proposition, however, scholars addressed how selection and causation processes might co-occur – that is, they attended to the possibility that mental illness might be associated with fewer economic resources, which in turn could increase one's symptoms. This is an important elaboration because it acknowledges that there are expected adaptations to acute stress and hardship that are universal. It is not difficult to imagine that people with physical disabilities might similarly experience greater functional disability when underresourced, at least to the extent that we would expect anyone without adequate resources to experience greater functional disability.

Additional research has considered whether the salience of selection and causation processes varies by disorder. This work has found support for both social causation and selection processes for most forms of mental illness, with the exception of schizophrenia (Dohrenwend et al., 1992). Building on this work, other research has examined factors associated uniquely or jointly with selection and causation processes over time. For example, childhood conduct disorder influences educational attainment, but it is not clear why, and so it is further uncertain whether later health outcomes derive from the experience of disorder in childhood, lower educational attainment, both, or neither (Kessler et al., 1995; Miech et al., 1999). What we can take from this work is its consideration of processes that are general versus specific to certain health conditions, and its recognition that minimizing causal relationships obscures the role of oppression and hardship in accounting for adverse health effects over time. This is an orientation to life course research that may resonate with disability researchers because it is motivated by addressing inequalities experienced by people with a typically chronic and often disabling impairment condition.

REFERENCES

Ben-Shlomo, Y., & Kuh, D. (2002). A life course approach to chronic disease epidemiology: Conceptual models, empirical challenges and interdisciplinary perspectives. *International Journal of Epidemiology, 31*(2), 285–293.

Berkman, L. F., Kawachi, I., & Glymour, M. M. (2014). *Social epidemiology*. Oxford University Press.

Bracke, P., Delaruelle, K., Dereuddre, R., & Van de Velde, S. (2020). Depression in women and men, cumulative disadvantage and gender inequality in 29 European countries. *Social Science & Medicine, 267*. https://doi.org/10.1016/j.socscimed.2020.113354

Braddock, D. L., Hemp, R. E., Tanis, E. S., Wu, J., & Haffer, L. (2017). *The state of the states in intellectual and developmental disabilities* (11th ed.). American Association on Intellectual and Developmental Disabilities.

Brown, R. L., & Moloney, M. E. (2019). Intersectionality, work, and well-being: The effects of gender and disability. *Gender & Society, 33*(1), 94–122.

Brown, R. L., Richman, J. A., Moody, M. D., & Rospenda, K. M. (2019). The enduring mental health effects of post-9/11 discrimination in the context of the Great Recession: Race/ethnic variation. *Society and Mental Health, 9*(2), 158–170.

Brown, R. L., Richman, J. A., & Rospenda, K. M. (2017). Economic stressors and psychological distress: Exploring age cohort variation in the wake of the Great Recession. *Stress and Health, 33*(3), 267–277.

Burgard, S. A., Brand, J. E., & House, J. S. (2009). Perceived job insecurity and worker health in the United States. *Social Science & Medicine, 69*(5), 777–785.

Burgard, S. A., & Seelye, S. (2017). Histories of perceived job insecurity and psychological distress among older US adults. *Society and Mental Health, 7*(1), 21–35.

Carpenter, L. M. (2010). Gendered sexuality over the life course: A conceptual framework. *Sociological Perspectives, 53*(2), 155–177.

Cochrane, J. H. (2011). Understanding policy in the Great Recession: Some unpleasant fiscal arithmetic. *European Economic Review, 55*(1), 2–30.

Dohrenwend, B. P., Levav, I., Shrout, P. E., Schwartz, S., Naveh, G., Link, B. G., Skodol, A. E., & Stueve, A. (1992). Socioeconomic status and psychiatric disorders: The causation-selection issue. *Science, 255*(5047), 946–952.

Elder, G. H. (1995). The life course paradigm: Social change and individual development. In *Examining lives in context: Perspectives on the ecology of human development* (pp. 101–139). American Psychological Association.

Ferraro, K. F., & Farmer, M. M. (1996). Double jeopardy, aging as leveler, or persistent health inequality? A longitudinal analysis of white and black Americans. *The Journals of Gerontology Series B: Psychological Sciences and Social Sciences, 51*(6), S319–S328.

Ferraro, K. F., & Schafer, M. H. (2017). Visions of the life course: Risks, resources, and vulnerability. *Research in Human Development, 14*(1), 88–93.

Ferraro, K. F., & Shippee, T. P. (2009). Aging and cumulative inequality: How does inequality get under the skin? *The Gerontologist, 49*(3), 333–343.

Fogg, N. P., Harrington, P. E., & McMahon, B. T. (2010). The impact of the Great Recession upon the unemployment of Americans with disabilities. *Journal of Vocational Rehabilitation, 33*(3), 193–202.

Fraser, R., Ajzen, I., Johnson, K., Hebert, J., & Chan, F. (2011). Understanding employers' hiring intention in relation to qualified workers with disabilities. *Journal of Vocational Rehabilitation, 35*(1), 1–11.

George, L. K. (1996). Missing links: The case for a social psychology of the life course. *The Gerontologist, 36*(2), 248–255.

House, J. S. (2018). Americans' changing lives: Waves I, II, III, IV, and V, 1986, 1989, 1994, 2002, and 2011. *Inter-university Consortium for Political and Social Research.* https://doi.org/10.3886/ICPSR04690.v9

House, J. S., Lantz, P. M., & Herd, P. (2005). Continuity and change in the social stratification of aging and health over the life course: Evidence from a nationally representative longitudinal study from 1986 to 2001/2002 (Americans' changing lives study). *Journals of Gerontology Series B: Psychological Sciences and Social Sciences, 60*(Special_Issue_2), S15–S26.

Hudson, C. G. (2005). Socioeconomic status and mental illness: Tests of the social causation and selection hypotheses. *American Journal of Orthopsychiatry, 75*(1), 3–18.

Iezzoni, L. I. (2011). Eliminating health and health care disparities among the growing population of people with disabilities. *Health Affairs, 30*(10), 1947–1954.

Johnson, J. G., Cohen, P., Dohrenwend, B. P., Link, B. G., & Brook, J. S. (1999). A longitudinal investigation of social causation and social selection processes involved in the association between socioeconomic status and psychiatric disorders. *Journal of Abnormal Psychology, 108*(3), 490–499.

Jones, B. S., & Box-Steffensmeier, J. M. (2004). Models for discrete data. In *Event history modeling: A guide for social scientists, analytical methods for social research* (pp. 69–84). Cambridge University Press.

Kalleberg, A. L. (2009). Precarious work, insecure workers: Employment relations in transition. *American Sociological Review, 74*(1), 1–22.

Kalousova, L., & Burgard, S. A. (2014). Unemployment, measured and perceived decline of economic resources: Contrasting three measures of recessionary hardships and their implications for adopting negative health behaviors. *Social Science & Medicine, 106*, 28–34.

Kalousová, L., & Burgard, S. (2022). Employment pathways during economic recession and recovery and adult health. *Journal of Health and Social Behavior, 63*(1), 105–124.

Kessler, R. C., Foster, C. L., Saunders, W. B., & Stang, P. E. (1995). Social consequences of psychiatric disorders, I: Educational attainment. *American Journal of Psychiatry, 152*(7), 1026–1032.

Mai, Q. D., Jacobs, A. W., & Schieman, S. (2019). Precarious sleep? Nonstandard work, gender, and sleep disturbance in 31 European countries. *Social Science & Medicine, 237*. https://doi.org/10.1016/j.socscimed.2019.112424

Miech, R. A., Caspi, A., Moffitt, T. E., Wright, B. R. E., & Silva, P. A. (1999). Low socioeconomic status and mental disorders: A longitudinal study of selection and causation during young adulthood. *American Journal of Sociology, 104*(4), 1096–1131.

Mirowsky, J., & Ross, C. E. (1989). Psychiatric diagnosis as reified measurement. *Journal of Health and Social Behavior, 30*(1), 11–25.

Moody, M. D., Brown, R. L., & Ciciurkaite, G. (2019). For better or worse: An assessment of the 'linked lives' concept and the race-based effects of partner stress on self-rated health among older adults. *Journal of Racial and Ethnic Health Disparities, 6*(4), 861–867.

O'Rand, A. M. (1996). The precious and the precocious: Understanding cumulative disadvantage and cumulative advantage over the life course. *The Gerontologist, 36*(2), 230–238.

Richman, J. A., Rospenda, K. M., Johnson, T. P., Cho, Y. I., Vijayasira, G., Cloninger, L., & Wolff, J. M. (2012). Drinking in the age of the Great Recession. *Journal of Addictive Diseases, 31*(2), 158–172.

Rugh, J. S., Albright, L., & Massey, D. S. (2015). Race, space, and cumulative disadvantage: A case study of the subprime lending collapse. *Social Problems, 62*(2), 186–218.

Shuey, K. M., & Willson, A. E. (2008). Cumulative disadvantage and black-white disparities in life-course health trajectories. *Research on Aging, 30*(2), 200–225.

Surn, A., & Khatiwada, I. (2010). The nation's underemployed in the Great Recession of 2007–09. *Monthly Labor Review, 133*(11), 3–15.

Turner, J. B., & Turner, R. J. (2004). Physical disability, unemployment, and mental health. *Rehabilitation Psychology, 49*(3), 241–249.

Vosko, L. F. (Ed.). (2006). *Precarious employment: Understanding labour market insecurity in Canada.* McGill-Queen's Press-MQUP.

THE DISABILITY GAP IN TIME USE BY AGE ACROSS THE LIFE COURSE

Carrie L. Shandra and Fiona Burke

AUTHOR BIOGRAPHIES

Carrie L. Shandra, PhD, is an Associate Professor of Sociology at the State University of New York at Stony Brook and past Chair of the Disability in Society section of the American Sociological Association. Her research is focused on understanding work (broadly defined) and life course inequalities in the United States, particularly as they occur during the transition to adulthood and among individuals with disabilities. Recent publications have appeared in *Social Forces, Journal of Marriage and Family, The Journals of Gerontology*, and *Social Science Research*.

Fiona Burke, MA, is a doctoral student in Sociology at the State University of New York at Stony Brook. Her research focuses on disability, medical sociology, gender, and caregiving.

ABSTRACT

How people spend their time is an indicator of how they live their lives, with time use over the life course conditioned both by age and by participation in age-graded institutions. This chapter uses nationally representative data from the pooled 2008–2020 American Time Use Survey (ATUS) to evaluate how time use in 12 activity categories varies by age, gender, and disability status among 137,266 respondents aged 15 and older. By doing so, we quantify the "disability gap" in time use between men and women with and without disabilities, identifying at what age and by how much people with disabilities experience time differentials in activities of daily living (ADLs), instrumental activities of daily living (IADLs), and other indicators of social participation. Results indicate that – at many ages – patterns of time use for people with disabilities deviate from those of people without disabilities, with more pronounced differences in midlife. Further, the magnitude of women's disability

Disabilities and the Life Course
Research in Social Science and Disability, Volume 14, 183–207
Copyright © 2023 Carrie L. Shandra and Fiona Burke
Published under exclusive licence by Emerald Publishing Limited
ISSN: 1479-3547/doi:10.1108/S1479-354720230000014011

gaps equals or exceeds men's for sleeping, and nearly all ADLs and IADLs, indicating that disability gaps are also gendered.

Keywords: Disability; life course; time use; social participation; gender; activities of daily living

How people spend their time is an indicator of how they live their lives, with time use over the life course conditioned both by age and by participation in age-graded institutions. Yet patterns of life course events like school enrollment, employment, independent living, partnership, and parenting look different for people with and without disabilities. Further, structural ableism excludes many people with disabilities from participating in the types of social institutions that facilitate these markers. Thus, daily time use is likely to vary by disability status and across early adulthood, midlife, and older ages.

At the same time, disability is not a monolithic experience and must be considered within larger frameworks of structural inequalities. As such, barriers to social participation faced by people with disabilities might be amplified when compounded with gender inequality (e.g., Garland-Thomson, 2002). Peoples' life courses and their time use are gendered, particularly when considering activities like care work, housework, and leisure (Moen & Spencer, 2006; Sayer et al., 2016). Men and women with disabilities experience different constraints in their everyday lives that likely impact time spent in daily activities.

This chapter uses nationally representative data from the pooled 2008–2020 American Time Use Survey (ATUS) (Hofferth et al., 2020) to evaluate how time use in multiple daily activities (sleeping, personal care, eating and drinking, household labor, purchasing goods and services, care work, paid work, education, leisure, television, civic and organizational activities, communications, and travel) varies by age, gender, and disability status among 137,266 respondents aged 15 and older. By doing so, we quantify the "disability gap" in time use between men and women with and without disabilities, identifying both the age period *when* and *by how much* people with and without experience differences in activities of daily living, instrumental activities of daily living, and other indicators of social participation.

LITERATURE REVIEW
Time Use and the Life Course

Broadly speaking, a life course perspective aims to understand how people live their lives, from childhood to older age, in historical time and place (e.g., Elder et al., 2003). Chronological age often plays a central role in life course questions, as age is structured by both social institutions and public policies (Settersten & Mayer, 1997). These age structures are often characterized by periods of education and training, family formation and child-rearing, employment, and retirement and leisure (Moen & Flood, 2013; Settersten, 2003). Such periods are neither lockstep nor universal, but suggestive of daily activity patterns in particular geographical and historical contexts.

A time use approach is especially useful for evaluating how people live their lives during particular ages, as time is a bounded resource, and time allocated to one activity carries opportunity costs of not engaging in other activities (Williams et al., 2016). For example, time spent in education is – on average – highest among people in their teen years, followed by those in their early 20s, and tapering off at midlife and older ages. Time spent in paid work follows a U-shaped curve, increasing through the prime working ages of the 40s and 50s and decreasing thereafter. Leisure time follows the opposite inverted U-shaped pattern, decreasing from the teen years through the apex of midlife before increasing again during retirement age (US Bureau of Labor Statistics, 2020).

A time use approach to understanding the life course also reflects activity participation – including activities that signal inclusion and independent living (Graf, 2008; Suh, 2016). Activities of Daily Living (ADLs) such as personal care time tends to be slightly higher in the teen and older adult years, while eating and drinking time tends to increase with age. Instrumental Activities of Daily Living (IADLs) like household labor and communication time tend to increase with age, while travel time decreases. Sleep tends to be slightly higher in the younger and older years, compared with midlife (Roman & Gracia, 2022; Marcum, 2013; US Bureau of Labor Statistics, 2020). Finally, care for others peaks during the 30s and 40s, while housework tends to increase with age – more for women than for men (Roman & Gracia, 2022; US Bureau of Labor Statistics, 2020).

These age differences are conditioned by socioeconomic background and by other social statuses. Many vary by gender, as women's investments in unpaid labor tend to exceed men's, and men's investments in paid labor tend to exceed women's (Sayer et al., 2016). Others are heterogenous by gender as well as employment status, marital status, parenting status, and residential status, which influence time in paid work, child care, and other nonmarket work (Anxo et al., 2011; Ice, 2022; Scheiner, 2016).

Disability and Time Use

Multiple major barriers may limit or constrain people with disabilities' participation in daily activities, regardless of age. First, people with disabilities report low levels of access to private vehicles, physical barriers to public transportation, and long wait times for paratransit – all of which can preclude social participation and the maintenance of personal networks (Bascom & Christensen, 2017). Second, inaccessible built environments in recreational and cultural spaces like fitness facilities, parks, community centers, and museums can make them unusable by people with disabilities (Lisney et al., 2013; Rimmer et al., 2017). Third, attitudinal barriers, including experiences of stigma and negative labeling, can deter people with disabilities from accessing activities outside the home (Balandin et al., 2006; Bedini, 2000). These patterns may increase the amount of time spent in "access work" to negotiate access to goods and services (e.g., Dillaway & Lysack, 2015), or preclude certain forms of social participation entirely.

Other barriers are unique to one's stage in the life course. Students with disabilities are less likely than students without disabilities to report participation in extracurricular activities like sports, academic teams, musical activities, and student government (Repetto et al., 2011). They report fewer friends, lower friendship quality, and higher levels of social isolation than those without disabilities (Bruefach & Reynolds, 2022; Tipton et al., 2013). And on average, adolescents with disabilities spend more time with parents and relatives than those without disabilities (Wikle & Shandra, 2022). These patterns may decrease the leisure and educational time of teenagers with disabilities, relative to their age peers.

Working-aged adults with disabilities may also experience unique forms of structural ableism. Employer bias, discrimination, lack of familiarity with disability accommodations, cost concerns, and fear of legal liability can exclude people with disabilities from participating in paid employment (Ameri et al., 2018; Kaye et al., 2011). One study of people's perceptions of interpersonal and institutional discrimination found greater levels among people with disabilities than those without, with people with disabilities in early midlife (40–49) reporting the highest levels of disrespect and harassment and the highest probability of discrimination by service providers, relative to people with disabilities at younger and older ages (Namkung & Carr, 2019). Workplace barriers and stigma both operate to exclude working-aged people with disabilities from the labor force.

Retirement age may have varying impacts on disability gaps in time use. People with disabilities aged 65 and above are more likely than those at all other ages to have health insurance coverage, a usual health care provider, and routine care – and are less likely to have unmet health needs because of cost (Okoro et al., 2018). Thus, eligibility for Social Security and Medicare may help shrink financial and health-related time use gaps between older adults with and without disabilities. Additionally, level of social support is also conditional on age, as Allen and Mor (1997) found that people with disabilities younger than age 65 reported higher levels of unmet need for cooking, housekeeping, shopping, and transportation than people with disabilities of age 65 or older. Similarly, older adults with disabilities report greater confidence in their social support system than younger adults with disabilities (Allen et al., 2000). These higher levels of support may attenuate the disability gap in ADLs and IADLs at older ages.

The introduction of expanded disability information in the ATUS in mid-2008 (Brault et al., 2007) has allowed scholars to estimate differences in time use between people with and without disabilities. Focusing on working-aged adults, Anand and Ben-Shalom (2014) find that – net of controls, and dependent on the type of disability – men and women with disabilities spend more time sleeping and in leisure and less time in paid work than those without disabilities. Men with disabilities spent less time on housework, while women with disabilities spent more. Focusing on parents, Shandra and Penner (2017) found that mothers and fathers with disabilities spent no less time on primary child care than mothers and fathers without disabilities, but they did spend less time on housework. Myers and Ravesloot's (2016) analysis finds that people with disabilities spend less time in transportation than those without. Yet none of these studies consider how age might condition the disability gap over the life course.

Gender and Disability

Peoples' life courses are gendered, shaped by structural constraints like state policies and employment practices that assume both a male breadwinner and an ideal worker (Acker, 1992; Moen & Spencer, 2006). This can be observed in gendered patterns of time use, particularly when considering activities like care work and housework (Sayer et al., 2016). On average, women spend more time on housework and care work throughout the life course, and men spend more time in market work (Anxo et al., 2011; Roman & Gracia, 2022). The birth of a first child signals a significant increase in women's time in housework, but men's time in housework remains unchanged (Baxter et al., 2008). At older ages, retirement tends to prompt greater convergence between men's and women's housework time (Leopold & Skopek, 2015). In sum, these gendered patterns are conditioned by employment and family statuses (and will be explored in supplemental analyses of this study).

Yet women with disabilities face multiple unique disadvantages relative to men with disabilities – particularly during working and child-rearing years. Men and women with disabilities have similar unemployment rates, but women have lower rates of labor force participation (US Bureau of Labor Statistics, 2022). Although the presence of a disability has greater earnings consequences for men than for women, women with disabilities have lower total income than men with disabilities and receive a greater proportion of income from government sources (Maroto et al., 2019; Pettinicchio & Maroto, 2017). Further, compared to men with disabilities (and women and men without disabilities), women with disabilities report less average work time (Anand & Ben-Shalom, 2014), lower occupational prestige, greater exposure to workplace stress, and are less likely to experience autonomous working conditions (Brown & Moloney, 2019). These greater workplace disadvantages might translate into a larger paid work gap between women with and without disabilities than men with and without disabilities.

Women with disabilities may also experience heightened caregiving expectations. Mothers with disability describe their adequacy as parents as under constant scrutiny, feeling additional pressure to convince others they are good parents. They invest a tremendous amount of (often hidden) labor to go above and beyond in impression management for themselves and their children (Frederick, 2017; Grue & Laerum, 2002; Malacrida, 2009). Fathers with disabilities also report difficulties being taken seriously as parents, as well as tension between their disability status and the breadwinning and physicality norms of hegemonic masculinity. Although some men renegotiate these norms to expand their caregiving responsibilities, others limit their involvement to avoid additional scrutiny outside the household (Kilkey & Clarke, 2010; Pini & Conway, 2017). Thus, we might observe a smaller caregiving gap between women with and without disabilities than men with and without disabilities.

DATA AND METHODS

ATUS is a nationally representative survey sponsored by the US Bureau of Labor Statistics that collects information on daily time use (Hofferth et al., 2020). Respondents aged 15 and over were chosen randomly from households that had undergone their final interview for the Current Population Survey (CPS), with the ATUS collected 2–5 months after the final CPS interview. The sample was randomized by day such that half the respondents reported on a weekday and half reported on a weekend day. Computer-assisted telephone interviewing was used to ask respondents to provide demographic information, as well as a detailed account of their activities during a 24-hour period beginning at 4:00 a.m. The "diary day" is the day about which the respondent reports, with pooled data from all available years in which disability questions are asked (2008–2020) resulting in an initial sample size of 146,446 diary days.

Detailed disability data were introduced in mid-2008, reducing the sample size to 137,933 diary days. Of the respondents with disability data, 667 were excluded due to interviewer-reported data quality problems. No other eligibility exclusions were made, leaving a total analytic sample of 137,266 respondents (76,273 women and 60,993 men) aged 15 and older. All analyses were weighted using corresponding module weights and Stata's subpopulation command (StataCorp, 2021).

Measures

Our choice of life domains is informed by previous analyses of disability and time use (Anand & Ben-Shalom, 2014; Verbrugge & Liu, 2014), and operationalized based on measures used in Bureau of Labor Statistics published tables and available in ATUS Data Extract Builder (Hofferth et al., 2020). Categories include sleeping, personal care (including grooming, self-care, and sexual activity), eating and drinking, household labor (including housework, cooking, and household management), purchasing goods and services, care work (of household and nonhousehold children and adults), paid work, education, leisure (including socializing, sports, and recreation), television, civic and organizational activities (including religious, voluntary, and civic participation), and travel (measured separately from each of its corresponding activity categories). We also discuss results for time spent in communications (nonwork telephone calls, mail, and email) in text. Together, these categories account for an average of 1,428 minutes among the women sample and 1,429 minutes of the men sample, out of a possible 1,440 minutes of the day. Further detail on the activity codes used in these classifications can be found in the Bureau of Labor Statistics' (2021) time use tables.

Disability status in the ATUS was measured in the CPS interview and designed to correspond to "four basic areas of functioning (vision, hearing, mobility, and cognitive functioning) that identified the largest component of the population of people with disabilities...[and] two key elements that could be used for monitoring independent living and the need for services" (Brault et al., 2007, p. 4). The analyses presented in the main tables use a dichotomous indicator that includes any of these disabilities ($N = 16,685$ total people with disabilities).[1]

We include indicators of life course and socioeconomic differences as covariates in regression models. *Age* differentiates between respondents who are 15–19, 20–29, 30–39, 40–49, 50–59, 60–69, and 70 or more years old. *Highest level of education* compares those with less than a high-school diploma or General Educational Development (GED), those with a high-school diploma or GED but less than a bachelor's degree, those with a bachelor's degree, and those with a postbaccalaureate degree. *School enrollment* compares those who were enrolled during the week prior to ATUS in high school or college with those who were not enrolled, not asked by the survey (ages 50 and above), or refused to answer. *Race/ ethnicity* compares those who identify as non-Hispanic White, Hispanic, non-Hispanic Black, and other non-Hispanic racial-ethnic groups. *Nativity status* compares those who are born in the United States, Puerto Rico, or US Outlying Areas or abroad of American parents to those who are foreign-born. *Employment status* distinguishes between those who are unemployed/not in the labor force to those who usually work part time (less than 35 hours per week) or full time (35 or more hours per week).

Household and geographic controls include *partnership status*, measured as no spouse or partner present, spouse present, or unmarried partner present in the household. Three separate dichotomous variables indicate the *presence of own children* aged 0–5, 6–12, or 13–17 in the household. *Number of household adults* is a categorical variable ranging from 0 to 4 or more. *Metropolitan residence* reports whether a household was located in a metropolitan area. *Annual family income* indicates those who reported less than $25,000, $25,000–49,999, $50,000–74,999, and $75,000 and above (CPS began imputing missing data for family income in 2010; missing values for previous years were replaced with the respondent's median income level by education, gender, and year). Models also control for survey year, whether the interview took place in summer, and whether the interview took place on a weekend or holiday.

Analysis

This chapter uses nationally representative data from the pooled 2008–2020 ATUS (Hofferth et al., 2020) to evaluate how time use in multiple facets of daily life (sleeping, personal care, eating and drinking, household labor, purchasing goods and services, care work, paid work, education, leisure, television, communications, and travel) varies by age, gender, and disability status among

---

[1]Disability prevalence in the unweighted sample varies by age group. Among women, these frequencies and within-age percentages are: $N = 114$ (3.3%) age 15–19, $N = 275$ (3.3%) age 20–29; $N = 547$ (3.9%) age 30–39; $N = 851$ (6.5%) age 40–49; $N = 1,736$ (13.8%) age 50–59; $N = 2,226$ (18.8%) age 60–69; $N = 4,188$ (33.1%) age 70 plus. Among men, $N = 153$ (4.1%) age 15–19, $N = 218$ (3.4%) age 20–29; $N = 397$ (3.6%) age 30–39; $N = 685$ (5.8%) age 40–49; $N = 1,330$ (12.2%) age 50–59; $N = 1,734$ (18.7%) age 60–69; $N = 2,231$ (29.4%) age 70 plus.

137,266 respondents aged 15 and older. By doing so, we quantify the "disability gap" in time use between men and women with and without disabilities, identifying *when* in the life course – and *by how much* – they experience differences in ADLs and other indicators of social participation.

Our first aim is to evaluate how time use varies across activity categories by age, gender, and disability status. We estimate the weighted mean number of minutes spent by respondents in each activity category and graph these results in Fig. 1, displaying minutes spent in each age category for four groups: women and men with and without disabilities. Our second aim is to evaluate if these patterns are explained or attenuated by life course and socioeconomic differences between people with and without disabilities. Tables 2 and 3 present results of ordinary least squares (OLS) regression models predicting minutes of time in each activity category, stratified by gender and controlling for the aforementioned covariates. Finally, our third aim is to quantify the "gap" in time use by disability status, comparing men and women with and without disabilities within the same age category, by interacting age with disability in each multivariate model. The results of these interaction terms are presented in Tables 2 and 3. We then use Stata's *margins* command to calculate the difference in predicted means (calculated as average marginal effects) between women and men with and without disabilities within each age group, and Stata's *contrast* command to construct confidence intervals and perform hypothesis tests. We visualize these differences as age- and gender-specific disability gaps in Figs. 2 and 3. Variance inflation factors (VIFs) were examined to assess multicollinearity in unweighted models, with mean overall VIFs less than 2.4. Influential cases were assessed in unweighted models using Cook's D (OLS) statistics; all values fell below 0.03.

RESULTS

Bivariate Analyses

Table 1 presents weighted distributional measures of age and sociodemographic differences in covariates, by disability status and gender. Statistically significant differences between adults with and without disabilities were examined using Stata's *lincom* command (StataCorp, 2021). Men and women with disabilities are significantly older, less likely to be Hispanic, more likely to be non-Hispanic Black, less likely to report that they are born outside of the United States, and more likely to report metropolitan residence. They have lower levels of education, lower income, and are less likely to report school enrollment or employment. Finally, they are less likely to live with a spouse or partner, live with fewer other adults, and are less likely to report the presence of their own children in the household.

Fig. 1 presents weighted means of daily time use by disability status, age, and gender. Statistically significant within-gender bivariate differences in time use emerge across the life course. Women and men with disabilities aged 30 and over spend more time sleeping than women and men without disabilities in comparable age groups. The same is also true for time spent in personal care (women

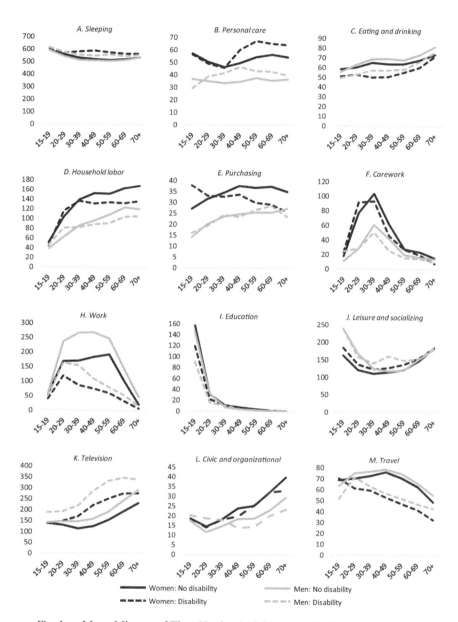

Fig. 1. Mean Minutes of Time Use by Activity, Age, Gender, and Disability Status. *Source:* American Time Use Survey. Results are weighted mean minutes per day in activities, by disability status, age, and gender.

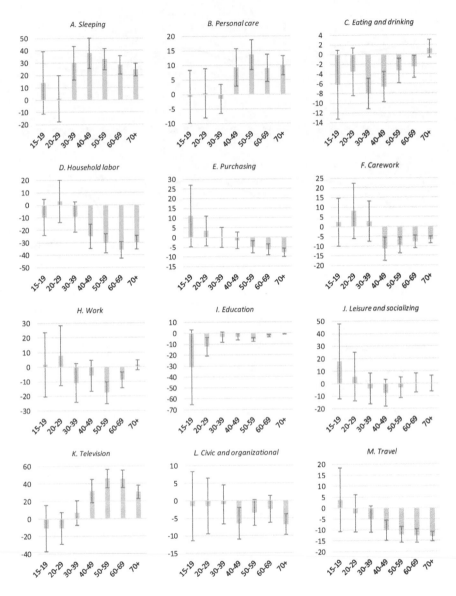

Fig. 2. Difference in Minutes Spent in Daily Activities for Women With Disabilities, by Age. *Source:* American Time Use Survey. Data shown are differences in minutes of time use between people with and without disabilities with 95% confidence intervals, calculated from multivariate models with all controls and interactions from Table 2.

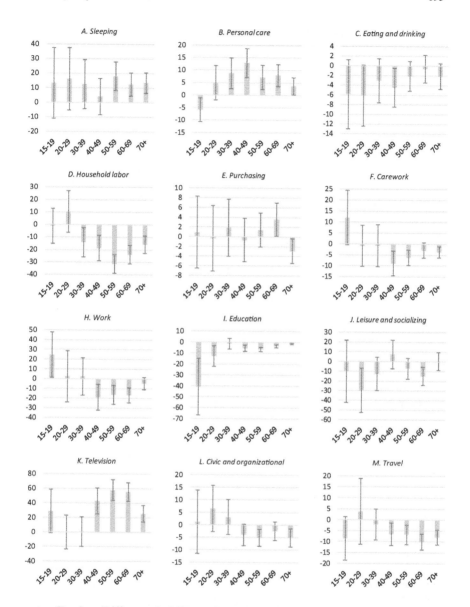

Fig. 3. Difference in Minutes Spent in Daily Activities for Men With Disabilities, by Age. *Source:* American Time Use Survey. Data shown are differences in minutes of time use between people with and without disabilities with 95% confidence intervals, calculated from multivariate models with all controls and interactions from Table 3.

Table 1. Distribution of all Variables, by Disability and Gender.

	Women			Men		
	Without Disability	With Disability	p Value	Without Disability	With Disability	p Value
Age						
15–19	51.0	1.2	***	6.7	2.3	***
20–29	12.1	27.7	***	11.4	3.2	***
30–39	20.6	5.5	***	19.9	5.9	***
40–49	18.6	8.6	***	20.6	10.2	***
50–59	16.4	17.5	**	17.7	19.7	***
60–69	14.5	22.4	***	13.9	25.7	***
70+	12.8	42.2	***	9.9	33.1	***
Race/ethnicity						
Non-Hispanic White	65.1	65.6		67.1	68.5	*
Hispanic	14.6	10.6	***	15.3	11.2	***
Non-Hispanic Black	14.8	20.7	***	12.1	17.4	***
Other	5.5	3.1	***	5.6	3.0	***
Nativity	14.9	7.9	***	15.5	7.0	***
Metropolitan residence	16.2	22.4	***	15.8	22.9	***
Highest education						
Less than high school	11.7	21.3	***	13.5	20.9	***
High-school diploma or GED	51.5	61.6	***	49.5	59.9	***
Bachelor's degree	22.6	10.9	***	22.6	12.0	***
Postbaccalaureate degree	14.3	6.3	***	14.4	7.1	***
Enrolled in school	9.5	2.3	***	9.2	2.6	***
Employment status						
Unemployed/not in the labor force	39.2	83.8	***	27.0	76.3	***
Usually works part time	17.0	6.8	***	9.4	7.7	***
Usually works full time	43.7	9.4	***	63.6	16.0	***
Family income						
Less than $25,000	21.3	54.9	***	16.0	43.6	***
$25,000–49,999	26.5	25.6		24.6	28.5	***
$50,000–74,999	18.4	10.0	***	20.1	12.9	***
$75,000 or more	33.8	9.5	***	39.4	15.1	***
Partnership status						
No spouse or unmarried partner in household	48.1	75.9	***	41.8	59.0	***
Spouse in household	48.1	22.3	***	54.2	38.5	***
Unmarried partner in household	3.8	1.9	***	4.0	2.5	***
Number of adults in the household						
0	32.0	61.7	***	26.8	47.2	***
1	52.5	29.5	***	56.7	41.4	***
2	11.0	6.4	***	12.2	8.4	***
3	4.6	2.4	***	5.3	2.9	***

Table 1. *(Continued)*

	Women			Men		
	Without Disability	With Disability	*p* Value	Without Disability	With Disability	*p* Value
Presence of own children 0–5	18.3	3.5	***	16.1	3.3	***
Presence of own children 6–12	22.0	6.5	***	19.1	5.6	***
Presence of own children 13–17	13.5	4.6	***	11.8	4.9	***

Source: American Time Use Survey. Data are weighted means (for linear measures) and percentages (for categorical measures). Difference between those with no disability and those with disability within each gender is significant at $*p < 0.05$; $**p < 0.01$; $***p < 0.001$ (two-tailed tests).

aged 40 and over; men aged 30–60). All but the oldest ages of women with disabilities and the youngest ages of men with disabilities spend less time eating and drinking. Women with disabilities aged 40 and above, and men with disabilities aged 50 and above, spend less time in household labor. Women with disabilities aged 50 and above, and men with disabilities aged 70 and more, spend less time purchasing. Women with disabilities aged 40–49 and 60 and above, and men with disabilities aged 15–19, 40–49, 50–59, and 70 plus spend less time in care work. Women and men with disabilities spend significantly less time in work than those without disabilities at ages 20 plus, as well as in education at ages 20–29 and 30–39. Women and men with disabilities aged 40–49 and 50–59 spend more time in leisure than those without disabilities in the same age groups, as well as watching television among women aged 20 and over and men of all ages. Women and men with disabilities of ages 30–39, 40–49, and 50–59 spend more time in communication. Women and men with disabilities aged 70+, and men with disabilities of ages 40–49 and 50–59, spend more time in civic and organizational activities. Finally, women with disabilities of all age groups except 15–19 and men with disabilities of all age groups except 20–29 spend less time in travel.

Multivariate Analyses and Interaction Results

Table 2 (women) and Table 3 (men) present linear regression models of minutes per day spent in daily activities, net of controls. Two models are estimated for each outcome: one with main effects of disability and age only (column A) and another that adds an interaction term between disability and age (column B). The coefficients for disability and age are presented for brevity.

Disability is significantly associated with nearly all time use outcomes in the main models (column A). It positively associates with sleep, personal care, and television for men and women. It negatively associates with eating and drinking, household labor, purchasing (for women), care work, work, education, leisure (for men), civic and organizational activities, and travel. Overall, younger ages (vs. the reference category of age 70 plus) tend to be associated with more sleep, education, leisure (for men), and travel. They tend to be associated with less time

Table 2. Ordinary Least Squares Regression of Minutes per Day Spent in Daily Activities – Women.

	Sleep		Personal Care		Eating and Drinking		Household Labor		Purchasing		Care work	
	(1.a)	(1.b)	(2.a)	(2.b)	(3.a)	(3.b)	(4.a)	(4.b)	(5.a)	(5.b)	(6.a)	(6.b)
Disability	27.7***	24.5***	9.1***	9.9***	−2.1***	1.2	−28.2***	29.9***	−5.2**	−7.8***	−6.7***	−6.8***
Age (reference = 70+)												
15–19	64.1***	63.3***	1.8	2.4	−11.6***	−10.3***	−84.5***	−85.8***	−0.2	−1.8	20.1***	19.8***
20–29	56.4***	55.8***	−3.8***	−3.2**	−14.3***	−12.9***	−40.2***	−42.0***	−0.2	−1.6	31.3***	30.9***
30–39	41.2***	39.4***	−4.7***	−4.0***	−13.6***	−11.9***	−22.4***	−24.0***	0.2	−1.1	39.2***	39.0***
40–49	27.4***	25.0***	−4.2***	−4.0***	−14.3***	−12.6***	−6.2***	−7.1***	2.3**	1.0	36.4***	36.8***
50–59	9.0***	6.8***	−2.6**	−3.0***	−12.4***	−10.9***	8.6***	8.3***	2.7***	1.6	26.8***	27.2***
60–69	1.0	−0.4	−0.2	0.1	−8.1***	−6.8***	7.3***	8.1***	2.9***	2.2**	15.4***	15.6***
Disability × Age 15–19		−10.5		−10.7***		−7.4*		20.3***		19.0***		9.2
Disability × Age 20–29		−23.4***		−9.5***		−4.7		33.1***		11.3***		15.0**
Disability × Age 30–39		5.5		−11.4***		−9.3***		20.5***		7.9***		9.6*
Disability × Age 40–49		13.5***		−0.7		−7.8***		4.9		6.3***		−4.7
Disability × Age 50–59		8.6**		3.7		−4.5*		−0.7		2.9		−2.8
Disability × Age 60–69		3.9		−0.9		−3.7*		−6.1		1.5		−0.9
Constant	523.9***	524.8***	50.6***	50.2***	63.5***	62.4***	154.0***	154.7***	32.5***	33.4***	18.5***	18.6***

	Work		Education		Leisure		Television		Civic and Organizational		Travel	
	(7.a)	(7.b)	(8.a)	(8.b)	(9.a)	(9.b)	(10.a)	(10.b)	(11.a)	(11.b)	(12.a)	(12.b)
Disability	−5.8***	1.3	−3.4***	−0.7***	−1.0	0.0	33.3***	30.6***	−4.5***	−6.8***	−11.5***	−13.1***
Age (reference = 70+)												
15–19	12.5***	14.8***	57.2***	59.2***	7.5*	7.3*	−73.0***	−72.4***	−17.1***	−18.0***	17.3***	16.1***
20–29	27.4***	29.9***	10.9***	12.3***	−17.0***	−16.7***	−38.8***	−38.4***	−20.1***	−21.0***	14.1***	13.1***
30–39	19.9***	23.2***	8.3***	9.4***	−25.5***	−24.7***	−30.8***	−30.9***	−19.0***	−20.0***	11.7***	10.8***

40–49	18.2**	21.3***	7.1***	8.2**	−31.3***	−30.2***	−27.7***	−29.0***	−14.9***	−15.6***	11.9***	11.2***
50–59	20.2**	24.7***	8.3***	9.7***	−33.0***	−32.2***	−24.0***	−26.9***	−11.3***	−12.3***	10.6***	10.1***
60–69	7.6***	10.8***	3.2***	4.0***	−21.4***	−21.3***	−8.2***	−11.5***	−5.5***	−6.7***	8.0***	7.6***
Disability × Age 15–19	0.3			−30.3*	18.0			−41.4***		5.3		17.0***
Disability × Age 20–29	6.5			−11.6**	5.8			−41.3***		5.3		10.7**
Disability × Age 30–39	−12.2*			−3.0	−3.9			−23.9***		5.8		8.0**
Disability × Age 40–49	−7.4			−2.7	−7.5			1.2		0.3		2.9
Disability × Age 50–59	−19.1***			−5.3***	−3.1			15.3**		3.4		0.9
Disability × Age 60–69	−10.3***			−1.9***	0.6			14.9*		4.4		0.3
Constant	74.5	72.3***	10.5***	9.6***	160.7***	160.5***	255.9***	256.6***	25.7***	26.4***	41.4***	42.0***

Source: American Time Use Survey.

Notes: Data shown are weighted linear regression coefficients and control for all covariates listed in Table 1, as well as interview timing (summer interview, weekend/holiday interview, and survey year); $^*p < 0.05$; $^{**}p < 0.01$; $^{***}p < 0.001$ (two-tailed tests). $N = 76,273$.

Table 3. Ordinary Least Squares Regression of Minutes per Day Day Spent in Daily Activities – Men.

	Sleep		Personal Care		Eating and Drinking		Household Labor		Purchasing		Care work	
	(1.a)	(1.b)	(2.a)	(2.b)	(3.a)	(3.b)	(4.a)	(4.b)	(5.a)	(5.b)	(6.a)	(6.b)
Disability	13.1***	13.5***	6.6***	3.7*	-2.3***	-2.1	-19.7***	-15.8***	0.4	-2.9**	-3.8***	-3.6***
Age (reference = 70+)												
15–19	55.3***	55.4***	0.7	0.3	-18.5***	-18.3***	-47.1***	-46.7***	-4.3***	-5.3***	14.7***	14.0***
20–29	33.8***	33.8***	-2.8**	-3.8**	-16.0***	-15.7***	-24.9***	-24.4***	-3.3***	-4.4***	12.5***	12.5***
30–39	21.4***	21.6***	-2.7**	-4.0**	-15.5***	-15.3***	-10.2***	-8.8***	-1.2	-2.3**	20.6***	20.7***
40–49	14.1***	14.8***	-2.3*	-3.8**	-14.0***	-13.8***	-1.8	-0.2	-0.1	-1.2	18.0***	18.6***
50–59	4.4*	3.9	-0.6	-1.8	-13.5***	-13.4***	10.0***	13.0***	1.5*	0.3	11.0***	11.5***
60–69	-4.7**	-4.5**	-1.5	-2.7**	-8.6***	-8.8***	13.1***	15.2***	0.8	-0.8	6.4***	6.4***
Disability × Age 15–19		-0.2		-9.6***		-3.8		14.7*		3.8		15.6***
Disability × Age 20–29		2.7		1.3		-4.0		26.2***		2.5		2.8
Disability × Age 30–39		-0.9		5.1		-0.9		1.7		4.7		2.8
Disability × Age 40–49		-9.4		9.2***		-2.3		-2.9		2.2		-5.2*
Disability × Age 50–59		4.6		3.5		0.0		-15.6***		4.3***		-2.6
Disability × Age 60–69		-1.0		4.3		1.5		-8.0		6.5***		0.8
Constant	536.6***	536.5***	33.6***	34.3***	66.7***	66.6***	91.0***	90.2***	18.0***	18.9***	6.7***	6.8***

	Work		Education		Leisure		Television		Civic and Organizational		Travel	
	(7.a)	(7.b)	(8.a)	(8.b)	(9.a)	(9.b)	(10.a)	(10.b)	(11.a)	(11.b)	(12.a)	(12.b)
Disability	-10.1***	-4.6	-4.9***	-1.2*	-6.6***	0.4	38.9***	25.6***	-3.1**	-5.1***	-7.3***	-7.9***
Age (reference = 70+)												
15–19	16.6***	16.7***	36.5***	39.5***	75.3***	77.7***	-137.0***	-140.7***	-5.8***	-6.6**	8.8***	8.6***
20–29	27.9***	29.5***	11.4***	12.9***	35.9***	38.8***	-72.6***	-75.8***	-11.6***	-12.5***	9.9***	9.2***
30–39	23.2***	24.9***	9.5***	10.6***	3.9	6.1*	-42.3***	-45.6***	-11.8***	-12.7***	6.3***	5.7***

40–49	22.8***	25.6***	9.0***	10.2**	−8.6***	−7.4**	−32.4***	−37.5***	−10.0***	−10.5***	4.8***	4.5***
50–59	16.4***	19.2***	9.6***	10.9***	−16.0***	−13.9***	−20.3***	−27.4***	−7.7***	−8.0***	4.8***	4.5***
60–69	6.4***	9.5***	4.3***	5.1**	−8.1***	−4.4	−5.9*	−13.3***	−4.4**	−5.1**	3.4***	3.7***
Disability × Age 15–19		29.3**		−39.7***		−10.6		2.9		6.2		−0.6
Disability × Age 20–29		7.0		−11.6*		−30.1**		−25.8*		11.6*		11.8
Disability × Age 30–39		6.9		−0.3		−13.1		−25.1**		8.2*		5.8
Disability × Age 40–49		−14.4*		−4.3***		6.9		17.3		1.1		1.3
Disability × Age 50–59		−11.8**		−5.3***		−7.6		32.3***		−0.1		1.1
Disability × Age 60–69		−12.3**		−2.4**		−15.4**		29.8***		2.7		−2.1
Constant	109.8***	108.6***	15.2***	13.9***	157.6***	155.5***	334.0***	337.4***	13.1***	13.7***	42.0***	42.2***

Source: American Time Use Survey.

Notes: Data shown are weighted linear regression coefficients and control for all covariates listed in Table 1, as well as interview timing (summer interview, weekend/holiday interview, and survey year); $^*p < 0.05$; $^{**}p < 0.01$; $^{***}p < 0.001$ (two-tailed tests). $N = 60{,}993$.

in household labor, purchasing (for men), civic and organizational activities, and television. Midlife sees the highest investments in care work and work, and relatively less time in personal care and communication.

The primary goal of these analyses is to quantify the "disability gap" in time use between men and women with and without disabilities throughout the life course, identifying *when* – and *by how much* – they experience differences in ADLs and other indicators of social participation. These results are calculated from models in Tables 2 and 3 and presented in Figs. 2 and 3 (respectively) for ease of interpretation. For example, Fig. 2 (Panel A) shows that women aged 40–49 with disabilities are predicted to spend 38 more minutes in sleep than women aged 40–49 without disabilities. An F test indicates that this value is significantly different than 0. The same value could be calculated by hand by adding the coefficient for the main effect of disability from Table 2 (model 1.B; β = 24.5) with the coefficient for the interaction term for disability and age 40–49 (β = 13.5).

Notably, differences in time use across three activities traditionally classified as ADLs – sleeping, personal care, and eating and drinking – are largest during midlife. Women with disabilities aged 30–39, 40–49, and 50–59 spend 30–38 more minutes sleeping and 3–8 fewer minutes eating and drinking, compared to women without disabilities in the same age group. Men with disabilities spend 18 more minutes sleeping than those without disabilities at ages 50–59 and four fewer minutes eating and drinking. Significant differences in personal care begin at ages 40–49 for women (9–14 minutes more) and 30–39 for men (4–13 minutes more).

Similar patterns can be found for the activities of household labor and transportation commonly classified as IADLs. Disability gaps in household labor emerge around the age of 40–49 for women with disabilities (25 minutes less), increasing to 36 minutes at ages 60–69. For men, differences in household labor begin at age 30–39 (14 minutes), increasing to 31 minutes at age 50–59. Differences in travel time emerge at ages 40–49 for women and men and persist at older ages (10–13 minutes for women; 6–10 minutes for men). Care work also follows this trend: both women (12 minutes) and men (9 minutes) with disabilities in the 40–49 year age range are predicted to spend fewer minutes in care work than those without disabilities in the same age category – differences that persist among older adults except men in the 60–69 year age range. Patterns for purchasing (another IADL) are more sporadic. Men with disabilities aged 60–69 are predicted to spend four minutes more than those without disabilities, and those aged 70 and over are predicted to spend three minutes less. Women with disabilities aged 50–59, 60–69, and 70 and over are predicted to spend five, six, and eight fewer minutes in purchasing than age peers without disabilities.

Significant differences for work (net of employment status) emerge for women of ages 50–59 (18 minutes less) and 60–69 (9 minutes less) and men of ages 15–19 (26 minutes more), 40–49 (19 minutes less), 50–59 (16 minutes less), and 60–69 (17 minutes less). Educational differences emerge for women aged 20–29 (12 minutes less), and age 40 and above (<1–6 minutes less) and for men at ages 15–19 (41 minutes less), 20–29 (13 minutes less), and 40 and above (1–6 minutes less). Only men with disabilities have a predicted gap in leisure and socializing time, and only for ages 20–29 (30 minutes less) and 60–69 (15 minutes less). For television, women and men with disabilities aged 40 and above spend more time than those without disabilities (30–46 minutes for women; 25–58 minutes for men). Women with disabilities spend less time in civic and organizational activities than women without disabilities at ages 40–49 (6 minutes) and at ages 70 plus (7 minutes), as do men with disabilities ages 50–59 and 70 plus relative to men without disabilities.

Supplemental Models

The primary goal of these analyses is to quantify the size and timing of the disability gap, irrespective of peoples' involvement in age-graded institutions; however, we also evaluate if and how these gaps persist among parents and those who are employed. These supplemental results stratify the sample to focus only on those reporting residential children and at least part-time employment.[2]

Mothers with disabilities sleep more than mothers without disabilities between the ages of 30 and 59, with no significant disability gap for fathers. They spend more time in personal care at ages 40–49 only, as do fathers with disabilities between ages 30 and 59. Mothers with disabilities spend less time in household labor at ages 40–49 only, whereas fathers spend less time at ages 30–39 and 50 and above. Care work differences emerge only for women aged 40–49 (12 minutes less) and men aged 40–49 (16 minutes less) and 70 and over (a statistically small group). Mothers with disabilities report fewer work minutes than mothers without disabilities at ages 30–39 and 70 plus whereas fathers with disabilities have no differences in work relative to fathers without disabilities. Mothers with disabilities have no differences in education time, and only fathers aged 20–29 spend less time. Leisure differences are nonexistent for mothers and for fathers, but mothers and fathers with disabilities of ages 30–39 and 40–49 spend more time watching television. Travel differences emerge for mothers aged 40–49 and 50–59, and fathers aged 30–39 and 40–49.

Among those who are employed, women with disabilities (but not men with disabilities) over age 60 sleep more than employed women without disabilities at comparable ages. Employed women with disabilities aged 30–39 spend less time in personal care and in eating and drinking (along with those aged 50–59), but employed men with disabilities aged 40–49 spend more time in personal care and the same amount of time eating and drinking. Only employed women with disabilities aged 70 plus spend less time in household labor, along with employed men aged 50–59. Employed women with disabilities aged 20–29 and employed men aged 30–39 and 40–49 spend less time in education. Employed men with disabilities (but not women) spend less time in leisure at ages 15–19 and more time in television at ages 50–59. Less communication is predicted for employed women with disabilities at ages 15–19 and employed men with disabilities at ages 50–59. Only employed women with disabilities aged 50–59 spend less time in

---

[2]Significant differences for parents aged 15–19 and 70 plus are not discussed, given statistically small cell sizes.

travel. Finally, employed men and women with disabilities spend the same time in care work and in work as employed men and women without disabilities.

DISCUSSION AND CONCLUSION

The "disability gap" in time use is well established, yet many studies treat disability as having constant effects on daily activities over the life course or over particular life stages. This study builds upon previous work by identifying the age periods *when* and *by how much* women and men with disabilities experience time use differentials in ADLs, IADLs, and other indicators of social participation. Our results identify heterogeneous associations between disability and multiple activity categories by age and by gender – some of which are attenuated by parenthood and employment and others of which are not.

To begin, bivariate results indicate that – at multiple ages – time use patterns for people with disabilities deviate from those of people without disabilities. For example, whereas sleep and personal care time are slightly higher in the teen and older adult years for people without disabilities, both are higher in midlife for those with disabilities. Household labor and purchasing time tends to increase steadily with age for people without disabilities and men with disabilities, but plateau (household labor) or decline (purchasing) for women with disabilities at midlife. Both work time and travel time drop off for men and women with disabilities after ages 20–29, instead of following the inverted U-shape for those without disabilities. Women and men with disabilities spend more time on communication and in leisure in midlife than those without disabilities, and more time in television at most ages. Eating, care work, and education mirrors that of people without disabilities, but at lower levels.

These and the multivariate results emphasize the importance of midlife as a stage in the life course where differences in daily life with and without disability become more pronounced. Although disability prevalence and severity increase with age (Taylor, 2018), many disability gaps observed here (net of controls) were absent or minimal in early adulthood and relatively smaller during the retirement years than in prime working and child-rearing years. This is true of sleeping, personal care, eating, care work, and work. These results align with studies indicating that experiences of disability stigma and discrimination are heightened among midlife working-aged adults (Namkung & Carr, 2019), and may also reflect the disproportionate stigma faced by midlife women and men when navigating parenthood (e.g., Frederick, 2017; Kilkey & Clarke, 2010). Further, midlife follows the "demographically dense" period often characterized by school-leaving, fertility, residential mobility, marriage, and paid work (Amato et al., 2016; Rindfuss, 1991). These statuses entail interactions with educational, financial, employment, and other social institutions that typically do not support individuals with less privilege (Settersten, 2012).

Notably, some – but not all – of these midlife differences disappear or attenuate when stratifying analyses by employment and parental status. For example, we do not observe disability gaps in work or care work among employed women and men with disabilities, but mothers with disabilities spend less time in work at ages 30–39, and mothers and fathers with disabilities spend less time in care work at ages 40–49. Employed women with disabilities spend less time in personal care and eating than employed women without disabilities at ages 30–39, but employed men with disabilities at age 40–49 spend *more* time than employed men without disabilities in personal care and equal time eating.

Our analyses demonstrate that disability gaps in time use are conditioned both by age and gender. Gendered experiences of disability – where gender shapes the experience of disability, and disability shapes the experience of gender – have been well documented, as have gendered experiences with structural ableism (e.g., Brown & Moloney, 2019; Deegan & Brooks, 1985; Dillaway & Lysack, 2015). In the context of time use, the magnitude of women's disability gaps equals or exceeds the magnitude of men's disability gaps for sleeping and nearly all ADLs and IADLs: personal care, eating and drinking, household labor, purchasing, communication, and travel. Women overall tend to spend more time than men on these activities, but time use differentials are greater between women with and without disabilities than they are between men with and without disabilities.[3]

These gaps weren't limited to midlife. We thought that students with disabilities' lower levels of school-based and peer-based social participation (Bruefach & Reynolds, 2022; Repetto et al., 2011) may decrease their leisure and educational time relative to their age peers. Although we found that young men with disabilities spend 41 minutes less in education than those without disabilities, no other differences in education, leisure, or communication were found in this age group. We also thought that having higher levels of social support and fewer unmet health needs in retirement and older ages (Allen & Mor, 1997; Okoro et al., 2018) might attenuate disability gaps in later life. This is observed in the relatively smaller disability gaps in sleeping, personal care, eating and drinking, and household labor (for men) – but differences in household labor (for women), purchasing, and travel are highest at older ages.

This study provides a starting point for quantifying disability gaps in time use by gender and over ages of the life course. Although the ATUS's large sample and nationally representative design provide many advantages, our study has several limitations. The ATUS is cross-sectional, meaning that results are correlational and should be interpreted as such. Additional information on the severity of disability, within-person variation in time use, or consistent health information – all relevant factors for understanding patterns of daily life (Cano & Gracia, 2020; Katz & Morris, 2007; Shandra, 2018; Verbrugge et al., 2017) – is not available. Neither is information about the age of disability onset, which is likely to further condition time use, as early onset is associated with independent living, marriage, education, and employment (Janus, 2009; Loprest & Maag,

---

[3]Interestingly, this trend tends to hold in the models stratified by employment but not those stratified by parental status, where women's and men's disability gaps are more comparable in size. These findings are worth exploring in future analyses, as other analyses with these data find that men with some types of disabilities spend more time in certain types of care work than men without disabilities (Shandra & Penner, 2017).

2007; Tumin, 2016). Further, individuals with earlier disability onset report better self-rated health and similar or higher social participation than those with later disability onset (Jamoom et al., 2008; Verbrugge & Yang, 2002). Disentangling age from onset effects would be a useful next step in this line of inquiry.

Finally, we utilize a measure of *any disability* here in order to reliably stratify results by gender, age, employment, and parenthood status. However, we acknowledge that experiences of disability are not homogenous and that time use varies by the type of disability (Shandra, 2018). For example, working-age men and women with physical disabilities spend less time in market work than those with cognitive and sensory disabilities. They spend more time in leisure and in tertiary activities like personal care. We urge the consistent inclusion of disability information in nationally representative data sources, so analyses can be adequately statistically powered to disaggregate types of disability, types of activities, and sociodemographic characteristics like age.

These results suggest multiple opportunities for future research. First, our focus is on broad conceptualizations of daily time use; however, many of the categories used here can be further disaggregated into components that have varying implications for the health and well-being of people with disabilities. For example, disability is positively associated with passive forms of leisure like watching television and negatively associated with social forms of leisure like attending events – patterns that are also conditioned by age (Shandra, 2020). Second, we do not consider the sequencing of daily activities, such as the distribution of time use over the day or the transition from one type of time use to another (Kolpashnikova et al., 2021) – an approach that may be particularly useful for understanding gendered and age-graded patterns of social participation. Third, we do not account for detailed information about household composition aside from controlling for number of household adults and the presence of household children. However, men and women have different patterns of coresidence with household dependents by age, and these patterns condition gender gaps in caregiving (Ice, 2022). Lastly, our analyses do not consider the potential interaction between disability and race – an understudied approach in sociology, yet one crucial to understanding disabled lives and advancing intersectional scholarship (Frederick & Shifrer, 2019).

REFERENCES

Acker, J. (1992). Gendering organizational theory. *Classics of Organizational Theory*, 6, 450–459.

Allen, S. M., Ciambrone, D., & Welch, L. C. (2000). Stage of life course and social support as a mediator of mood state among persons with disability. *Journal of Aging and Health*, *12*(3), 318–341.

Allen, S. M., & Mor, V. (1997). The prevalence and consequences of unmet need. Contrasts between older and younger adults with disability. *Medical Care*, *35*(11), 1132–1148. https://doi.org/10.1097/00005650-199711000-00005

Amato, P. R., Booth, A., McHale, S. M., & Van Hook, J. (2016). *Families in an era of increasing inequality*. Springer.

Ameri, M., Schur, L., Adya, M., Bentley, F. S., McKay, P., & Kruse, D. (2018). The disability employment puzzle: A field experiment on employer hiring behavior. *ILR Review*, *71*(2), 329–364.

Anand, P., & Ben-Shalom, Y. (2014). How do working-age people with disabilities spend their time? New evidence from the American Time Use Survey. *Demography*, *51*(6), 1977–1998.

Anxo, D., Mencarini, L., Pailhé, A., Solaz, A., Tanturri, M. L., & Flood, L. (2011). Gender differences in time use over the life course in France, Italy, Sweden, and the US. *Feminist Economics*, *17*(3), 159–195.

Balandin, S., Llewellyn, G., Dew, A., & Ballin, L. (2006). We couldn't function without volunteers': Volunteering with a disability, the perspective of not-for-profit agencies. *International Journal of Rehabilitation Research*, *29*(2), 131–136.

Bascom, G. W., & Christensen, K. M. (2017). The impacts of limited transportation access on persons with disabilities' social participation. *Journal of Transport & Health*, *7*, 227–234.

Baxter, J., Hewitt, B., & Haynes, M. (2008). Life course transitions and housework: Marriage, parenthood, and time on housework. *Journal of Marriage and Family*, *70*(2), 259–272.

Bedini, L. A. (2000). "Just sit down so we can talk:" Perceived stigma and community recreation pursuits of people with disabilities. *Therapeutic Recreation Journal*, *34*(1), 55–68.

Brault, M., Stern, S., & Raglin, D. (2007). *Evaluation report covering disability* (p. 4). American Community Survey Content Test Report.

Brown, R. L., & Moloney, M. E. (2019). Intersectionality, work, and well-being: The effects of gender and disability. *Gender & Society*, *33*(1), 94–122.

Bruefach, T., & Reynolds, J. R. (2022). Social isolation and achievement of students with learning disabilities. *Social Science Research*, *104*, 102667.

Cano, T., & Gracia, P. (2020). The gendered consequences of parental separation for parents' and children's time investments: A longitudinal study. *SocArXiv*. https://doi.org/10.31235/osf.io/8j37s

Deegan, M. J., & Brooks, N. A. (1985). *Women and disability: The double handicap*. Routledge.

Dillaway, H. E., & Lysack, C. L. (2015). "Most of them are amateurs": Women with spinal cord injury experience the lack of education and training among medical providers while seeking gynecological care. *Disability Studies Quarterly*, *35*(3), 231–257.

Elder, G. H., Johnson, M. K., & Crosnoe, R. (2003). The emergence and development of life course theory. In *Handbook of the life course* (pp. 3–19). Springer.

Frederick, A. (2017). Risky mothers and the normalcy project: Women with disabilities negotiate scientific motherhood. *Gender & Society*, *31*(1), 74–95.

Frederick, A., & Shifrer, D. (2019). Race and disability: From analogy to intersectionality. *Sociology of Race and Ethnicity*, *5*(2), 200–214.

Garland-Thomson, R. (2002). Integrating disability, transforming feminist theory. *NWSA Journal*, *14*(3), 1–32.

Graf, C. (2008). The Lawton instrumental activities of daily living scale. *AJN The American Journal of Nursing*, *108*(4), 52–62.

Grue, L., & Laerum, K. T. (2002). Doing motherhood': Some experiences of mothers with physical disabilities. *Disability & Society*, *17*(6), 671–683.

Hofferth, S. L., Flood, S., Sobek, M., & Backman, D. (2020). *American Time Use Survey data extract builder: Version 2.8* [dataset]. IPUMS.

Ice, E. (2022). Bringing family demography back in: A life course approach to the gender gap in caregiving in the United States. *Social Forces*, *101*(3), 1143–1170. https://doi.org/10.1093/sf/soac041

Jamoom, E. W., Horner-Johnson, W., Suzuki, R., Andresen, E. M., & Campbell, V. A. (2008). Age at disability onset and self-reported health status. *BMC Public Health*, *8*(1), 1–7.

Janus, A. L. (2009). Disability and the transition to adulthood. *Social Forces*, *88*(1), 99–120.

Katz, P., & Morris, A. (2007). Time use patterns among women with rheumatoid arthritis: Association with functional limitations and psychological status. *Rheumatology*, *46*(3), 490–495.

Kaye, H. S., Jans, L. H., & Jones, E. C. (2011). Why don't employers hire and retain workers with disabilities? *Journal of Occupational Rehabilitation*, *21*(4), 526–536.

Kilkey, M., & Clarke, H. (2010). Disabled men and fathering: Opportunities and constraints. *Community, Work & Family*, *13*(2), 127–146.

.iikova, K., Flood, S., Sullivan, O., Sayer, L., Hertog, E., Zhou, M., Kan, M.-Y., Suh, J., & Gershuny, J. (2021). Exploring daily time-use patterns: ATUS-X data extractor and online diary visualization tool. *PLoS One, 16*(6), e0252843. https://doi.org/10.1371/journal.pone. 0252843

Leopold, T., & Skopek, J. (2015). Convergence or continuity? The gender gap in household labor after retirement. *Journal of Marriage and Family, 77*(4), 819–832.

Lisney, E., Bowen, J. P., Hearn, K., & Zedda, M. (2013). Museums and technology: Being inclusive helps accessibility for all. *Curator: The Museum Journal, 56*(3), 353–361.

Loprest, P., & Maag, E. (2007). The relationship between early disability onset and education and employment. *Journal of Vocational Rehabilitation, 26*(1), 49–62.

Malacrida, C. (2009). Performing motherhood in a disablist world: Dilemmas of motherhood, femininity and disability. *International Journal of Qualitative Studies in Education, 22*(1), 99–117.

Marcum, C. S. (2013). Age differences in daily social activities. *Research on Aging, 35*(5), 612–640.

Maroto, M., Pettinicchio, D., & Patterson, A. C. (2019). Hierarchies of categorical disadvantage: Economic insecurity at the intersection of disability, gender, and race. *Gender & Society, 33*(1), 64–93.

Moen, P., & Flood, S. (2013). Limited engagements? Women's and men's work/volunteer time in the encore life course stage. *Social Problems, 60*(2), 206–233.

Moen, P., & Spencer, D. (2006). Converging divergences in age, gender, health, and well-being: Strategic selection in the third age. In *Handbook of aging and the social sciences* (pp. 127–144). Elsevier.

Myers, A., & Ravesloot, C. (2016). Navigating time and space: How Americans with disabilities use time and transportation. *Community Development, 47*(1), 75–90.

Namkung, E. H., & Carr, D. (2019). Perceived interpersonal and institutional discrimination among persons with disability in the US: Do patterns differ by age? *Social Science & Medicine, 239*, 112521. https://doi.org/10.1016/j.socscimed.2019.112521

Okoro, C. A., Hollis, N. D., Cyrus, A. C., & Griffin-Blake, S. (2018). Prevalence of disabilities and health care access by disability status and type among adults—United States, 2016. *Morbidity and Mortality Weekly Report, 67*(32), 882.

Pettinicchio, D., & Maroto, M. (2017). Employment outcomes among men and women with disabilities: How the intersection of gender and disability status shapes labor market inequality. In *Research in social science and disability* (Vol. 10, pp. 3–33). https://doi.org/10.1108/S1479-354720170000010003

Pini, B., & Conway, M.-L. (2017). Masculinity and fathering in the lives of rural men with a disability. *Journal of Rural Studies, 51*, 267–274.

Repetto, J. B., McGorray, S. P., Wang, H., Podmostko, M., Andrews, W. D., Lubbers, J., & Gritz, S. (2011). The high school experience: What students with and without disabilities report as they leave school. *Career Development for Exceptional Individuals, 34*(3), 142–152.

Rimmer, J. H., Padalabalanarayanan, S., Malone, L. A., & Mehta, T. (2017). Fitness facilities still lack accessibility for people with disabilities. *Disability and Health Journal, 10*(2), 214–221.

Rindfuss, R. R. (1991). The young adult years: Diversity, structural change, and fertility. *Demography, 28*(4), 493–512.

Roman, G. J., & Gracia, P. (2022). Gender differences in time use across age groups: A study of ten industrialized countries, 2005–2015. *PLoS One, 17*(3), e0264411.

Sayer, L. C., Freedman, V. A., & Bianchi, S. M. (2016). Gender, time use, and aging. In *Handbook of aging and the social sciences* (pp. 163–180). Elsevier.

Scheiner, J. (2016). Time use and the life course: A study of key events in the lives of men and women using panel data. *European Journal of Transport and Infrastructure Research, 16*(4), 638–660.

Settersten, R. A. (2003). Age structuring and the rhythm of the life course. In *Handbook of the life course* (pp. 81–98). Springer.

Settersten, R. A. (2012). The contemporary context of young adulthood in the USA: From demography to development, from private troubles to public issues. In *Early adulthood in a family context* (pp. 3–26). Springer.

Settersten, R. A., & Mayer, K. U. (1997). The measurement of age, age structuring, and the life course. *Annual Review of Sociology*, 233–261.

Shandra, C. L. (2018). Disability as inequality: Social disparities, health disparities, and participation in daily activities. *Social Forces, 97*(1), 157–192.

Shandra, C. L. (2020). Disability and patterns of leisure participation across the life course. *The Journals of Gerontology Series B: Psychological Sciences and Social Sciences, 76*(4), 801–809. https://doi.org/10.1093/geronb/gbaa065

Shandra, C. L., & Penner, A. (2017). Benefactors and beneficiaries? Disability and care to others. *Journal of Marriage and Family, 79*(4), 1160–1185.

StataCorp. (2021). Stata statistical software: Release 17. In StataCorp LLC.

Suh, J. (2016). Measuring the "sandwich": Care for children and adults in the American Time Use Survey 2003–2012. *Journal of Family and Economic Issues, 37*(2), 197–211.

Taylor, D. M. (2018). *Americans with disabilities: 2014* (pp. 1–32). US Census Bureau.

Tipton, L. A., Christensen, L., & Blacher, J. (2013). Friendship quality in adolescents with and without an intellectual disability. *Journal of Applied Research in Intellectual Disabilities, 26*(6), 522–532.

Tumin, D. (2016). Marriage trends among Americans with childhood-onset disabilities, 1997–2013. *Disability and Health Journal, 9*(4), 713–718.

U.S. Bureau of Labor Statistics. (2020). *American Time Use Survey – 2019 results*. U.S. Department of Labor.

U.S. Bureau of Labor Statistics. (2021). *BLS 2021 – American Time Use Survey – May to December 2019 and 2020 results*. U.S. Department of Labor.

U.S. Bureau of Labor Statistics. (2022). *Persons with a disability: Labor force characteristics – 2021*. U.S. Department of Labor.

Verbrugge, L. M., Latham, K., & Clarke, P. J. (2017). Aging with disability for midlife and older adults. *Research on Aging, 39*(6), 741–777.

Verbrugge, L. M., & Liu, X. (2014). Midlife trends in activities and disability. *Journal of Aging and Health, 26*(2), 178–206.

Verbrugge, L. M., & Yang, L.-s. (2002). Aging with disability and disability with aging. *Journal of Disability Policy Studies, 12*(4), 253–267.

Wikle, J. S., & Shandra, C. L. (2022). Social contact and family contact for youth with disabilities. *Youth & Society*, 44118. https://doi.org/10.1177/0044118X221074717

Williams, J. R., Masuda, Y. J., & Tallis, H. (2016). A measure whose time has come: Formalizing time poverty. *Social Indicators Research, 128*(1), 265–283.

INDEX